# STATE AND SOCIETY IN CHINA'S POLITICAL ECONOMY

# STATE AND SOCIETY IN CHINA'S POLITICAL ECONOMY

---

## THE CULTURAL DYNAMICS OF SOCIALIST REFORM

CHIH-YU SHIH

LYNNE RIENNER PUBLISHERS

BOULDER
LONDON

Published in the United States of America in 1995 by
Lynne Rienner Publishers, Inc.
1800 30th Street, Boulder, Colorado 80301

and in the United Kingdom by
Lynne Rienner Publishers, Inc.
3 Henrietta Street, Covent Garden, London WC2E 8LU

**Library of Congress Cataloging-in-Publication Data**
Shih, Chih-yu, 1958–
    State and society in China's political economy : the cultural
dynamics of socialist reform / Chih-yu Shih.
      p.  cm.
    Includes bibliographical references and index.
    ISBN 1-55587-580-7
    1. China—Economic policy—1976–   2. Socialism—China. 3. China— ·
Cultural policy. I. Title.
HC427.92.S5377  1995
335.43'45—dc20                           94-23749
                                                CIP

**British Cataloguing in Publication Data**
A Cataloguing in Publication record for this book
is available from the British Library.

Printed and bound in the United States of America

    The paper used in this publication meets the requirements
⊗  of the American National Standard for Permanence of
    Paper for Printed Library Materials Z39.48-1984.

    5  4  3  2  1

*To Eva, Alison, and Albert*

# CONTENTS

# PREFACE

In May 1989 I wrote an article on the decline of China's moral regime. On June 4 the Tiananmen massacre took place. I packed up my paper and sent it to the *American Political Science Review*, which rejected it three months later. Although it received positive comments from one reviewer, the other two questioned the usefulness of the notion of morality in political analysis. In the same year, the editorial board of the University Press of Kentucky turned down a book-length manuscript I coauthored with Jonathan Adelman. Despite two reviewers' recommendations for publication, the press decided that we should not have assumed that Chinese were different from Americans or Russians in their war behavior. I have since become accustomed to such comments. Editors have often asked me to drop the philosophic section of a paper but to keep the analytical part. The moral problematic that I, as a native Chinese, am familiar with seems to be either exotic or irrelevant to my American colleagues. And when I returned to Taiwan to teach in 1990, I was shocked to find that even some of my colleagues in Taiwan could not speak without using the jargon they had learned in the United States.

I had a similar experience with the manuscript that became this book. Two reviewers suggested I discard the discussion of morality; they found the rest of the book enlightening. I felt as if I were left headless, though: I had written the book just to argue that China's moral regime had declined and that this was a permanent decline, not a cyclical phenomenon. This had been the theme of my 1989 paper as well. (By the way, the paper was finally published by *Comparative Political Studies* in 1994, five years after I had completed it.) Citing the reviewers' agreement on the point, the publisher insisted that I drop the first half of the book. I had to invent a new problematic, if not to satisfy the readers, at least to soothe my own empty soul. I felt obliged to tell myself why I wrote this book, having left behind the real reason. When the third reviewer okayed the third draft, I felt, ironically, a kind of loss.

The annual Sino-American Seminar of 1994 was held in Taipei. I gave a paper on the flexibility of Chinese foreign policy. I deliberately chose the topic to suggest that Chinese and American scholars viewed the issue quite differently. Since my return to Taiwan in 1990, numerous students had asked me about consistency in policy. Yet during my previous three years in the United States, not one student had ever raised the issue. In private Harlen Jencks told me that he had only one Taiwanese student ask him the same question. I think that the lesson is that Chinese students are concerned whether their government (or any government) is morally consistent. The state is not conceptually separate from society in China, thus there is no unique set of moral principles that the state follows in dealing with external affairs. Although my purpose was to show that different societies come up with different questions, two American scholars told me after the panel that they found my analysis and case studies useful (I used the Shanghai Communiqué and Sino-British talks on Hong Kong as my cases) but asked why I wasted good case studies in responding to such a nontheoretical question!

In spring 1994 I began to teach a course on the epistemology of China studies at National Taiwan University. My key point was that research in China studies is not only a matter of the object under study but, more importantly, the life experiences of the researchers. The approach to which we are accustomed in comparative analysis (including systems analysis, state-society differentiation, institutional incentive mechanism, game matrix, and authoritarian transition) reflects our own concern for the individual's role in the political process. The problematic points to the opportunity for and constraints on enhancing the quality of political participation. We who are used to the democratic life-style (or myth) want to know if we represent the norm in the world. My students once joked that democracy and authoritarianism were like a CPA's two ties, and we were studying how alternately wearing the two ties determined the CPA's auditing behavior.

Another analogy is even more dramatic. Say I want to study how the color of Deng Xiaoping's socks affects Deng's policy decisions each day. Ten years later I decide that it should not be the color but the length of his socks. Another ten years later, I realize that it may be the materials of the socks. Then one day a friend tells me my socks are determining *my* daily behavior: I am crazy about basketball, so whenever I wear a pair of long, white, cotton socks, I am excited throughout the day because I know I am going to play ball that day. The point is I thought Deng was just like me, conditioned by my socks, forgetting that my socks are reflective of my own obsession with basketball. Scholars who see no alternative to American democracy tend to watch for China to adopt an institution that glorifies the participation of individuals in political processes. They want China to wear American socks, so to speak. (For three months after I presented that analogy in class, students greeted me by asking what socks I had on that day.)

The key is the way problems are presented. In the American problematic, affect is not an issue. For those in the field, it may be difficult to appreciate a situation without talking about hatred, dedication, integrity, and so on. American scholar Martha Cottam criticizes Cold War studies for ignoring the affective factor, regretting that political science becomes an intellectual entertainment. Indeed, without an affective notion such as hatred, it is unlikely that one can get a whole picture of an event like the Cultural Revolution. The problematic in China is consistently the reconciliation between collectivistic and individualistic interests, from the dynastic court officials through Sun Yat-sen, Mao Zedong, and Deng Xiaoping, to Jiang Zeming, Li Peng, and Zhu Rongji. The approach to this exercise has undergone tumultuous changes over generations, but the problematic remains. And it is this problematic, I believe, that blocks the communication among American scholars as well as between my American-trained colleagues and myself.

Each kind of problematic incurs its own style of human pretension. The individualistic problematic leads to an institutional pretension that people strive for their own interests. They either do not have or do not need a collective identity; they are independent personalities. The collectivistic problematic suppresses personal needs in an archetypal drama of self-sacrifice: People live meaninglessly outside the realm of collectivity. Consequently, citizens coming from the two extremes would ask very different questions about their private problems. Reform in China can therefore accommodate entirely opposite assessments. On the one hand, Americans wonder if the Chinese will become just like them, expecting a middle class to emerge in Chinese society. This perception is in striking contrast with the assessment during the antiwar 1960s, when U.S. radicals praised the Cultural Revolution to shame their own society. On the other hand, the Chinese are busy manipulating nebulous policies so as to gain windfall profits while ostensibly maintaining their dedication to collective interests. To show their sincerity, they maneuver to stage a show of antispiritual pollution once in a while, even against their own material interests. They claim that interests at all levels are served this way.

This book is no longer a complete presentation of the Chinese problematic that I once wished it to be. Instead, I have come to pretend that there is no such difference in problematic or that such difference is not pertinent. I have dropped the word *morality* in as many places as possible. I cut the first half of the book dealing with the morality issue. But to be fair to the readers, I have here described the process I went through and compel myself to rethink. This question of interaction among cultural problematics has become my personal puzzle.

Some words of acknowledgment are necessary here. It is perhaps too late to thank my family, especially my parents, who constantly worry about my radical remarks and errant academic projects. Chinese workers, managers, and party cadres who candidly expressed their feelings about reform and other matters made the greatest contribution to this book. Others who have read the whole or a part of this project and kindly helped me improve my thoughts are Yang-shan Chou, Cheng-tsong Huang, Elizabeth Perry, Lucian Pye, Peter Van Ness, Yu-shan Wu, and Jialing Zhang. Martha Cottam (whom I have met only once in the past four years) continues to inspire me with her work on political psychology. Brantly Womack enlightened me enormously during his short visit to Taipei in summer 1994. Martha Peacock considerately downplayed the reviewers' criticism and successfully kept the project alive. I find her to be the most trustworthy editor I have met so far in my career, East as well as West. Lily Ling, Chao-chi Shan, Kim Chang, and Eliza Lee together called back my lost confidence in a two-day workshop in Hong Kong in summer 1994. Finally, participants in a workshop on indigenous psychology at National Taiwan University and students in my seminars on China's political economy in these past few years have provided me with support and criticism. As a Chinese, I believe it is imperative to let the readers know that they, though they remain nameless, also compose an important part of the collective effort this book represents.

# State and Society in China's Political Economy

# 1

# INDIGENOUS SOCIALISM: CULTURAL TRADITION VERSUS SOCIALIST IDEOLOGY

## CULTURAL STYLE

To understand reform in China is to feel it. But it seems that empathy is a factor virtually overlooked in current research on political economy. Recently, however, some scholars have begun to appreciate the Confucian motivation of economic development in East Asia.[1] But the implicit assumption that culture is an independent variable and development a dependent variable may be somewhat misleading. The positive relationship between the two factors can be further questioned in the case of China, the birthplace of Confucianism. Chinese experience suggests the possibility that culturally sensitive development strategies may, when they fail, lead to cultural changes. Those of us who normally try to control the culture variable, not at all interested in empathizing with the practitioners of the Chinese political economy, do not see this link.

In an age of turbulence, changes in social, political, and economic parameters require us to reorganize our cognitive order to appreciate the bewildering changes and adapt to them.[2] It is critical to social coordination that people share some views of political economic history to make their acceptance of current political economic order sensible.[3] Without such common perspectives, social coordination would become exhausting and political control costly—and our research would be spurious. In this book I study how the Chinese themselves make sense of past political economic order and how they proceed to understand the process of modern socialist development. In short, by showing how the Chinese interpret political economy, I hope to contribute to a general understanding of China's political economy. I go on to explore the possible impacts that the tradition-socialism bifurcation in the Chinese worldview may have had on China's political economic practices. This process of bifurcation started at the turn of the century as traditionalists and modernists seem to have adopted two incompatible systems of reasoning. When the communist regime was founded in 1949, the issue became more precisely one of tradition versus socialism.

1

Of course Chinese cultural elements were by no means homogeneous even before the rise of modern productive forces. As the twentieth century dawned, a seeming heterogeneity affirmed itself rather acutely. Richard Wilson sees this bifurcation occurring among traditional, modern, and revolutionary values;[4] in another work I develop a cybernetic model of cultural alternation among hierarchical, equal, and revolutionary worldviews;[5] Suzanne Ogden simply describes the struggle as reflecting a contradiction among cultural, developmental, and political necessities;[6] Peter Van Ness traces the communist experience back to three indigenous ideological views of economics, including central command, marketeer, and mass line.[7] Nevertheless, there is something non-Chinese in these combinations of worldviews that raises the issue of cultural change.

The most significant of these non-Chinese elements had to be party-state socialism. To understand how this particular non-Chinese element has been received in Chinese culture requires some basic elaboration on what is traditionally Chinese. In the academic cliché, this has to do with the interaction between state-enforced ideology and society-inherited tradition. Although the argument exists that typical Chinese can accommodate incompatible thought systems at the same time without necessarily experiencing dissonance,[8] most still believe that the introduction of Western factors into Chinese culture must prompt some conscious adjustment before both Chinese and non-Chinese elements can coexist. Literature suggests that this state-society, or socialism-tradition, interaction has displayed certain patterns of change and continuity. Against these patterns one may detect the kind of continuity that current reform has succeeded and the kind of change that it must reflect.

## POLITICAL ECONOMY BEFORE REFORM

On the issue of the continuity of style in political economy, Western literature provides at least four useful perspectives: patriarchal rule, human feelings, inner drive, and state corporatism. Patriarchal rulers justify themselves not by their professional knowledge but by their intrinsic goodness and moral leadership. The institutionalization of this patriarchal clan-type practice, however, has obstructed socialist development primarily because patriarchal leaders use every avenue available to them to channel assistance (public resources) to their own relatives.[9] Cultural variables therefore contribute to the widespread economic phenomenon of feudal corruption and backdoor business, those aspects of Chinese culture least supportive of modernization.[10] This combination of tradition and socialism can nevertheless be desirable in terms of bringing supposedly incompatible values together. The emergence of the so-called communist gentry in the Chinese countryside attests to this unique adjustment in rural leadership. They continue their past practice as general leaders yet at the same time are consciously and particularly benign toward people within their own circles.[11]

The communist gentry faces incentive problems in its attempt to mobilize out-group members to work for socialism. Most importantly, since the ruled do not appreciate and thus do not trust socialist leadership—which is ideally based on class as well as fairness—but expect that the cadres act according to traditional nepotic practices, the cadres who respond favorably to this expectation in order to rule effectively lose credibility under socialism.[12] People are convinced that leaders must treat their own followers exceptionally well. As a result, the ostentatious fairness of rule under socialism also loses credit and a paradigm of pragmatism arises to replace it. The contradiction therefore occurs not only between socialism and tradition but also between the peculiar synthesis of tradition and socialism and its pragmatic substitute. The patriarchal clan system, which protects the vested interests of local leadership by utilizing socialism to benefit in-groups, ironically undermines the legitimacy of that system.

This intriguing development of Chinese politics exacerbated the self-contradictive nature of the synthesis of socialism and tradition. The patriarchal clan system reached an absurd stage during the Cultural Revolution when Mao, as personal leader, replaced the synthesis of socialism and tradition to become the symbol of political legitimacy. Once political legitimation began to depend on personalized, ambiguous Maoism, practical synthesis of tradition and socialism became nearly irrelevant, as Mao could be quoted to humiliate virtually anything or anyone. Maoism was so comprehensive and ambiguous that all existing worldviews, including both socialism and Confucianism, no longer made sense. This process most certainly expedited the rise of pragmatism in the postrevolutionary period.[13]

Pragmatism is said by some always to have been an intrinsic part of Chinese culture. In a comparison of the kind of pragmatism that bred familistic utilitarianism and the more individualized, self-centered strain of pragmatism common today, clear differences emerge. Familistic pragmatism is a product of patriarchal clan rule, which makes a sharp distinction between treatment of in-groups and out-groups. To apply in-group norms to out-group connections requires a certain degree of manipulation of human feelings. While socialism discourages the invocation of emotion, socialist governments are well aware of its importance. Emotional manipulation can incur in-group affection and sometimes transform a purely equity-based, instrumental relationship into a semi–in-group relationship.[14] Through the manipulation of feelings, public out-group norms and private in-group norms can coexist in spite of their obvious inconsistency. In this sense pragmatism refers to flexibility in people's behavior in order to suit the context.

Pragmatism after the Cultural Revolution has more to do with the movement away from control of human feelings. Management grounded in exploitation of emotions would tend toward nepotism, coordination of activities through interpersonal connections, and insistence on the unification of ownership and management. Management evolving away from the traditional style would, on the contrary, willingly employ out-group workers, coordinate through institutionalized operating procedures, and divorce management from ownership.[15] Pragmatism in the latter sense has serious political implications, since people would no longer regard patriarchal clan rules as a valid portrayal of social relationships and would start contemplating their own socioeconomic surroundings as the source of life's meaning. Consequently, a regime whose legitimacy was based upon patriarchy would lose its leverage in attempting to mobilize social support by invoking the importance of self-sacrifice.

The decline of the emotional element in social contacts also undermines the classic foundation of neo-Confucianism. Today's neo-Confucianists vehemently dispute Max Weber's notion that the Chinese lack an inner drive to overcome the outer world. From the Weberian point of view, Chinese philosophy is most interested in achieving a harmonious relationship with nature, while modernization in the Western sense requires the conquest of nature.[16] Neo-Confucianists have recently documented in detail that people in East Asia (including both China and Japan) are indeed equipped with the kind of inner drive that Weber held was nonexistent in China.[17] The Chinese adopt the so-called affective model, which motivates one to glorify one's family.[18] In Japan the sphere of influence of this affective model is even wider, for the Japanese feudal tradition incorporates outsiders as in-group members relatively easily; this is the so-called *iemoto* model.[19] Group orientation prompts one to become industrious as well as frugal and hence effectively contribute to collective economic development.

Under socialism, this neo-Confucianist stress on harmony with nature is particularly pertinent. Socialism is preoccupied with the notion of class unity. This aspect can attain ready support from a Confucian tradition whose adherents pursue a spirit of oneness and egalitarianism.[20] Furthermore, Chinese individuals need to prove their ability to suffer hardship and advance group interests to be accepted as worthy group members. This psychological propensity to prove such an aptitude inspires them to work harder and learn more eagerly in comparison to their Western counterparts.[21] This is the Chinese sense of predicament that comes from within. If the Chinese began to subscribe to individualistic pragmatism, their inner drive would lose its traditional vigor.

Still, socialized production on a truly massive scale provides some neo-Confucianists with a new sense of hope. Since China has historically had a fear of failing to control worldly desires, modern technological forces present the opportunity for neo-Confucianists to ignore the inducement of such desires: These would be met by an abundance of material goods and would thus not inject confusion into a harmonious relationship with nature.[22] It would appear, then, that socialism would stand a much better chance of thriving under neo-Confucianism, owing to a Chinese mind-set that is already prepared for class unity bred in a sense of oneness.

Moving beyond the Chinese inner world to view the structure of Chinese society, one can argue that East Asia (and China in particular) generally adopts the institution of state corporatism.[23] Socialist China typically emphasizes the importance of harmonizing interest relationships among individuals, their enterprises, and the state.[24] Chinese leaders are required by Confucian ethos to ensure the welfare of all their subjects as a way of embodying the Confucian sense of equality. Under socialism, the state organization is as encompassing as it is under corporatism. Interest group activities, however, are minimized because of a collectivist culture in which self-interest is not a legitimate policy concern.

State corporatism can curb the "unsound" development of pursuit of personal interest at the expense of public interest. Yet the state deliberately brings in modern values to counter traditional feudal thoughts. In other words, the synthesis of socialism and tradition can be beneficial as well as malignant. Whether or not each can be utilized to its full potential with minimal detrimental effects depends on the state.[25] State corporatism buttressed by Confucianism is said to contain the optimal possible combination.

In summary, before reform started in the 1970s, socialism and Chinese tradition had interacted with each other and obviously impacted upon the meaning of both. Although this book will touch upon the contents of traditional cultural norms and socialist state ideology (as the works cited in this chapter have done), the main focus will be their interaction. This approach attests to the changing political economic context of China under reform. In order to emphasize the meaning of reform, we should abandon any neat labeling and categorizing mechanism. Reform is neither a revitalization nor a betrayal of state/socialism (or society/tradition). Rather, reform continues to provide a realm for socialist ideology and cultural tradition alike to contribute to the current style of political economy, albeit with a different focus.

## THE CHANGING CONTEXT OF REFORM

Before I examine the political economy of reform in the following chapters, I review in this section how the Chinese literature has treated the changing contexts in terms of cultural, moral, political, and ideological style.

## The Evolving Cultural Context

Regarding the cultural dimension, the majority of scholars in China acknowledge that Confucianism survives in the symbiosis of good and bad.[26] Some feel that the Chinese people hold a love-hate attitude toward Confucian tradition.[27] It was Mao, in fact, who once suggested that one must summarize Chinese heritage from Confucius to Sun Yat-sen before one could successfully sinify Marxism.[28] Following in his footsteps, Zhang Jian struggles to identify the modern implications of Confucianism. According to Zhang, filial piety and loyalty are virtues conducive to the development of modern productive forces. In Zhang's final analysis, the household responsibility system, widely applied since 1978, activates the Confucian concern for family that has become the upper structure of socialist productive relations.[29]

The traditional mode of production, however, persists in many parts of society, and this is conceived of as composing an antiprogressive, self-enclosed system.[30] In concurrence, others point to central economic planning as a modern incarnation of the feudalistic drive for unity, and the epidemic presence of political authority as the re-creation of the image of omniscient feudalistic leadership.[31] A successful reform movement has to demolish both images in order to undergo "a thorough operation of the Confucianistic feudal system."[32] This may not perceptually counter socialism, for Lu Xun recorded in his famous story of Ah Q that one must refuse to test one's self-image in the objective world so as to "see the world as shaped and transformed by some subjective creation and imagination."[33]

In the current round of reform, the most important task is the development of productive forces. In this regard most believe that Confucianism does not have to be a negative element.[34] Literature attests to the Confucian notion of expediency and utilitarianism.[35] In fact, Confucius himself discussed commerce and taxation on a number of occasions. Jiang Jianqiang summarizes some of the more interesting remarks.[36] His philosophy that the prince can get rich only if everyone else is rich is identical with the tenets of supply-side economics. Reform in China makes a similar appeal through financial decentralization, which enables unbudgeted monies to flow and form a market outside the planning system.

Since the thrust of reform is to facilitate the flow of commodities, scholars fathom the compatibility between traditional culture and market, with some paying special attention to the mentality of competition.[37] In the past Confucianism promoted agricultural development and restrained commercial activities to some extent. Through political and family relations, however, Chinese entrepreneurs always avoid the test of the market.[38] Accordingly, for socialism to liberate productive forces in the current round of reform, it must break the linkage between party and enterprise and separate political, cultural, and commercial activities.[39]

In general, those who criticize tradition generally anticipate its decline, while others hold a somewhat more ambivalent attitude. Those who favor Marxist guidelines commonly believe that the solution lies in the liberation of productive forces. Once this is accomplished, individuals will be naturally emancipated and individual, collective, and social interests can parallel one another on the road to modernization. Culturally speaking, some scholars thus praise tradition for allowing individuals to derive meaning from the collective yet benefiting the collective by encouraging individuals to decide for themselves how to make their contribution.[40] In later chapters I demonstrate this to be the thinking of reformers. Those who appear sympathetic with Western individualism predict that tradition will survive with some individualistic elements assimilated into Chinese culture. One thing that seems certain to all scholars is that even if individual identity continues to show dependence, or what was once assertive again becomes submissive, culture as a whole has definitely changed.

Wang Huning summarizes ten cultural changes: from revolutionary to constructive, from politically to economically oriented, from holistic to individualistic, from unidimensional to multidimensional, from spiritual to material, from principle-oriented to practice-oriented, from goal-driven to procedure-driven, from idealistic to realistic, from single-sourced to pluralistic, and from derivative to innovative.[41] Obviously, even those who are extremely critical of tradition treat the field much more seriously than their counterparts did during the Cultural Revolution. Antitradition no longer reflects the drama of revolution or political self-interest. Similarly, those who urge revitalization of Confucianism do not display ethnocentrism or xenophobia. Instead, some even dare nurture the vision that individuals will decide what tradition means in the current age.

## The Evolving Moral Context

Under reform there has been a consistent move away from the moral incentive first toward the coercive and then toward the material incentive. Moral decline in politics is a long process that has the following signs. First, the supreme leader loses his ability to reign through collectivistic pretension.[42] Power is based either upon coercion, when resources are available, or compromise, when they are not.[43] Since leaders' pretensions of selflessness are not as important as before, the need to maintain a unified leadership around a supreme figure no longer exists.[44] In short, coercion predominates persuasion,[45] factionalism begins to undermine unity,[46] power talks replace preceptive talks,[47] and profit making prevails over concerns for production.[48]

Second, the local leaders no longer serve as local educators. Not only does corruption become widespread; it is even openly acknowledged. In Chinese society local leaders defer to party cadres who replaced the gentry class to become the kernel of the preceptive regime.[49] Cadres cease to protect the image of a selfless regime and instead straightforwardly abuse power. They do not depend on the regime to resist pressure from the masses but selectively recruit citizens (often relatives and friends) as the recipients of favors and rally local support to resist central interference. Unlike the traditional gentry class, cadres are no longer on the side of the regime.

Third, the masses are no longer willing to respond to leaders' calls for spiritual purification and political rectification. Material interests dominate the way individuals plan their lives. Competition for narrow personal interests overwhelms concern for collective interests. The moral alienation of the masses can also be reflected in vandalism against public objects, waste of public resources, and refusal to cooperate in the execution of public projects.[50]

As reform started in the 1980s, many young Chinese simply lost their sense of direction. Responding to Pan Xiao's discussion of the meaning of life in *Zhongguo Qingnian*, for example, Zhao Lin wrote: "My world view was completely transformed; in the past I had been full of yearning and love of life; now I have come to hate life. . . . I submit rather that it was the inevitable result of a long period of imprisonment of the self by the Chinese people. It was the inevitable result of society's opinions of using the whole to suppress the individual."[51]

The 1983 campaign against spiritual pollution and the 1987 campaign against bourgeois liberalization purported to consolidate collectivistic consciousness. They received little attention even from party members.[52] Extravagance was another commonplace phenomenon in the 1980s.[53] Contrary to most observers' belief that there is an overconcentration of power in China, a well-known economist worries that corruption will aggravate the "social demise of the power-thirsty." He believes the Cultural Revolution created a power vacuum in politics. Individual demands for power thrive because "using power for oneself becomes a social custom," and once one acquires power it seems possible to acquire anything. It is as if "everyone is an official," and hence no one truly possesses power. He finds during this dangerous interlude that "society may possibly slide into the abyss of the alternation between corruption and anarchism."[54] Party cadres have yet to resume their preceptive leadership after the Cultural Revolution. On the contrary, some continue to use power for selfish purposes, while others compete with the masses for resources in order to get rich.[55] Corruption that erodes the economic interests of the masses is resented most,[56] but perhaps more dramatic and alarming are reports of corruption involving children of high-level party leaders. The masses no longer voluntarily succumb to cadres and leaders, for social status does not connote superiority.

One clear sign of moral decay in the 1980s was the surge of legalism at the political center in contrast to the spread of democracy in society. The Chinese mass media in the 1980s were choked with demands that criminals be dealt with severely; most serious is the advocating of punishment for political dissidents. Reformers and conservatives alike agree on this point.[57] The 1989 talks concerning neoauthoritarianism, the concept of instituting enlightened despotism in China, were the highlight in a series of calls for order and discipline. It was reported that both Deng Xiaoping and then general secretary Zhao Ziyang supported this position.[58] Later that year, the ruthless massacre in Beijing manifested the extreme side of coercion.

That power talks should replace preceptive talks is not a phenomenon exclusive to the political center. Citizens no longer expect leaders to be moral superbeings. Instead, calls for checks and balances on power, freedom of speech, and citizen participation form the core of a countertheory. Citizens have learned to create their own moral power by setting the stages for self-directed rituals.[59] It would appear thus far at least that the moral regime in China has experienced permanent decline. The decline does not result from short-term pragmatism, because the individual has gradually come to challenge the collectivity as the sole point of life.

## The Evolving Political Context

Concerning the political dimension, the style of factionalism has undergone subtle yet important changes. Common sense has it that Chinese politicians are extremely sensitive to political signs of factionalism.[60] One's policy position is determined by the ideological implications of a disputed issue within one's faction. The nature of those implications is generally decided by faction leaders. Factionalism is not based on the articulation of particular interests but by complicated human factors. The Chinese spend a good deal of time and energy on a policy's ideological implications; the faction's mastermind is constantly preparing a moral coup. Furthermore, once a faction is defeated, the victors denounce the policies of the vanquished as if the losers were thoroughly depraved and lacking in any virtue or validity whatsoever. Such comprehensive denunciation reinforces the collectivistic aspect of the purge as good versus evil.[61]

During the Cultural Revolution factional struggles became public, resembling an open struggle between the dowager's family and eunuchs under a young emperor. The difference, of course, is that the Cultural Revolution reached every corner of urban society and many parts of the rural world, whereas the old-fashioned fight was always limited to the court. This difference in extent resulted in serious pattern changes. The most profound was that people could no longer assume that decaying politics could be rescued by a selfless hero; the selfless leader proved unable to rule. After the Great Leap Forward, policy disputes had become the forum for factional struggles carried out beneath the surface, and economic policy had taken on the role of ultimate importance.[62] All right-wing revisionists were rectified during the Four Modernizations campaign; all those labeled capitalist roaders were no longer capitalist roaders; and many of the policies they had once advocated were adopted to suggest the mistakes of the Gang of Four. The Four Modernizations was thus not just an economic campaign, it was also an ideological war against the Cultural Revolution.[63]

Reform politics in the 1980s moved factionalism away from its traditional mode. Reform politics has been constrained by an economic logic that originated in the Four Modernizations. The notion of reform arose because the Four Modernizations was unable to break through the rigidity of the existing central planning system. Starting in 1984, the center made a few bold moves simultaneously: initiating financial decentralization, which gave more discretion to local governments and enterprises; increasing autonomy for socialist enterprises; and so on. All factions face the same pressure to continue reform policy because enterprises of all scales that benefit from the reform will probably support continued reform. It is unlikely that any factional struggle can target reform directly.[64] In addition, cadres and children of party leaders have been the first to utilize the opportunities available under reform to get rich. Since economics is no longer a useful channel to express factional struggle,[65] it has become more difficult for politicians to hide factionalism behind policy debates or to protect the appearance of harmony.

In 1986 the reformist faction lost Hu Yaobang; in 1989 it was Zhao Ziyang. Hu and Zhao, just like Hua Guofeng, were able to keep their personal integrity after losing power. Although there was pressure from the winning faction to destroy their images, this did not happen; nor did the winners override the economic policy lines of Hu and Zhao. Both lost power for not handling the student movement well enough. The irony is that each time, the student movement was denounced as reflecting bourgeois liberalization, yet neither Hu nor Zhao was forced to wear that label, and both were permitted merely to step down—a sign that political and ideological positions are now separated from reform.

This development has three important implications. First, if a regime remains concerned about the pretense of harmony, factional struggles will have to be disguised in policy areas other than the economic, probably in the fields of arts and literature. Indeed, dissident writers who believed that the party was unable to handle the required reforms were purged.[66] Li Reihuan, however, suggests that issues of socialist civilization should be handled according to local features (*yindizhiyi*), avoiding the need to force everyone to conform.[67] As a result, policies would seem alternately to be opening up and cracking down. Second, factionalism in the name of socialist civilization has failed to provide a collectivistic pretension that can explain to the public how socialism matters. If the debate on socialist civilization is to clarify the nature of supreme harmony, it only demonstrates that this debate is irrelevant for those engaging in economic reform. Third, and perhaps most important, factionalism without the disguise of harmony or a publicly recognized set of criteria to make moral judgments has to be carried out in a straightforward fashion. That is, for the public, factionalism does not mean policy debate, it means an outright power struggle among politicians. In other words, politics does not lead to socialism.

## The Evolving Ideological Context

According to the Chinese scholarly literature, the theory of the primary stage of socialism, which the Chinese Communist Party proposed at the Sixth Plenary Session of the Eleventh Party Congress, aimed precisely at providing legitimacy for the regime to engage in reform and focus attention on upgrading productive forces.[68] In fact, the most fundamental Chinese characteristic in the primary stage of socialism is identified as low productivity.[69]

The theory of the primary stage of socialism thus highlights the significance of promoting the commodity economy, that is, the market economy, as the instrument to emancipate potential productive forces in society. In order to have a state enterprise respond to the market, it must be held accountable for its own profits and losses.[70] This in turn requires enterprise reform. The most controversial proposals are those that touch upon ownership of the means of production. Scholars and some national leaders have recently recognized the need to formulate a new property law to allow private enterprises to compete with their public counterparts in the marketplace.[71] Individualized craft work, localized consumer goods, and small-scale supplements to urban industry can even adopt the institution of private ownership.[72]

Since managers in public enterprises have to motivate workers by some means of profit incentive, workers in these sectors are undeniably better off than other workers in terms of stable wages, fringe benefits, and regular bonuses. Strong concerns are raised regarding the legitimacy of these workers in benefiting from their position in the name of public ownership. In other words, the continued application of public ownership does not guarantee the integrity of socialism. Here, the contradiction between public ownership and private profit incentive appears unmanageable. Some scholars regard this as a short-term anomaly and would not upend socialism, at least philosophically. This is because the use of labor forces is a process separate from the growth of labor forces, and labor forces are not spent entirely on reproducing labor forces; laborers must get reimbursement in some form in order to compensate the exhaustion of their personal consumptive materials in nonreproductive activities.[73]

Political legitimation under reform, however, differs significantly from traditional practices in other aspects. In China's patriarchal tradition the regime was not supposed to be concerned about productivity. In contrast, primary-stage socialism attends exclusively to productivity. On the one hand, in regulating the market the regime would certainly incur tacit resistance from society, which is tantamount to denying the regime's superiority. On the other hand, the regime's possession of economic resources would unavoidably entice actual decisionmakers in the bureaucracy to abuse their access to such resources by engaging in illegal business practices.[74] This would also damage the regime's credibility as a representative of collective interests in the market. Political legitimation of any sort is not pertinent to individual pursuit of material welfare in the market. On the contrary, it is exactly the lip service paid to socialism that protects one's economic behavior. Building spiritual civilization thus becomes an intrinsic part of legitimation under reform.[75]

Second, if one acknowledges that historical evolution involves objective laws, then political leaders' intentions cannot be critical in determining the nature of the regime.[76] The regime and individuals alike must fulfill their historical duty to develop productive forces. In short, the regime is not superior to individuals in moving history forward. Theoretically, therefore, primary-stage socialism, as Deng Xiaoping once declared, deprives the regime of its monopoly over truth. In the traditional patriarchy only the gentry came to know heavenly reason, and such knowledge could not be denied by commoners, rich or poor. In contrast, the Communist Party's claimed dedication to socialism is not intrinsic to upgrading productivity, but productivity can determine if the regime correctly enacts its role.

Finally, China's Confucian tradition always had supreme leaders perform public rituals and pose as models for commoners to emulate—commoners had no role to play in ritual politics. In contrast, socialism in the primary stage requires individual workers to perform the historical function of development. Individuals' value to society is measured by the product of their work, not their intentions. Consequently, leaders' own motivations are no longer germane to political legitimation.

The Communist Party artfully distinguishes between politics and economics and claims partial detachment from the market. This reinterpretation of the state in the market may have played a key role in successfully rescuing the regime from its legitimacy crisis in the aftermath of the Cultural Revolution, for the state can no longer be held exclusively accountable for an individual's lot in life. The state becomes a competitor rather than a leader, an interest pursuer rather than a moral rectifier.

## THE INTENT OF THIS BOOK

Western as well as Chinese literature on Chinese culture seems to suggest that socialism and tradition together were responsible for causing certain political economic problems. As reformers addressed these problems, Confucian values, authoritarian rules, factional plays, and socialist theory continued to constrain the experiences of reform in China, except that socialism and tradition now seem to be on the same side—the collectivist side—in opposition to the other side—the individualistic side. The difference between the traditional value of harmony and the socialist norm of class struggle obscures their common puzzle: how to deal with individual incentives.[77] It is against these cultural, moral, political, and ideological backdrops of collectivism versus individualism that I begin my exploration of the meaning of China's economic reform.

The style of China's political economy lies in the ironic symbiosis of socialist norms, now consistent with traditional obsession with collective interests, and the mobilization of individualized working incentives. Self-consciousness thus becomes a key element, either in reminding those engrossed in profit making of the ultimate socialist cause or in pushing those seeking shelter under state planning to embrace the market challenge. The rest of this book is devoted to making sense of the state-society symbiosis in China's political economy, explaining how it is likely that China's reformers have theoretically allowed and encouraged a typical Chinese to be socialist and profit-driven at the same time.

In Chapter Two I examine nascent economic conceptions, particularly the notion of opportunity cost. In Chapter Three I contend that the central planners are caught in a legitimacy crisis today because they cannot prove why the central government is relevant to the market, and in Chapter Four I describe how and why state planners circulate the idea of corporate purchase. I go on to argue in Chapter Five that the supposed cultural and ideological constraints on the growth of the consumer goods market are spurious. Chapters Six through Nine are a report on field research in a large Chinese factory. I conclude with two middle-level officials' observations on China's political economic development, an open-ended conclusion intended as a reminder to students of China's political economy that we have much more work to do before we can become comfortable with our subject matter.

In essence, the style of Chinese political economy is shaped by China's cultural tradition and socialist ideology. Therefore, the style of current reform has to do with how the reformers secure traditional and socialist concerns for collective interests when promoting a market economy based upon individualized calculation. Readers are thus encouraged to come back to the problematic of collectivism versus individualism while going through the details of reform practices. This same problematic appears again and again in the discussion of the state-society relationship between the center and the localities, the planners and the enterprises, the state enterprises and the social producers, the rich and the stringent consumers, and the managers and the workers. I hope this book will enable students of China's political economy to feel the dilemma and empathize with those who are constantly under pressure from both directions, above and below, state and society. What appears to an economist to be purely rhetorical or superficial often goes far deeper for the Chinese.

# 2

## CALCULATED SOCIALISM: NEW ECONOMIC CONCEPT

Traditionally, the Chinese political regime rarely discussed issues of policy in a public and calculated manner lest this give the impression that the regime was concerned more with material interests than moral integrity. In economics a decision to allocate resources would by definition incur an opportunity cost, for resources so dispensed could not contribute to other useful ends, hence the loss of opportunity to achieve such ends. If the loss of potential value in achieving other ends exceeds the value of those ends pursued, the decision is not rational. In China the regime does not usually justify resource allocation by juxtaposing expected benefits and opportunity costs, for the regime presumably cares only about right and wrong.[1]

There are two cultural premises that establish the environment in which opportunity cost of resource allocation can become a legitimate policy concern. First, at least two value systems provide alternatives in terms of who should get what, how, and when. Second, there is some objective standard to compare the alternatives. In reality, a traditional regime did not normally allow itself to be torn between two value systems. Its supreme leadership relied heavily on a single moral code. The consequential lack of pluralism stifled the rise of the notion of opportunity cost. In addition, the monetary gauge that serves to compare alternatives in modern times was not fully developed in the past, so the regime's spiritual values could not easily be translated into mundane terms. This further complicated the calculation of opportunity cost.

In this chapter I trace the rise of the notion of opportunity cost in China's socialist reform and discuss the implications of this particular economic concept for the Chinese style of political economy.

### THE NOTION OF OPPORTUNITY COST IN HISTORY

Although there was little systematic discussion of the notion of opportunity cost during the dynastic period, similar concepts are nonetheless scattered throughout the classic literature. In political life, for example, subjects of the emperor constantly found themselves struggling between requirements of loyalty to the emperor and filial piety, *zhong xiao buneng liangquan.* The former required one to overcome all fear of losing one's life on the battlefield, while the latter directed one to survive in order to continue the family line. With regard to economic policy, Mencius once urged the prince to avoid extracting labor from the agricultural population, noting the tradeoff between public construction and private field cultivation. An old Chinese saying that one cannot have both bear paw and fish (two of the finest delicacies) at the same time is constantly used to illustrate such a dilemma.

Notwithstanding the apparent appreciation of value tradeoff in daily life, the ideal Chinese society embraced the myth of a regime reigned by a supreme leader dominating in a monolithic ethical system. Signs of pluralism, whether indirect, implicit, or unintended, would challenge the superiority of leadership. For a poor peasant, detailed calculation of petty interests could be critical to surviving a bitter winter. This is exactly why the regime could not afford to present itself in a similarly calculative image, lest peasants see that the regime ran contrary to those interests pertinent to the peasants' survival. In other words, if the regime could prove that it had no concern for its own material interests, it would be unlikely that the regime would become the target of rebellion even during the most difficult times.[2] Because of this consideration alone, the regime had to wrap itself in a lofty image in allocating resources. It could achieve this more easily if leaders could consciously ignore the application of the opportunity-cost argument in the public forum.

It goes without saying that policymakers must have had some form of calculation in mind. Sima Qian, a noted Confucian official in the Han dynasty whose work is still widely read today, pointed out in one of his memoranda that an investment review must weigh the prevailing interest rate against the expected rate of return and ensure that the latter is greater. At other times he implicitly applied the notion of opportunity cost to review the efficacy of public ownership of the means of production.[3] Policy disputes, though, seldom centered on economic rationale in the ensuing dynasties. Historically speaking, economic policy disputes split classic Chinese economists into two camps: advocates of a free economy and the legalists. Both sides were preoccupied with the legitimacy of the regime.

For those of the school of free economics, which began to attract disciples during the warring states period (which ended in 221 B.C.), the prince and the gentry could calculate only the interests of the people and would not jettison their principled neutrality while making such calculations. According to Xun Zi, the true gentry enriched underheaven without bettering themselves. This does not mean that the gentry could not pursue material interests, only that these interests were so minor and insignificant that they were as transient as clouds in the sky. Since the Confucian value system contains no plural elements, Confucian officials could not and should not measure the value of being a member of the gentry or following dao in material terms (whatever the definition).

The free economics school argued that taxation as well as state extraction of societal resources pitted the commoner against the emperor. This would have caused serious problems because the emperor did not really enjoy firm control over all of underheaven. If the emperor openly pursued material interests, how could he possibly entice society to refrain from doing the same thing, most notably when his bureaucracy was fragile and outnumbered? On the contrary, if the noble refrained from pursuing his own personal interests, according to Xun Zi, the country would be rich anyway. Although this line of argument was echoed by the supply-side economists 2,000 years later, this early rationale was ethical, not economic. For enrichment should be regarded as the effect rather than the reason. The rationale of the free economy was not to expand the economic pie but to substantiate the virtue of the gentry—in other words, to bring harmony to underheaven, where gentry and commoners could coexist peacefully.

Some legalists, who favored a ruler's economy, contended that the prince could rule only if the state enjoyed economic monopoly. Shang Yang believed that if people were wealthy, they would not need to respond to the rule of the prince. Moreover, if the prince allowed society to possess wealth, the rich could become more powerful than the ruler. It would be they, not the prince, who would manipulate the majority through economic sanctions. The ruler's economy would enable the prince to make the rich poor and the poor rich—a compliant mass of commoners. The rationale for adopting the ruler's economy was therefore *not* to expand the economic pie. Rather, the ruler's economy aimed at improving political functionality. Even Dong Zhongshu, one of history's most famous Confucian officials, once urged the emperor to utilize the commoners' selfish nature by employing an economic carrot-and-stick approach. The ultimate goal was unambiguously their political loyalty.

The notion of opportunity cost was not present in the age-old debate between these two schools. Legalists would sacrifice people's happiness without reservation, for their happiness was regarded not as a value but primarily as a threat. There was no opportunity cost lost in that the sole objective was consolidation of the regime. By contrast, the free economics school espoused decentralization of financial control in the belief that the nobility would feel indifferent as long as underheaven was ruled in harmony.

The priority of values hence seemed obvious to all discussants. As a result, ancient Chinese economic thought that guided public policy was the combination of these two schools of thought. On the one hand, the government was urged to keep taxes on agricultural products low (the free economy) and taxes on commerce high (the ruler's economy). And of course the state maintained true monopoly in the highly profitable trades. The peasant's (and later landlord's) sovereignty in production and the state's monopoly in commerce were paradoxically parallel. This laid the foundation for what modern economists would criticize as a Chinese economy that stagnated for the better part of two millennia. This irony, however, is precisely that stagnation is a sign of harmony and unity. Thus stagnation was not considered an opportunity cost. Efficient allocation of resources to achieve higher development was typically irrelevant in the official position. Official concerns were for peace and harmony between court and commoner and, more importantly, the freedom of the emperor to act if necessary under the pretension that he could not possibly do so selfishly.

That the notion of opportunity cost was not officially present in Chinese public policy is not the same as saying the concept absolutely did not exist. In fact, the Chinese regime developed a unique way of handling via alternate channels what would have been regarded as opportunity cost. One method was to consider all policy issues against the criterion of harmony. All that contributes to harmony is acceptable. In this regard, calculation in material terms would challenge the image that the gentry have no material interests and would thus work to undermine harmony. The act of calculation itself would imply a moral problem. In considering stagnation, for example, one should stress its effect on the diminished possibility of the rise of a competing source of authority in society. Likewise, stagnation suppressed luxurious life-styles, kept peasants in the field, and assisted in spiritual rectification. It appeared that there was absolutely no cost.

The second defense mechanism was to acknowledge that a competing value did exist but to refuse to recognize that the current resource allocation caused it any disadvantage. Some Chinese scholars call this "spiritual victory," referring to subjective reinterpretation of an objective phenomenon to make acceptable that which was previously unacceptable.[4] In a typical example, a court official who abides by the code of filial piety must mourn over his parents' grave for three years. He would have to forgo this virtue, however, if the emperor called him to fight on a faraway battlefield before this period had passed. Here, the official was said to have converted the virtue of filial piety into the virtue of loyalty (*yixiao zuozhong*). In such a manner, the official perceptually maintained his virtue of filial piety, although he left unperformed its most important ritual.

In Chinese history utilitarianism rarely enjoyed attention in official economic philosophy, as all cost-benefit argumentation was forced to pass some Confucian test. For example, Li Anshi urged Emperor Xiaowen of the northern Wei dynasty to adopt an "equalizing" land policy. The rationale he originally presented was that such a policy would help utilize land resources more efficiently, as tillers without land could work in unused fields. Emperor Xiaowen finally accepted the proposal but used another rationale. The emperor proposed to "strive for harmony under heaven by enriching the commoners. This could not be achieved if those without died fighting over land or became vagrants for lack of food."[5] A Confucian emperor should have accepted the policy of land equalization rather easily since Confucianists have long recognized that commoners must be motivated by material incentives. In addition, as the court's annual revenue was primarily extracted from the agricultural sector, it was perfectly acceptable to discuss land policy in such contexts. Yet the Wei court did not phrase its policy rationale this way at all.

Interest calculation appears to be an equally dreadful deed in modern times. The Chinese Communist Party (CCP) launched land reform shortly after coming to power in 1949. The economic implications of such reform, though, were not even publicly addressed. The major appeal was to strike against the exploiting landlord class, and the campaign was referred to as liberation of the peasant class, not of the agrarian labor force. In other words, communism was more than just an economic plea. Although the peasant's concern was primarily economic, Mao's ideology contributed to the sense of virtue of the peasantry, which helped them accept organization led by party cadres.[6] From the party's point of view, official economic argumentation became moot: "Communist virtue aims at unifying all workers in their struggle against all exploitation and all principles serving petty private ownership. . . . Virtue should improve the level of development in all human society, assist in the working class's emancipation from exploitation . . . and consolidate and complete the ideal of communism. These are the foundations of communist virtue."[7]

Indeed, the notion of opportunity cost was missing in Chinese political tradition; consequently, decisions of resource allocation could not be examined against a materialist criterion. Allocating resources was a matter of right and wrong, and every policy option was introduced in moral terms. In order to prove sincerity toward the moral goal one's policy supposedly promoted, one would have to worry only that too little was achieved or further investment came forth too slowly. This style of devotion through increased investment (in time and energy) was what Confucius himself encouraged. He urged the gentry to do the proper thing, even if they knew this was unfeasible and would not bring about concrete results. While economists use opportunity cost to determine the rationality of a decision, Confucianists use opportunity cost to measure the value of their goal. High opportunity cost does not bother Confucianists; on the contrary, lack of opportunity cost causes them considerably more anxiety. Opportunity cost is the sacrifice they make, and the greater their sacrifice, the more dramatic their devotion. This mind-set is clearly not conducive to economic efficiency.

When China was opened up by the Western powers during the late Qing dynasty, a policy debate ensued upon the proper strategy for meeting the Western colonial powers. The outcome reconfirmed the existing single hierarchy of the value system. Although all agreed that China had to "use one barbarian against the other," the court mainstream insisted that the ultimate purpose was to protect the Chinese system. The term *barbarian* avoided the connotation that learning from the West was an act of submission—there could be no compromise of China's supremacy in virtue! It was not until the Boxer Rebellion that China completely acknowledged the superficiality of its alleged superiority. The adjustment was drastic and *essentially Chinese* in style. Many declared complete Westernization as if there had been nothing in tradition worthy of recognition. Within this context, the May Fourth movement demanded thorough renovation of Chinese culture. For those participants, the cost of burning the classics and breaking the civil exam system was zero, inasmuch as tradition as a whole had proved unable to meet the challenge of the modern age.

Even the moderates refused to note the possible costs involved in cultural renovation. Their view that both Western and Chinese cultures have inherent strengths and that the best strategy is to graft Western strengths onto Chinese culture is still popular today. Many Chinese scholars today juxtapose what they consider to be the most desirable aspects of both cultures and claim that their combination would ensure China a bright future.[8] The primary assumption of these mainstream thinkers (who still dominate in China) is that the correct and sincere attitude of philosophers alone can determine the fate of cultural development. Few if any address the issue of cost in cultural renovation; as they see it, preserving all good elements and jettisoning problematic ones does not appear to compromise credibility. This approach suggests an excessive need for simplicity and a desire for all-encompassing answers. Lucian Pye observes the psychological drive for simplicity in China:

> The Chinese practice of settling for single explanations reflects in part a pronounced preference for an orderly scheme of things, for a clear hierarchy of values, and a desire that human relationships be unambiguous so that where people stand on issues can be clearly understood. Multiple explanations suggest confusion and raise anxieties. To open the door to alternative explanations is to tolerate unbecoming controversy. The disinclination to seek ever more complex explanations of events is a way of preserving social harmony and realizing consensus, values that are important in Chinese political culture.[9]

After the communists came to power, Marxism and Maoism replaced Confucianism as the state ideology. The previous style of resource allocation—or, more precisely, the traditional justification for that allocation policy—survived. It was, however, the Maoist strategy of the united front rather than Marxian ideology that best indicated the traditional obsession with moral appearance. According to the united front strategy, the revolutionary should always identify one primary target in each specific historical period and develop cooperative relationships with other, secondary enemies. The united front strategy would thus serve to convert secondary enemies. Besides, the true revolutionary would never ignore them for long after the primary enemy was overthrown, if their conversion proved unsuccessful. In this sense a tolerant policy toward secondary enemies and resource allocation would not jeopardize the integrity of the revolutionary force.

Compromise on the revolutionary front against secondary enemies like kulaks, the national bourgeoisie, or the petty bourgeoisie was henceforth not a compromise at all. Temporary abandonment of revolution against these class enemies connoted no cost for Mao. This method of always singling out the primary target and cooperating with secondary enemies clearly displayed the traditional proclivity toward a simplified hierarchy. Mao helped his comrades conceptualize the compromise toward minor enemies in the united front through this reinterpretation:

> For the sake of long-term cooperation, each participating party in the united front should provide assistance as well as make concessions to one another. This must be executed in an active manner, not in a defensive manner. . . . There should be mutual concession. No one undermines the force of the others. . . . This involves a retreat in preparation for a future leap forward and is consistent with Leninism. We should not consider concession as a defensive move, for Marxism and Leninism do not permit this attitude. . . . Every concession, retreat, defense, and pause we make to either enemies or allies must be part of a revolutionary policy and should be an inevitable process built in the historical revolutionary development. They compose part of a chain that is a sinuous [but shorter] route rather than a straight [but longer] one. In one word, it is vigorous.[10]

Like all revolutionary regimes, Mao's leadership in the aftermath of the revolution was forced to deal with the dilemma of choosing between loyalty and expertise. The problem arose when it became obvious that many professionals recruited by the new regime necessarily came from strata that had once served the old regime, thereby carrying the ideological stigma of the outcast regime. The mass leader who actually led the revolution could no longer provide effective leadership with enthusiasm, loyalty, and sacrifice. Technocrats in China, however, never completed their duty, as they owed their legitimacy to some public image that only a revolutionary could bestow. The force of revolution periodically tried to indoctrinate the professional strata.[11] They did this without reference to the possible loss of time and resources in various historical campaigns. Neither slower development of productive forces nor the resultant incapacity to improve planning techniques could shake the ideological criterion used by the revolutionary. One heard complaints only in private; there could be no public debate over the opportunity benefit thus forgone in all these campaigns.

Officially, therefore, the costs of technological retardation and wasted time were not considered costs at all. Rather, these sacrifices evidenced commitment to ideological purity. The regime engaged only in the kind of economic development conducive to the spread of the Maoist notion of equality and continuous struggle. There was no common denominator that could convert the measurement of gross national product (GNP) into revolutionary terms. The most important focus had to be the style of development rather than its results. It would become a sign of opportunism to use expense in terms of lost development potential to measure the value of a certain development approach. In Mao's well-known thesis on the ten contradictory relationships, which include the dyad of investment and consumption, his solution was not to choose the one of higher value (whatever the criterion). Instead, he argued that there was a way to resolve the contradiction and reach a mutually complementary solution. The communists refused to acknowledge the existence of opportunity cost in every policy just as their predecessors had done.

The Great Leap Forward campaign of 1958 clearly elucidates this characteristic, as hundreds of thousands of peasants were encouraged to invest in economically meaningless backyard furnaces. In its wake many regretted the waste thus caused. The sense of regret misses the point. What motivated the practice of backyard furnaces could not be economic rationality; it had to be a drive for spiritual purity. While the labor-intensive sectors could be a rational focus of China's economic development, Mao's emphasis was nonetheless on the "all-round socialist workers." He was forced to deny the inevitable tradeoffs among four simultaneous goals: quantity, speed, quality, and economy. Mao placed high credit on human devotion, which proved confidence and then invited more waste. The blind spot in this type of regime was that the notion of opportunity cost could not serve as a legitimate argument. Those who tried to use it, like Deng Zihui, had to be purged.

## THE EMERGENCE OF THE OPPORTUNITY-COST CONCEPT

Since economic growth was not considered a value in the past, it was perfectly acceptable for the current regime to monopolize commercial activities. In the 1950s the CCP introduced the concept of development and indeed released a portion of the agrarian labor force. In fact the party launched the Great Leap Forward exactly in order to achieve rapid development; the failure of the campaign was rooted in the failure of such development. Since the regime acknowledged this failure at the Lushan conference of 1959 by formally examining the lack of material growth, the regime must have noticed the relevance of materialism in its pursuit of the communist ideal. The failure of the campaign became a warning sign of the possible failure of communism. Communism, as a divine goal, was accidentally measured in material terms. If communism and development were thought mutually congruent in the first place and the goal of development was presented as the mundane side of communism, the 1958–1959 failure must have forced the public to realize that there was a contradiction between communism as a sacred goal and development as a secular desire. To save confidence in communism would thus require some success in development. The value of communism became measurable! (The same line of reasoning should be applicable to the former socialist economies in Eastern Europe.)

The process of transformation was nonetheless prolonged. Communist ideology prescribed that all investment be measured in terms of labor time and that only narrow differentials be permitted in valuing such. This way the central planning system severed the link between the quality and price of a product—the planner rather than the market decided its price. Consequently, it made the calculation of opportunity cost meaningless. In an extreme case allocating resources to different sectors made no difference in aggregate nominal value, since all measurements were in labor time and wage rates were essentially flat, thus making the calculation of opportunity cost virtually impossible. Nobel Prize winner K. Arrow proved that pricing in socialist systems through labor cost would naturally push the central planner alone to determine the goal of production, as consumer expectations could not be reflected in prices.[12]

When the communist regime was established in 1949, economic development remained an issue of identity. The First Five-Year Plan, kicked off in 1953, was basically a Soviet concept that placed primary stress on heavy industry. The heavy industry bias of this first plan was twofold: the traditional obsession with spiritual purity void of the concept of opportunity cost, with industrial development as the symbol of socialism; and the socialist decision to ignore economic efficiency in terms of maximizing consumer satisfaction, whereby opportunity cost could not be measured by definition.

Objections raised by the noted economist Deng Zihui indeed challenged the rationality of central planning, criticizing the centralizing tendency of the First Five-Year Plan. His critique involved the notion of opportunity cost. Basically, Deng believed that the first plan overinvested in a few select sectors at the expense of others, reflecting "a most detrimental view of doctrinism and subjectivism that accentuated centralization and precluded decentralization."[13] Deng pointed out overinvestment in food and cotton production in the agricultural sectors, warned against the tendency to overlook diversity in regions, and reminded the planner of lost opportunities to produce other, more region-oriented products.[14] Deng also raised the issue of simultaneous, balanced development of commerce, transportation, and cooperative culture.[15] At face value the Great Leap Forward was a decentralizing movement. The resultant overcentralization in local planning centers, though, more than offset the decentralizing effects Beijing intended. Each region was expected to attain self-reliance and thus engage in numerous productive tasks that could be better accomplished elsewhere. Promoting regional specialization would have been political suicide under such circumstances.

The failure of the Great Leap Forward led to a few adjustments, and all seemed to acknowledge the exorbitant opportunity cost incurred in the campaign. In addition to installing the responsibility system, widely known in the 1980s, the central planners made five other major modifications. First, workers in the cities were shifted back to the villages in order to improve productive forces in the agricultural sector and ease pressures on the planners to feed swelling urban populations. As a result, China's urban population dropped by 26 million between 1960 and 1963. Second, the central planners pared investment in local capital to the point where the rate of capital accumulation dropped from approximately 40 percent in 1960 to 10 percent in 1962. Third, investment in steel and coal was curtailed as more funds were shifted to the petrochemical industry. Fourth, investment in agricultural machinery was increased while rural extraction was scaled back. In order to further ease pressures on food, the central planners both raised the purchase price for food products and turned to imports during the early 1960s. Finally, they adopted stringent financial policies and set high prices for nonessentials.[16] The lesson of the Great Leap Forward is that economic development must follow the law of proportionality, which is beyond human determination or subjective will. Achievement of proportionality, though, requires knowledge of the productive functions of various goods—and how could the planners know these without pricing via the actions of the market?

## THE OPPORTUNITY-COST CONCEPT DURING REFORM

The Great Leap Forward triggered discussion on the meaning of proportionate development (*anbili fazhan*). Scholars first raised the issue in 1959 and maintained that "proportionate development is the precondition for high-speed development."[17] Proportionality is not the same as opportunity cost. Nonetheless, demands for proportionality were a response to ideo-logical and political biases in investment decisions and were thus also de-mands for resource reallocation. Reallocation would require calculation of cost and benefit, hence the demands of proportionality were conducive to the notion of opportunity cost. Unfortunately, the political atmosphere dur-ing the aftermath of the Great Leap Forward did not allow this type of dis-cussion to spread. The mass media in the 1960s continued to praise the masses for having "no fear of lacking capacity but fear of lacking visions." The scholarly reminder of proportionate restraint was subdued under the propaganda of subjective activism (*zhuguan nengdong*).[18] It was only after the Cultural Revolution that cost conception became a legitimate argument under Deng Xiaoping's urge for pragmatism. The debates on resource al-location in the new environment have taken three standpoints: among eco-nomic sectors, among regions, and between the state and enterprises.[19]

The allocation controversy may arise among economic sectors because of the concomitance of a large amount of stocked machinery in one sector and rising demands for new investment in another. This paradox explains why actual aggregate supply is far above nominal aggregate supply in China.[20] One cannot easily and successfully entice producers to make full use of idle machines simply by entitling them with the goods thus manu-factured. Overstock of machinery is a matter of the socialist predilection for quantity rather than quality and is a typical sign of overlooking oppor-tunity cost. This is because there is no financial penalty for money-losing enterprises that tend to invest more than they need in order to satisfy mar-ket demand. As a result, there are numerous signs of waste in lethargic en-terprises, and the government has no idea how much investment support enterprises really need without some sort of performance check by a self-regulating market.[21] In order to realize opportunity cost, Li Yining, a well-known Chinese reform economist, urges that the market be allowed to de-termine prices. The market and the plan compose what he calls a dual economic mechanism. Li portrays the ideal relationship between the plan-ners and the market: "The market guides the economic adjustment of en-terprises. This is the primary adjustment, upon which the government may embark upon the second-round adjustment. The government's adjustment must be the second-round adjustment and would be exercised only when the primary adjustment fails to work or when it cannot possibly work. . . . The primary adjustment is always there and is everywhere while the sec-ond-round adjustment may or may not even exist."[22]

Li, like many economists in other socialist states, wants to limit the role of government in pricing decisions. Others have gone further. Toward the end of the 1980s, "horizontal linkage" (*hengxiang lianhe*) became a new catchphrase in the reform circle. It drives at the need to break admin-istrative and regional confinements in order for enterprises to expand their sphere of activities if they are capable of doing so. Accordingly, enterprises are encouraged to cooperate in developing cross-sector or interregional joint ventures.[23] Obviously, this sort of tolerance targets both the central planner, whose base is in ministerial administrative echelons, and the local planner, whose base is in regional as well as administrative echelons. In order to crack the protective bottlenecks guarded by superior administrative organs, a few localities have initiated trial runs of enterprise purchase and bankruptcy laws. Profiting enterprises are encouraged to take advantage of cheap capital, land, and labor force released from money-losing enterprises. Each of these measures is intended to improve economic efficiency by raising consciousness of opportunity cost via the market.[24] The concern for efficiency in this sense is nourished not by socialism but by the market.

The political implication is dramatic. The central planner, that is, government leadership, is no longer able to pretend to have a superior knowledge of the road to socialism, now objectively defined in terms of development. On the contrary, it is precisely the leadership that has caused inefficiency in material terms. The planning system cannot detect opportunity cost, nor can it correct the problem. The widely acknowledged problems of the planning system, though, are not the central message. What is most significant is that the government has publicly recruited the market to rescue itself and openly praised criteria of efficiency in order to expose and explain the problem to the masses. The role of the government is no longer as leader but as a relatively strong *competitor* in the market at best. If socialism cannot survive without the market, it must be measured against an objective set of criteria common to the market, such as GNP, inflation, wages, and employment. The legitimacy of leadership would in turn be a matter of performance rather than intention and a matter of quality service rather than lofty rhetoric.

From a different vantage point, those who advocate stronger horizontal linkages may indeed aim at resource reallocation among regions. They are critical of previous calls for autarky at the national, provincial, or even the lower-brigade levels. They maintain that the drive for "completeness" within each individual economic unit lost sight of the diversified nature of each locality. The result was productive inefficiency precipitated by an overproduction of nonspecialized goods. Development strategies in the 1960s were guided by the notion of three-line construction (*sanxian jianshe*), which divided the country into three areas according to political and strategic considerations. By contrast, central planning in recent years has encouraged each locality to develop a specialization in line with its natural environment. Under such a premise, one group of scholars has become particularly worried about northern and northeast China and Guangxi Province, where short-term products are developed to generate quick profits without utilizing the natural strength of the region. This has accelerated the "opportunity cost in the agricultural sectors."[25]

In order to facilitate more horizontal linkages, many cities have been selected as new plan centers. The idea is to develop the economic potential of each locality based on its own unique conditions, thus broadening economic reach. The central planner has therefore intentionally established planning boards in these new centers and directly assigns capital and raw materials from Beijing without going through administrative channels.[26] Horizontal linkages are utilized to generate market pressure so that opportunity cost can be exposed.

Academic seminars in the latter part of the 1980s evidenced the emergence of a new trend toward research in horizontal linkage. Economic efficiency has become an obsession in academic circles of late. Zoning is now a subdiscipline in macroeconomic studies, with some arguing that China should be divided into coastal, center, and western regions, each at distinct economic stages and each led by the area to its east.[27] Others promote the idea of dividing China into five zones in order to achieve further specialization.[28] Still others want to see China concentrate only on coastal areas in order to generate foreign reserves for use in its future development. Some refer to this as the international circle with two heads outside China (*liangtou zaiwai*, the import of capital as one head and export of products as another).[29] Finally, there is the suggestion that inland areas should enlist the support of foreign capital and technology through the medium of the coastal areas. This is the so-called two-radial fan (*liangge shanmian*) theory, with one receiving capital from all over the world, the other spreading multiplied growth inland.[30]

The discussion of regional specialization inevitably raises the question of the superiority of administrative leadership. The challenge is particularly acute as it applies market criteria to review traditional planning rationale. The administrative leadership is typically clothed in socialist rhetoric, while new economic management scholarship embraces the market, thereby introducing a brand new identity. Successful leadership is no longer defined as the good intentions of someone well versed in socialist ideology. Administrative leadership has little control over market criteria. The problem does not lie in the loss of control, since this may also imply the discharge of responsibility for economic failure—which is not necessarily a bad development. The problem arises as administrative leadership confronts the crisis of losing the definition of leadership in the classical sense. If resource allocation is no longer under their control, traditional regional planners would no longer be capable of acting like leaders.

This sense of crisis explains in part why regional leaders have striven to institute all sorts of administrative barriers to prevent economic integration, which would cut across their administrative boundaries. Scholars refer to these regional groupings as blocs (*kuaikuai*) as opposed to sectors (*tiaotiao*, referring to the control by the ministers at the center). In order to develop overall control, regional leaders regularly pursue all-round development of their region at the expense of comparative advantages that individual regions enjoy. The impact of this mind-set is impressive, as statistics suggest that the Hoffman coefficient, which measures the similarity among industrial structures of different regions, is as high as 0.98 among China's provinces,[31] a sign of virtually zero specialty. This regional tendency to oppose horizontal linkages is primarily aimed at protecting the administrative leadership but has to be carried out by competing control over resource allocation. This drive for firmer control over resources stands in stark contrast to the traditional understanding of leadership, which is supposedly indifferent to material goods. Such competition likewise makes the center as well as the regions appear egotistical.

To a certain extent, administrative regionalism recognizes the notion of opportunity cost, only differently. For provincial leadership, it is important that the pursuit of horizontal linkages does not harm control over the province. The major concern is to keep resources inside the province. Gain in other provinces would almost automatically appear as loss in one's own. While the aforementioned economic zoning adopts a comprehensive viewpoint to measure the economic efficiency of the entire country, regionalism adopts a provincial view to measure the loss of economic resources in a particular region. Regionalism thus becomes a barrier to economic zoning based upon specialty. Nevertheless, both perspectives must measure how well or where resources are allocated and hence signal the change of political logic in China. Public concern before reform was mainly for the image of the regime, whereas during reform it has become the ability to control resources.

The same can be said about the mind-set of planners working for ministerial departments (i.e., *tiaotiao*). The debate over the nature of reform as capitalist or socialist precisely reflects the tenacity of the planning system within each ministerial organization. Technocrats working for planning boards at the center are basically cynical about reform, for it simply allows enterprises too much leeway in allocating resources, hurting planning, the essential characteristic of socialism. Just as regional leaders strive to maintain control over resources, ministerial technocrats also display the proclivity toward firmer control. The cultural dilemma of the planners is identical with that of the regional leaders: Each must jettison the traditional image of leadership as having no interest in material goods. If central planners must control resources to prove the integrity of the planning system and regional leaders must control resources to prove the integrity of provincial leadership, the planning system and the provincial leadership are no longer neutral arbitrators in the competition for larger shares under heaven.

The last standpoint of resource allocation deals with the tug-of-war between planners and state-owned enterprises. An especially sensitive feud is over taxation and profit-sharing mechanisms. The bargaining over tax rates and the amount of profit apportioned to enterprises concerns the tradeoff between accumulation and consumption. The Soviet model extracted all profits earned by enterprises and reallocated them according to an investment priority determined by the center. As reform in China continues, different voices are beginning to be heard. The noted economist Tong Dalin warns against the danger of "drawing a parallel between consumption and squandering" and urges the planner to explore "the inner drive" for productive forces in consumption. He cautions his readers that consumption and accumulation have a "proportional relationship" and that consumption should be "the foundation and stepping stone of economic planning." So the key to reform is to enrich enterprise workers.[32]

Accordingly, economic development and the search for equality are no longer equivalent goals of socialism. Economic development is defined in terms of the pursuit of material interests. This is actually acceptable in the sense that China's political tradition indeed requires the regime to enrich the commoners. However, socialist ideology continues as the state ideology. This fact alone would require the government to control at least a certain amount of resources in order to claim that the means of production are still in the hands of the public. The contradiction between the ideological need to possess resources and the economic need for their release reveals the predicament of the regime: It must do both in order to survive.

The controversy over tax rates and profit-sharing ratios illustrates this predicament. Enterprises in China have invariably adopted generous bonus policies. When enterprises are allowed a greater share of profit, the implication is obvious: an increasing demand for consumer goods and increased inflationary surges through the market. The center therefore struggles to walk a tightrope of allowing a higher rate of sharing and stipulating that enterprises must reinvest a definite proportion of profits before making deposits in the bonus account. The predicament lies in the regime's embarrassing dispute with enterprises over the details of what enterprises should do with their profits. Since enterprises clearly represent the material interests of their workers, this constant dispute inevitably suggests a departmentalist tendency on all sides, a tendency the regime has denounced since its first days in power.

Although this same sort of dispute existed before the initiation of reform, the fight over resources is now an open secret as enterprises support the worker against the planner. The process is further exacerbated by the fact that reform was initiated virtually overnight without clear enunciation of the rules of the game. In 1983 the planner tried to substitute a new taxation system for the original profit-sharing system governing regime-enterprise relations. The resulting dispute over how to measure the tax base, however, continues to rock the increasingly shaky cooperation between state and enterprise during the course of reform. The current system is designed to separate profit from tax. On the one hand, the state ideally has a fixed share of profit since the state is the investor. The enterprise, on the other hand, must pay taxes for its portion of shared profits. Nonetheless, prolonged negotiation is unavoidable, particularly between the planner and the most profitable enterprises.[33]

Theoretically, enterprises belong to the proletarian class and are not endowed with the right to share profit. The original rationale for substituting a taxation system for the state monopoly was to enliven enterprises' consciousness of cost through a profit-sharing arrangement, ergo a portion of state profit is treated as enterprise profit. As long as enterprises are owned by the state, this arrangement should be acceptable even to hardline conservatives. The reformist economist Yue Fubing, though, remains bitter on this point. He holds that the state, as shareholder, and enterprise, as manager, are equals in this one-on-one interaction. The means by which the new taxation system allows the shareholder to tax the manager is an unheard-of practice that demotes the latter to the role of junior partner. Yue insists that the entire rationale behind reform is to liberate enterprises from the planning system, whereas the new taxation system gives the planner the right to interfere in the enterprise's internal management. Additionally, the goal of reform is to separate politics from economics, yet the new system combines the two more closely.[34]

Indeed, decentralization through profit sharing aims at providing enterprises with material incentives. The planner nonetheless has to maintain financial leverage in order to remain the sole critical allocator. The state must decentralize the financial system in order to uncover ulterior costs incurred in inefficient enterprises. The state cannot trust enterprises totally, though, and it chooses to rely on financial instruments like profit sharing and taxation. Profit sharing alone cannot guarantee the state the ability to influence enterprises, for hard bargaining goes on continuously at all levels. Taxation, the rate of which is universally determined and applied, was once thought of as a cure for the process of endless bargaining. But experience shows that the taxation system continues to be undermined by detailed bargaining. Enterprises fight to get tax breaks and privileges and use auditing tricks to help shrink the tax base.

Over the long run, the trend toward more material-based economics is undeniable. Planners, sectoral managers, regional leaders, enterprises, and even individuals can now communicate with one another using one criterion, which is cost related and spiritually irrelevant. The integrity of the central planning system must be evaluated by lower economic units according to the cost effect on their slice of the economic pie. The state cannot simply boost socialism while promoting a divergent economic goal and expect to be obeyed. The state must appear as interested pursuer, as other economic units come to regard the state as precisely another competitor. Although each unit has its own distinctive concerns, each is cost-conscious. The state worries about the size of the national economic pie; the provinces, their provincial economic pies; and enterprises, their own economic pies. The notion of opportunity cost is splitting the reliance on state collectivism.

## CONCLUSION

The recurring policy debate since the late 1980s over the Three Gorges Dam project has reflected the rising concern over opportunity cost. The debate crested in 1992 during the annual meeting of the Political Consultation Conference and the National People's Congress, where opposing sides listed the pros and cons of the project. The supporters of the project estimate lost opportunity benefits in terms of potential electricity the dam could provide if the project is scuttled or even delayed. Their opponents question the rationality of the project by estimating how much funding the project could achieve elsewhere and how much ecological damage the project is expected to cause. To my knowledge the dam project is the first time in China's history that a policy issue has been openly debated in terms of cost and benefit. This approach of arguing policy should be taken as an indicator of a changing style of politics.

Opportunity cost is a natural concept that is not exclusively an analytical tool of professional economists. Selling a policy by comparing potential benefit and opportunity cost, though, is certainly not the style of the traditional regime. The agricultural cooperative movement in the early 1950s was opposed by Deng Zihui and his colleagues precisely for its unnoted but potentially significant opportunity cost. It was nonetheless the failure of the Great Leap Forward that formally introduced the notion of proportionate development to China's public policy. The contemporary obsession with development that was ushered in with the demise of the Cultural Revolution has opened the door to all kinds of cost-related arguments in public forums. That the notion of opportunity cost becomes a legitimate point in debate constrains the regime from an overdependence on moral incentives for resource mobilization. Even spiritual goals would have to pass the test of cost examination. Within this context, socialism in China can survive only if it also acquires some sort of mundane function that either generates material gain or curtails cost for the people.

# 3

# MARKET SOCIALISM:
# MACROECONOMICS WITH CONSCIENCE

Throughout China's economic history the central government has invariably played a leading role. Modern scholarship on Chinese economic history, though, has yet to discover a common set of macroeconomic policy instruments that previous dynasties applied consistently; early macroeconomic theory in China was rudimentary at best. Nonetheless, it is the consensus that the government had significant influence over the course of development (or stagnation, for that matter).

Past governments were highly concerned with the availability of productive factors and circulation of goods, the most critical productive factors being land and labor. Dynastic rulers regularly relied on the labor force of the commoners for public construction as well as services for the emperor. In certain periods commoners were permitted to substitute taxes for labor obligations, as such obligations were generally more despised and feared than taxes. Historical texts note a wide variety of methods for evading labor requirements. Land policy, in contrast, impacted upon the peasants' work incentives in the field and hence reflected upon government revenue, leading to constant struggle among dynastic officials over strategy in this arena. This rise and fall of dynasties often reflected the change or continuity of certain land policies. Fundamentally, land policy was aimed at preventing mergers in order to guarantee that the peasantry had access to land and would yield ample revenue. Classic wisdom held that land policy was the key to political stability and economic prosperity.

Concerning the circulation of goods (i.e., commerce), dynastic rulers invariably adopted a form of the ruler's economy (which was a loose version of command economy).[1] Nationalized commerce was considered the solution to mercantile exploitation of the peasant class. The scope of nationalization included salt, iron, alcohol, natural resources (mountains and rivers), and so on, which, in conjunction with labor obligations, were crucial factors in determining the rate of accumulation. Dynastic courts resorted at times to printing money for short-term financial crises; at other times they went as far as collecting taxes on razors (for shaving men's heads) to catch those who sought to avoid labor obligations by taking refuge in the monasteries.

Another popular economic tool of dynastic rulers was the establishment of commodities banks, especially food banks. Almost all dynasties had some sort of food bank in order to control food prices by selling in times of scarcity and buying during times of overproduction. In reality, however, food banks never really worked as expected because of poor system design and corruption. Such problems were particularly acute considering the standard practice of regional nobles to undermine and benefit from the court's taxation in kind, and landlords and merchants who made economically detrimental land purchases. The competition between regions and center was equally acute as each dynasty entered its inevitable phase of decline.

The court itself spent chiefly on activities that did little to stimulate economic accumulation: housing and feeding troops and bloated staffs, building city walls, upgrading imperial residences, traveling, and recreation. Midlevel and local officials took advantage of this loosely structured command system to squeeze resources from below and keep them from above. Their enrichment was more a result of manipulation than of market operation. Most unfortunate to the development of capitalism was that these local forces rarely engaged in economic activities outside the scope of land purchases. The rise and scope of commerce were determined by the limited capacity of local banking and confined to sectors such as rice and fabric; profits were generally invested in land.[2]

The communist regime did not transform the traditional economic style when it first came to power. The new government emerged from a split political system composed of local strongmen. Economic control through command was reinstalled gradually as the regime consolidated its political power. In one sense, however, the communist regime was historically innovative in that it was highly concerned with capital accumulation. This emphasis on economic growth did not negate egalitarian concerns but stimulated dispute as to whether central or local authorities were more appropriate as the locus for development initiative. The decentralizing pull was already articulated during the Great Leap Forward and the Cultural Revolution. After a short interlude, reform economists began publicly to encourage economic actors at lower echelons to take the initiative. In the following section I discuss whether the deeply rooted philosophy of the ruler's economy has undergone irrevocable reformation.[3]

## MACROECONOMICS UNDER MARKET SOCIALISM

The aggressive planners of China's command economy extracted resources directly from the agricultural sectors and redistributed them to support industrialization. Extraction took three forms. First, the planners arbitrarily kept agricultural prices low and prices for manufactured goods and machinery high, and this price differential promoted capital accumulation in industry. This practice is untraditional to a limited degree since the past rationale for the existence of food banks was to prevent food prices from dropping too low. Nonetheless, the bank also had the traditional function of thwarting inflation and dissuading commercial interests from profiteering from food exchanges. Dynastic rulers must have considered profiting from such market manipulation as did their communist successors, only not for purposes of industrialization.

Second, the planners requested taxes in kind, including both foodstuffs and raw materials for light industry. Third, the planners regularly employed agrarian labor forces to build dams and roads and engage in small-scale, labor-intensive workshops. These two latter forms of extraction are typical. Like their dynastic predecessors, the communists intended to regulate the use of land and labor, but in this case the regime was able to achieve more because of its enlarged and effective political authority. In the cities the planners directly manipulated worker wages. Since most workers had a peasant background, the wage control was a kind of extraction (though to a lesser degree) of agrarian resources. In short, the scope, the willingness, and the capacity of the economic planners dramatically superseded that of the dynastic courts. The continuity lies in the regime's gesture of seeming selflessness in caring for public welfare and suppressing private commercial activity.

At some point in the 1980s, the communist regime formulated a theory of the commodity economy in the belief that the command economy was incapable of promoting productive forces. The continued use of the traditional command economy in its first few decades enabled the regime to translate its epochal apprehension for development into real policy action, yet ironically exposed inherent weaknesses. Decentralization was first tried in the 1950s, when it appeared that the production of raw materials had approached a bottleneck. Decentralization, though, is not the same as using the market. The experience of the Great Leap Forward suggests that decentralization can lead to highly centralized local plan centers. The issue in decentralization is therefore not how efficiency is improved but how the regime could deliberately encourage decentralization without jeopardizing its political control.

Reform in the 1980s triggered the use of the market to cure efficiency problems caused by overcentralization in each region. In this way the ability to regulate from the center has been further weakened. This is completely at odds with traditional practice, since the dynastic courts never surrendered economic command without having first lost political control to regional strongmen; the regime today remains the only supreme political authority as the legitimacy of the command economy gradually diminishes.

One must note the possible political effects here. In an extreme case if the market alone could provide for the public welfare as the regime originally intended, then it would no longer matter how the regime chose to present itself to the public, for the intention of the regime would no longer be germane to the improvement of public welfare—the integrity of the regime would be irrelevant.

Without being politically subdued, the regime takes voluntary action in decentralizing financial power and, later, letting market pressure reflect the change of political economic logic. Although decentralization and deregulation have so far been limited to the economic arena, it is precisely this separation of economics from politics that deserves attention, for the regime has moved beyond the constraints of millennia of economic thought as a newly invoked socialist theory of the command economy revokes the tenets of that system. As the regime constructs a theory of decentralization and relinquishment (*fangquan rangli*) to oppose the planner's sovereignty, it permits the separation of economics from politics.

*Fangquan rangli* has been the synoptic slogan for socialist macroeconomics since the 1980s. *Fangquan* refers to financial decentralization and *rangli* the actual receipt of profits by people. A close examination of so-called socialist macroeconomics, though, reveals ubiquitous parallels to neoclassical economics in the West. An economics textbook published by the CCP Central Party School (Zhonggong zhongyang dangxiao) details at least four necessary foundations.[4] First, major efforts must be made to achieve equilibrium between aggregate demand and supply, taking into account such issues as inflation, sectoral balance, and balance of foreign exchange. Second, the government should promote the development of productive forces in society and enable the national economy to grow steadily. Third, the government should attempt to improve economic efficiency. Finally, the government should make sure people can gradually raise their standards of material life.

This material life includes consumptive capability as well as the basic necessities of food, clothing, shelter, and transportation. There is also a cultural aspect to material life: education, recreation, and sanitation. Social security is also considered a key element that is measured by indicators such as rate of employment and life expectancy.[5] In terms of goals these concepts are certainly not unique to socialist or command economies.

A relatively effective way to achieve equilibrium is to allow the market to operate on its own; economic reform must therefore begin by restricting the planning system. The new economic philosophy is so entirely different from that of the command economy that only "in a specifically determined period should the state maintain direct control over a small number of priority projects, specialized industries, and precious but scarce goods."[6] The new philosophy holds that the guidance authorities provide should be just that: unbinding suggestions. Regulation by the planners should accordingly be executed indirectly through managing economic levers well known in the West, such as the discount rate, tax rates, interest rates, and budgeting.

Even these levers must be controlled by decentralized economic units. It is argued that the best guarantee of scientific macroeconomic management is democratization of policymaking, for "centralized policymaking is often subject to the detrimental intrusion of individual planners' prejudices."[7] In practice democratization refers to the notion of separation of management from ownership. The rationale of democratization is the belief that the enterprise knows the market best and should be encouraged to adjust its investment policy accordingly, so that national resource allocation at the macroeconomic level may satisfy the requirements of efficiency. To take the argument one step further, democratization in its ultimate form would mean consumer sovereignty:

> We cannot help but make that market choice made by consumers an increasingly important constraining factor in resource allocation. In a sense, under the conditions of the commodity economy, the sum of market choices consumers make reflects the movement of societal demand that ultimately prescribes the direction of movement in national resource allocation. Although the degree to which consumption demand guides resource allocation varies with periods and types of state, the general requirement that resource allocation must comply with consumer choice is irrefutable. Therefore, research on the relation between resource allocation and the economic system under socialism must embark upon the search for consumers' behavioral patterns in the socialist context. Consumers' choices define the goal of resource allocation. . . . This way, resource allocation effectively accommodates consumers' choices.[8]

In order to empower enterprises to respond flexibly to the market, the state also needs to enable them not only to use resources based upon their own market judgment but also to generate enough resources to enable them to grab market opportunities. This requires a looser financial policy whereby enterprises can acquire easier credit from banks. In fact, up until 1984, the four specialized banking systems had generated credits three times that of the central bank.[9] Later policy concerns arose on suspicions that the specialized banking systems were subject to administrative interference by their superiors and were using newly acquired permission to grant credit to provide improperly approved loans to well-connected enterprises. One solution is to have banks accountable for their own profits and losses, thus forcing them to be cautious in their selection of patrons. In reality, establishing such accountability remains difficult after decades of extreme centralization. Political interference in financial affairs was standard practice long before these specialized banks were opened under reform.

As a result, abuse of credit sparked serious inflationary pressures on several occasions in the 1980s.

One easy answer lies in the liberation of interest policies. Scholars criticize past interest controls as consistently "rigid" and "highly centralized." This deprived the planners of the freedom to implement a stable monetary policy. Reform requires a floating rate. Theorists contend that a floating interest rate policy would serve to absorb funds in the private sector and compel enterprises to think twice before using their connections with banks to rescue money-losing businesses. The catchwords they would suggest are self-regulation (*ziwo jingying*) and self-renovation (*ziwo gaizao*).[10]

Closely associated with *fangquan* of the banking system is the theory of regionalism. Regional economic development under the socialist command economy was formerly subject to two forms of constraint. One constraint originates in the regional strategic preoccupation with autarky over specialization. The other constraint is related to a sectoral strategic concern that reflects the departmentalist interests of each state ministry. The former constraint appears to be a natural tendency that has survived, even flourished, across dynasties and regimes. The communists subdued regionalism for a brief period only to have it explode during the course of the Great Leap Forward. The latter constraint is said to be rational, as China lacks economic managers and has therefore had to depend on a small number of technocrats to lead China out of its underdevelopment.[11]

Under reform, economists maintain that regionalism should be recognized to the extent that regional specialization utilizes regional strengths. Obviously, local elites are in a better position than the central planner to realize regional strengths. The central planner apparently appreciates this approach and establishes new localized plan centers that belong to both the sectoral/ministerial plan system and the regional/provincial plan system. The new plan centers are primarily cities; some are mammoth enterprises. They currently receive planned materials directly from the central plan without going through regional or sectoral planning boards. On the contrary, it is required, at least theoretically, that traditional planning boards provide assistance to these new plan centers in order to help them develop independently.

Specialization is often a critical element in realizing market efficiency. The communist regime fully utilized its power as a central planner first to enforce decentralization and then to move beyond decentralization in search of specialization. The regime henceforth constricts its own capability, symbolized by sectoral technocracy, in favor of a locally based, elite-oriented development route. Likewise, the central bank establishes branches wherever there is a local plan center just to guarantee that the new plan center is equipped with sufficient financial instruments to initiate plans, lead industry, and construct supporting facilities and other basic infrastructure. The thinking behind such economic philosophy is akin to that which prompted the establishment of an economic axis in some Latin American countries.[12]

Apparently, the Chinese state has no intention of giving up its socialist commitment to both development and egalitarianism. The aforementioned goal of macroeconomic management mentions the material life of people. Would *fangquan rangli*, which encourages decentralization and regional specialization and recognizes consumer and enterprise sovereignty, lead to results in direct opposition to the overall, long-term goal of equilibrium, growth, and equality? More importantly, why would low-level economic units regard the regime as a relevant actor in the market?

## POLITICAL IMPLICATIONS OF *FANGQUAN RANGLI*

China's guiding economic principle during reform has been that the state regulates the market and the market directs enterprises. In other words, the levers available to the state in the market should be economic and indirect. This would make China appear capitalistic, and, in fact, Deng Xiaoping's public plea in 1992 boldly to adopt capitalist measures has inspired reform-oriented officials and scholars to proclaim a more liberal interpretation of socialism. In this regard socialism can no longer be indicated by economic measurements and has to be identified somewhere else—for example, by the intention of its economic actors. The communist regime is fully aware of the importance of rectifying people's preferences and intentions as a unique way of preserving socialism.

Intention produces goals. Theoretically speaking, capitalist states are run by the bourgeoisie, and their market operation must, by definition, serve bourgeois interests. In socialist China, in contrast, economic regulation in the name of all laborers cannot possibly be aimed at anything other than public welfare, as China's bourgeoisie perished decades ago. In practice, though, intention may hardly matter. Since the price of a product is largely determined by the market, laborers must abide by the iron law of prices. They cannot satisfy their preferences simply by arbitrarily setting prices low. In actuality, they would instead have to pay *more* to reveal their preferences and, as a rule, restrain their preferences as prices climb.[13] The intentions of economic actors before entering the market and policy goals that meet such intentions are therefore not pertinent to market operation.

Nonetheless, socialist producers must logically differ from bourgeois producers. If one believes that the latter breed of entrepreneurs is constantly conscious of the need to accumulate capital and this affects their market behavior, those with socialist goals should also be able to do the same, simply with opposing preferences. A socialist state may actually satisfy its preferences better than a bourgeois government, which has access to materials and profits only through the market, because the socialist state itself is both economic manager and owner of raw materials. Exactly because no bourgeoisie controls the means of production, the socialist state is constantly able to bear in mind its most important mission of reconciling individual and collective interests and short-term and long-term causes. It is in charge of the overall direction of state development:

> [The state] prescribes the guiding strategy, principle, and policy of economic and social development; systematically executes specific economic and social goals of enriching resources, technology, industries, and knowledge; organizes and accommodates endogenous and exogenous needs of regions, sectors, and enterprises to grow and cooperate; reconciles interest relationships among the state, enterprise, and individual; provides overheads of information, consultation, technology exploration, education and training, social security, etc.; stipulates, supervises, and executes economic laws and regulations; and establishes fundamental economic order.[14]

At first sight such remarks may appear to be from one of East Asia's other developing capitalist-oriented states. One might wonder if China's socialism is simply more Asian than socialist. Thanks to public ownership of the major means of production, though, the Chinese socialist state may actually get involved in economics to a much greater extent than other Asian states. At least it is assumed natural for the state to think so, as Jiang Zeming once wanted the state to constrict investment in local capital; to control consumptive pressures; to perform well its tasks of inspection of tax records, financing, pricing, and crediting; to secure the supply of necessities; to form self-regulative mechanisms inside each enterprise; to actively carry out pioneering housing reform; to create conditions favorable for economic management and regulations; and to intensify the "double-growth, double-savings" campaign.[15]

The aggressiveness of the planners does not promise that economic actors in society will comply, since planners would also like to protect the integrity and independence of a market in which a plan has no legitimate role. Advanced economic scholarship thus focuses its attention on the socialist conscience as well. The rationale of plan management shifts noticeably. Some point out that a plan should impact not by legally, administratively, and politically restraining economic actors' market behavior but by molding their preferences and values. There are two approaches to successful preference management. First, planners give up the traditional practice of directly issuing plan commands to the enterprise. Instead, they simply propose options. The plan is therefore a "soft plan" and budgeting therein is "soft budgeting." Theoretically, it is up to the enterprise to decide to what extent it will follow the proposal thus delivered. Second, the Communist Party empowers the enterprise to instill a sense of socialist duty in the laborer. Enterprises acquire their mandate to persuade workers to engage in projects that best satisfy long-term collective interests.

Soft planning is nonetheless a kind of planning and inconsistent with the logic of the market. Chinese scholars hence struggle to distinguish between a soft plan and the traditional hard plan. They say a soft plan provides direction and is "the prime foundation of healthy national economic development."[16] More importantly, its major contents comprise "proposals that forecast, refer, and guide according to the laws of commodity exchange and price." A soft plan's function, therefore, is to assist in "reconciling the activities of individual economic actors with the overall bearing of national plans by persuading and influencing those economic actors to hedge against market uncertainties."[17]

The intriguing aspect of soft planning is precisely its noncoercive nature. The enterprise receiving a soft plan is encouraged to revise the plan according to market information it collects in the process of executing the plan. In other words, a plan tells what the planners think feasible and agreeable. The enterprise cooperates because the planners have a grasp of the overall economic picture and supposedly know more about market trends, based upon their capacity for information collection. Ideally, following the soft plan gives the enterprise an edge in the marketplace since individual enterprises do not usually have the ability to collect, systematize, and interpret broadly scattered market information.

Before a plan is assigned and all available tax privileges are legalized, the planners and the enterprise must negotiate. This tedious process, however, may enhance the socialist conscience of the enterprise as it strives to internalize the plan's rationale. Of greatest importance is the recognition that planners may make mistakes, or at least the market trends they spot may shift. Planners thus depend on the enterprise to take the pulse of the market by generating information through revisions to the original plan. The soft plan raises the annual objectives of the enterprise, and the enterprise revises such goals via implementation. The soft plan is soft because planners realize there is an objective limit to knowledge and they cannot possibly have sovereignty in the market as traditionally assumed but must rely on the enterprise to detect current market trends. While each individual enterprise is concerned only with its own profits and revising the part of the soft plan related to its own production lines, planners have the advantage of a comprehensive communication network in their soft plan system.

Whether or not the enterprise is obliged to negotiate with the planners if the enterprise has access to market information and, more importantly, resources seems not to be exclusively an economic or even legal issue.

Preference management, therefore, cannot simply go through the soft planning system alone but must be conducted on the condition that the soft plan is politically irresistible. Planners are legitimate, though indirect, actors in the market because they cannot be exploiters. Just imagine what pretexts an enterprise could enlist to justify its rejection of a plan without incurring a negative image.

To preserve socialism, planners must enhance the socialist conscience and guarantee that the enterprise is endowed with a socialist worldview. For this purpose, there must be mechanisms that serve to bring together the concepts of interest as held by the state, the enterprise, and its laborers. In the past this was the exclusive domain of the party leadership. The state has recently endeavored to consolidate the convergence of all these perceptions as the market becomes more germane to decisionmaking in the enterprise and as the party's role of indoctrinator fades. The idea is to have the enterprise internalize the state's concept of interest. The enterprise is expected to bear in mind the principles of socialism while making investment and bonus decisions. This is what Chinese scholars repeatedly cite as the principle of self-consciousness (*zijue yuanze*).

Several methods are employed to rectify *zijue yuanze*. First, the plan must be written against market information, and there should be no predetermined time for reaching the final stage of communism. There is therefore no need for a business to demonstrate dedication to communism by rapid advancement in that direction. That the planners are not exploiters is alone considered sufficient proof of the strength of socialism in China. Nowadays neither economic backwardness nor temporarily sluggish growth can be used to insinuate the failure of socialism. With this understood, planners can proceed to collect as much information as possible to assist in objective economic forecasting. Ostentatious reports of achievement become unnecessary to establish the legitimacy of an enterprise.

For this reason, factual statistics are now considered one of the most important foundations of policy analysis. The National Bureau of Statistics and its regional divisions have participated in UN statistical systems that enable planners to analyze the vicissitudes of consumption and investment throughout banks' accounts. China has also taken advantage of modern satellite facilities to link with numerous international science and technology information centers.[18] These statistics are the sum total of individual economic decisions taken in the market. As long as planners faithfully reflect the market situation, their proposals to enterprises will likely contribute to the enterprises' capacity for profit. In actuality, enterprises and consumers in the market ultimately determine the contents of the plan. Planners perform the role of inductive media.

Second, the state can make direct investment from the center. Each sizable investment that a state-owned enterprise makes in a locality spontaneously captures local attention. As local enterprises respond and start peripheral supporting industries, the state investment multiplies its economic effects. State investment of this magnitude is referred to as dragonhead (*longtou*) investment, which economists believe can stimulate local investors to more effectively "use their natural environment self-consciously and in an orderly fashion."[19] Also, the state owns mineral resources and is able to influence investment decisions of collective enterprises. Collective, private, and individual enterprises generally maintain contractual relations with state-owned enterprises. This guarantees that as long as general managers at state enterprises maintain a socialist conscience, actions taken by other enterprises cannot conceivably stray too far away from the socialist track.[20] The drawback, then, is that these market-oriented extrastate enterprises may not achieve socialist consciousness simultaneously.

Third, there are numerous legislative, judicial, and administrative channels through which planners can straightforwardly engage in preference management. Planners may make clear their own preferences and simply direct subordinate enterprises to enforce them. This approach violates the integrity of the market and so should not be employed regularly. The availability of these channels, though, is "the essential hallmark of the socialist market as opposed to the capitalist market."[21] In short, the need to enliven enterprises does not justify complete freedom. Because enterprises are rarely penalized for bad management by being declared insolvent, planners must remain in ultimate charge lest enterprises wastefully abuse the soft budgeting system.

Administrative interference by the state should be considered an act to rescue enterprises from illegal practices under general market failure, a condition that remains epidemic in most state-run enterprises. Among these practices are the often-cited problems of overinvestment, investment overlap, generous bonus policies toward money-losing enterprises, and so on. The goal of such interference should be to restore market order, yet the difficulties in attaining such a goal are monumental.[22] There is no guarantee, for example, that the state manager would respect the market any more than would the enterprise manager. Likewise, administrative interference defeats the purpose of making enterprise managers conscious of the market, though they may bitterly appreciate the existence of the omniscient socialist planner. Finally, interference of this sort stirs up grievances among labor and is harmful to consolidation of regime legitimacy in the long run.

The most effective although not necessarily most economically efficient instrument to rectify *zijue yuanze* is leadership provided through the party network in each enterprise. Successful political rectification not only contributes to the socialist conscience of enterprise workers but may also enhance the profitability of the enterprise through tax breaks and the training of market-oriented managers. Obviously, the Communist Party holds the sole legitimate claim to being the supreme educator in today's China, granted the general trend of moral decline in that society. Since the first introduction of reform, the party's political leadership in the market has become subtle and intriguing:

> Generally speaking, the party is the tool of ruling. However, only at the top level does this general rule completely show. Economic entities like enterprises do not perform the general political function of the state machinery, so the party organization in the enterprise cannot be analogous to party committees in the central and local governments, nor can their influence be comparable to each other. In the enterprises it is the general manager who is in charge. He cannot possibly leave party leadership behind, though. It does not matter how the general manager is selected in the enterprise; he will have to execute the state plan and state laws, orders, and regulations. . . . All this suggests that the general manager, totally responsible for business management and sometimes not even a party member, cannot substitute for the leadership the party provides for the enterprise. What has changed is the style and content of that leadership.[23]

The most important task for party organs within enterprises today is to produce good party workers to serve as models in factories. They must also work on the thought and ideology of enterprise cadres and workers. These party members remind the enterprise that state regulations should be faithfully observed. Their task is "difficult but crucial."[24]

Although planners remain powerful actors in the market, their interference presumably requires economic justification under reform. The chief characters in the realm of central planning have gone through a stark transformation. The plan must represent more than a show of planner sovereignty and the assignment given the enterprise through bargaining. The soft planning system is the combination of material incentives (tax privileges), coercion (administrative interference), and persuasion (party leadership), which is aimed at helping the enterprise internalize the plan and perpetuate its socialist conscience.

For thousands of years, Chinese regimes feigned no conflict of interest with the people in order to justify their command economy (or the ruler's economy). They traditionally suppressed commercial interests and dreaded market calculation; it would only be natural for reform in Communist China to begin to depart from this practice. The regime hesitates in the face of the market, preferring the enterprise to handle the market on its own. Past regimes pretended economic selflessness to enforce the ruler's economy; today's regime prepares to forgo its total command while preserving its spiritual pretension. The task that remains is to prove that political leadership and economic command can be separated yet remain mutually congruent.

## IRREVOCABLE *FANGQUAN RANGLI*

*Fangquan rangli* contributed to the rise of regionalism in the late 1980s, which critics call the feudal lord economy (*zhuhou jingji*). They claim that such regionalism splits the national economy just as princes over 2,000 years ago split the feudal Zhou dynasty. Feudalism was characterized by geographical demarcation within a nation, each bestowed to a prince. Feudal lord economy refers to local elites' utilizing administrative barriers to protect the tax base of their respective regions. These administrative barriers prevent economic actors from purchasing goods outside their own provinces, so that all possible profits generated in the area remain in the area. Economists acknowledge that the feudal lord economy would help capital accumulation within the region over the short run but would eventually become "detrimental to regional development," for it "blocks the formation of a nationwide market" and thus limits the potential for growth in all regions.[25]

One solution is to establish new, lower-level plan centers, primarily in municipalities. It is predicted that these new plan centers would cut across traditional administrative demarcations. Once they receive independent assignments from the central planner and acquire stable institutional accesses to resources, rational enterprises would pursue new connections with these centers, and traditional regionalism would thus be rendered meaningless.[26] Others are uneasy about the possibility of the central planner's losing control over these new municipal centers, which it is claimed will become new regional blocs to thwart national economic integration.[27] Scholars may disagree on some details, but most concur that problems arise from regionalism, be it provincial or municipal. One group of economists aims to thwart partial regionalism by encouraging comprehensive regionalism, believing it would compel regions to realize the merits of integration:

> For a while, the boundaries between central and local government were obscure. The central government is reluctant to acknowledge that localities have relatively independent interests. This leads to the oblivion of provincial economic entities. The center grabs everything and the localities follow heedlessly, creating colossal blindness and permanent imbalance in the evolution of local economic structures. Regional advantages are lost as a direct or indirect consequence. Henceforth, the local government must take over duty from the central government as director of local economic structural adjustment. This should precisely be the approach. Local governments can develop their own economic resources more efficiently, reduce past blindness, and avert massive periodical fluctuation and local economic imbalance.[28]

If the regime encourages localities to pursue purely economic interests in the name of government, though, it in fact violates the traditional expectation that the regime alone knows where the public interest lies. In fact, the creation of an office in charge of interprovincial commerce illustrates the Chinese socialist planner's lack of trust in local judgment.[29] Partial decentralization allows localities the opportunity to abuse the advantage thus gained in order to protect their myopic, departmentalist interests; thorough decentralization negates the leadership provided by the regime in Beijing. Decentralization therefore reflects the predicament the regime faces:

> Since reform started, all measures of reform have been introduced under the promotion and recognition of the center. However, decentralization produces numerous competitors against the center. Consequently, in the arena of economic competition there exists a never-ending battle between the local and central teams. The central team rarely triumphs as a competitor since it alone has to cope with all local teams. Although the central team sets the rules of the game and plays the role of referee, it always loses. The central team thus revises the rules and comes back again for another round of competition. This begets complaints from the local teams.[30]

The recommendation here is that the central team withdraw from competition and become a professional full-time referee, the thought being that the center can establish itself as an economic authority in such a manner. Only then can the regime keep the process of decentralization from "continuously splitting the government into parts."[31] This solution does not answer the fundamental question regarding the source of economic authority. Whoever is to protect the market must enjoy a powerful economic position. If the center withdraws from the market, how can it thus protect the market? Furthermore, without a position in the market, how can the center be influential in broadcasting socialist concerns?

*Fangquan rangli* is also reflected in the rise of rural enterprises. Villages and towns in which small enterprises have begun to thrive have a long way to go before they reach a level of prosperity—a full 70 percent of these locations are still below that level. This situation hinders the healthy development of the commodity economy, since products cannot possibly be sold outside the localities in which they are produced. This lack of integration among small localities means that rural enterprises invariably engage in investments that "blindly overlap" and are of poor quality. The goods they produce have no market in urban centers, and the local market is monopolized to such an extent that urban goods cannot penetrate. This conflict of interests between urban and rural enterprises has been described by many as "acute."[32]

Rural businesses consume resources that would supposedly be used more efficiently by urban industry. They dominate markets that would rightfully belong to urban products, yet they are small and flexible enough to deflect all possible retaliations by more advanced and larger enterprises. Regardless, the government supports the continued development of rural businesses and requests that party and government organizations at all levels "actively provide guidance and support with enthusiasm."[33] It appears clear that the damage these enterprises have inflicted on the hallmark of socialism, the state-owned enterprise, is intentionally tolerated. The government must encourage rural businesses in order to absorb surplus labor from the villages, preventing rural immigration to urban areas, a source of social instability. The political consequence is that the regime is unable to cope with the conflict of interests thus generated and so alternatively offer support to all sides.

The lifting of *fangquan rangli* to the status of official policy opens another Pandora's box, and decentralization takes on a momentum of its own. Despite the tremendous socialist legacy, the regime, together with local governments and enterprises, cries out for further decentralization as if the central plan were the source of all evil. The Great Leap Forward attempted to penetrate the countryside and recruit local leaders to serve central interests; ironically, local elites gained the opportunity to expand local interests and precipitate regionalism.[34] The stress on market mechanisms during reform furthers regionalism as *fangquan* empowers local governments and enterprises. While central planning was originally blamed in order to introduce market mechanisms, actual developments have made regionalism the biggest winner.

The government is unable to rein in financial power already decentralized for two reasons. First, the government does not have a theory that would convince central planners that returning a measure of power to the center would resolve the problem of economic stagnation, which plagued the nation before the 1980s. Second, local forces that enjoy access to resources are no longer totally dependent on the center; hence they are ready and willing to resist any attempts at recentralization. It is logical to assume that the use of market mechanisms does not have to harm the socialist character of the regime as long as the means of production are still theoretically in public hands. Regionalism, however, undeniably damages the sense of being socialist, since the pretension that the regime represents one proletarian class and symbolizes a harmony of interests within that class is shattered in the face of regionalism. *Fangquan rangli* is destructive exactly because this policy invites regionalism through the market.

## CONCLUSION

In Chinese history it was truly rare for a regime voluntarily to give up economic power when its hold on political power was firm. Economic levers were always considered essential to successful ruling not just because commoners responded to economic carrots and sticks but also because the regime did not want to encourage the pursuit of commercial interests in society. Since the regime did not pursue selfish interests, challengers who did so were forced initially to deny the regime's moral superiority, thus undermining the regime's political legitimacy. In the 1980s the communist regime voluntarily bestowed command of economic development to lower economic units and initiated an irrevocable process of decentralization.[35]

The current regime has struggled to avoid the political implications of reform, instead striving to separate economics from politics. This has been achieved through the assumption that labor with a socialist conscience could continue to honor the leadership provided by a Communist Party whose power has been seriously curtailed in a market now subject to the preferences of labor. The irony is twofold. The regime cannot be certain that labor indeed possesses this socialist conscience unless the workers are willing to forgo market interests in certain cases and support state plans at their own expense. This would pit the state against labor and offset any demonstration effect on laborers' socialist conscience that their sacrifice could provide. Second, the state still relies on economic strength to enforce its socialist plan, but this incurs certain responsibilities if the plan fails to boost development. Although responsibility for economic failure can now be transferred to economic actors who make initial economic decisions, this implies that the regime is unable to lead.

From the local perspective, the market has been introduced to resist state interference. This is not necessarily a negative mind-set as long as each locality does not also impose regional barriers to hinder economic integration. Macroeconomic textbooks constantly refer to self-consciousness to remind economic actors of the existence of the market as well as their socialist duty. But if it hopes to enhance a socialist conscience, the Communist Party never advocates the separation of party and enterprise even as it lauds the separation of politics and economics and government and enterprise. The crisis the Communist Party faces today is therefore much more complicated than the fight against capitalism that most commentators have assumed. It is a matter of regime legitimacy in terms of maintaining the relevance of the Communist Party in the arena of market socialism.

# 4

# ENTERPRISE SOCIALISM:
# THE PRODUCTION-FACTORS MARKET

In the modern age, exchanges of goods and services occur primarily on the price-based market, whether that market is competitive, monopolized, or well planned. Although producers in the market provide a wide range of commodities, in this chapter I focus on the supply of productive factors, including labor and capital goods, in socialist China. For the most part, *capital goods* refers to productive factors such as stock, machinery, steel, and raw materials. I define the supply of capital goods more broadly to include enterprise sale. Since the modern market creates demand for large supplies of goods, enterprises as producers inevitably command a considerable amount of capital, raw materials, and labor in order to respond to planners' demands. The rise of the state-owned enterprise on a national scale signifies China's departure from a traditional natural economy. However, the mode of macroeconomic management in China today continues to involve central command, a style of management that has been blamed for instigating nearly 1,000 years of stagnation.

There are nonetheless fundamental differences in the socialist and traditional modes of production. For one, Beijing's legitimacy lies in maintaining a socialist demeanor, which to a great extent involves the use of central planning. The socialist regime must *actively* intervene in economic affairs in order to fulfill its claim to being a proletarian government. In contrast, the ruler's economy in dynastic periods aimed essentially at restraining private entrepreneurship rather than expanding the government's own role in economic development. Another difference is that Beijing has the nontraditional task of promoting growth within the competitive, productive atmosphere of international development in general and East Asian development in particular. In comparison, dynastic regimes faced no external competition and were perfectly comfortable preaching the norm of harmony as opposed to competition in virtually all fields, including economic activity.

The command economy in socialist China thus requires conscious state effort to expand and utilize the economies of scale in modern productive processes. Since China subscribes to socialism, Beijing must also plan where and how all these huge suppliers acquire their raw materials. In the first few years of their experiment, leaders in Beijing were able to accumulate a fair amount of capital for public distribution, and some coastal cities indeed enjoyed planned stability in the supply of productive factors. Toward the end of the First Five-Year Plan, however, planners noted emerging bottlenecks in raw material supply. The original economic rationale of the Great Leap Forward was precisely to mobilize surplus labor through the growth of village factories in order to sustain overall industrial development.[1] This obviously deviated from the traditional style of command economy.

Traditional regimes always based their political legitimacy on an image of selflessness. At least two elements of that image concern us here.[2] First, there was formerly a comprehensive symbiosis of moral authority and political authority that in effect created a monolithic power. Second, this symbiosis of authority reproduced itself through compliant local leaders who helped cultivate the image of the central regime in exchange for support in maintaining credibility in their own localities.[3] Both elements are severely challenged in the current round of reform, especially in the planners' efforts to reconstruct the capital goods market. This is the focus of the present chapter.

It is not unlikely, however, that reform will bring the Japanese model of business relationships to mainland China. As Chinese state-owned enterprises begin to issue stock and as thousands of nonurban businesses begin to serve as contractors for state-owned enterprises, there is a considerable possibility that Chinese reform will mimic the Japanese developmental scheme. Nevertheless, a closer look at differences in cultural legacy may lead to the conclusion that China is not and will not become Japan.

Most discussion of Chinese economic reform with regard to the supply system neglects such cultural repercussions, for reform itself is fundamentally an endeavor to break the rigidity of the past state-monopolized supply system and to accommodate a much looser system of multiple channels. This recognition of multiple channels and market efficiency, however, boosts the status of large state-owned enterprises to such an extent that they themselves generate support and trust among their immediate local constituency, undercutting the central planner's credibility as supreme mover; the notion of authority then becomes complex and differentiated. Furthermore, deregulation in the capital goods market introduces the notion of a profit criterion into economic management, itself detrimental to the integrity of the monolithic normative system. Profitability now serves as an alternative, if not contending, standard. Finally, smaller village factories begin to rely on extraplan sources of capital goods supply. The scope of the planners' moral authority is thus no longer comprehensive or sufficient, even theoretically, in providing working incentives.

## THE CHINESE AND JAPANESE MODELS COMPARED

Literature on Japanese development points out that linkages between large and small Japanese enterprises carry a Confucian legacy.[4] Conventional wisdom cites the grouping of large enterprises into *zaibatsu* in Japan to illustrate the strength of the business conglomerate.[5] The uniqueness of Japanese practice is grounded in a kind of relationship that moves far beyond that portrayed in the written contract. The relationship involves moral and affective elements cemented in the genuine sense of mutual obligation. A contractual relationship is not evaluated purely in terms of profitability; on the contrary, loss of profit would not normally lead to the automatic termination of an existing relationship.[6] Relationships, once established, are in and of themselves values to be preserved. Essentially, the value of a stable contractual relationship involves long-term trust and mutual affinity.

A large Japanese enterprise must survive in two types of socioeconomic network. At the top it joins a financial group wherein each member holds stock in other concerns, likely to include banking, insurance, the automobile industry, department stores, transportation, and so on. Mutual share purchases thus guarantee market share for everyone within the group in the individual enterprise's respective industry even during periods of economic turndown. At the lower echelons, a large enterprise maintains complex relationships with contractors and subcontractors who provide necessary parts and supplies. Reciprocal interactions of this sort foster caring and loyalty. Many contracting firms are owned by retired former employees of the original enterprise who subcontract to their relatives and friends. When the market softens, an enterprise has little choice but to continue to rely on this web of contractual relationships.

Obviously, an enterprise that exists in such a complex socioeconomic network would not be able to base its sourcing and financial policy purely on market information. Each has to take into account the collective of which it is a part. In the long run, therefore, entrepreneurs in crisis would know that they could enlist assistance from a number of relations who would be willing to share the burden.[7] For this reason alone, each partner and member would certainly contribute to the growth of the collective with more care, and the products they provided one another would necessarily be of a better quality. This is productive efficiency as opposed to allocative efficiency, the latter form being what market economists are nearly exclusively accustomed to and obsessed with.

Some claim that the Japanese model reflects a Confucianism rooted in feudal legacy. Compared with European feudalism, Japanese feudalism was less concerned with class status than domanial membership. Historically, the Japanese peasantry was as much constrained by its loyalty to lords as its lower-class standing. In other words, vertical, sectarian relationships (e.g., domain, school, company) prevailed over horizontal, class relationships (e.g., landlord, feudal lord, capitalist).[8] Consequently, norms like loyalty, filial piety, and benevolence obscured others like class solidarity. Many Japanese observers believe that Japanese interenterprise structures mimic such traditional feudal structures. How different, however, is this unique version of Japanese feudalism from corporatism, which also stresses hierarchy within economic sectors as opposed to class solidarity?

Corporatist hierarchy is composed of members who belong to like industrial sectors, whereas Japanese financial groups involve members from differing sectors. Membership in a Japanese group is not determined by one's membership in a productive sector. As a matter of fact, companies belonging to the same productive sector—for example, Honda and Toyota in the automobile industry—are likely to be head-on competitors because of their association with different financial groups. As a result, contractors and subcontractors affiliated with these top competitors are presumably fierce rivals. Adversarial relationships may, however, change with the context. Japanese scholars caution foreign observers about the Japanese preoccupation with the "locus of battle."[9] In domestic politics, for example, the navy and army were rivals, yet in the international arena they were allies. The locus of the battlefield determines whether individuals, companies, or financial groups are competitors or allies.

Japanese business culture therefore reflects a historical legacy that differs from both the European style of feudalism and the Chinese brand of Confucianism. In Japan, unlike Europe, antagonistic class relations were not easily developed, thanks to the influence of Confucianism; unlike China, however, the object of loyalty in Japan was contingent on where the battlefield was, obviously owing to Japan's feudal tradition. In China, by contrast, the emperor was the exclusive recipient of loyalty. This last distinction between China and Japan may be one of the keys to understanding why the Chinese socialist emphasis on the collective and the Japanese feudal emphasis on the collective may create different results.

In Chinese tradition the emperor was the supreme ruler, in theory unrestrained by the lords and generals of his dynasty. Unlike the Chinese emperor, the Japanese emperor was a symbol of unity merely in theory but not in practice. The Japanese emperor could not use his own force to guarantee unity—this had to be achieved by the feudal lords and their subjects, each following his own set of norms of benevolence and loyalty. Whether the Japanese emperor could survive political turmoil depended on whether unity could be cemented at the lower levels. In contrast, this kind of unity between local leader and people would have been regarded as a serious threat to a Chinese emperor, for the emperor played the role of sole paramount arbitrator.

In addition, reorganization of economic and political forces in Japan affected only the eventual locus of battlefield without alluding to the emperor's symbolic status as the representative of Japan. In China reorganization of economic and political forces would inevitably suggest the decline of the supreme leader and insinuate his incapacity to reign over the Middle Kingdom. Consequently, competition in the political economic system would leave a Japanese emperor's symbolic status intact but undermine a Chinese regime's legitimacy.

Within the context of Chinese culture, current economic reform that emancipates thousands of state-owned enterprises and allows them to compete in the market has serious political repercussions. Many Beijing reformers even encourage these enterprises to establish business alliances and break the long-established plan system. In Japan realignment of business relationships can be psychologically shocking in the short run but nonetheless provides new niches for workers, contractors, and companies once a certain battle is over. In the long run a Japanese business may continue its semifeudal arrangement, as the Japanese are psychologically and culturally prepared to transfer loyalty as the context demands. In China realignment of business relationships would be psychologically shocking in the long run, as the planners' version of socialism is no longer the only legitimating instrument of national resource allocation. The Chinese will have to wonder if the socialist regime planners represent can continue singularly to determine the criteria for legitimacy. Financial groups help the Japanese to find modern substitutes for feudal domains. A similar type of grouping would destroy the Chinese sense of harmony symbolized by a single ruler.

## CHINESE REFORM IN THE
## PRODUCTION-FACTORS MARKET

One goal of the current round of reform in China is to provide business leaders with cost incentives so that enterprises will enhance efficiency in allocating resources. Cost incentives cannot be imposed unless there is a competitive capital goods market. In the early stages of reform, the responsibility system was introduced to establish profit incentives. The responsibility system was first applied to agricultural sectors, and the results were impressive. Under the system producers are allowed to own and sell goods as long as they satisfy a quota planners assign. While the responsibility system indeed provides sufficient profit incentive for some enterprises to boost efficiency, the system basically "responds only to the problem of hierarchical profit sharing between the state and the enterprises without alluding to capital goods reallocation, whereby enterprises expand and grow through horizontal connections" among enterprises, sectors, and areas.[10] In short, there is little cost incentive in the design of the responsibility system.

The problem is of course built into the planning system, in which enterprises are categorized into sectors (*tiaotiao*) according to central ministerial administration and blocs (*kuaikuai*) according to localities. Enterprises cannot formulate their own sourcing policy. *Tiaotiao* and *kuaikuai* superiors not only control the timing, price, and amount of raw materials each enterprise can acquire but also buyers and amount of goods for sale from each enterprise. The funding problem fares worse. The enterprise is supposed to turn in all profits that are theoretically a part of revenue. If the enterprise manages to save resources and somehow accumulates its own capital, the usual solution is to stock it away as inventory. At the end of 1988, for example, one-third of fixed capital in state-owned enterprises was idle.[11] Nevertheless, when particular enterprises expand, they rarely if ever utilize inventory accumulated elsewhere. An enterprise seeking growth usually receives permission and then raw materials from its own *tiao-kuai* source. This means that new investment by the state is made when a good deal of state-owned machinery lies unused elsewhere.

Planners have long noted this problem in the lack of flow of capital goods. It was not until the Thirteenth Party Congress in 1987 that Zhao Ziyang took the first step toward a solution. At that gathering the Chinese Communist Party decided to allow smaller state-owned enterprises to be sold to collective enterprises and individuals. In this decision the party made two clarifications:

> First, as to the flow of productive factors in the socialist commodity economy, one important mechanism is to facilitate the holistic flow of multiple productive factors. This way the internal structures of originally stocked productive factors can be maintained and be more efficiently utilized and can serve as the base for enhancing efficiency in the consumer goods market. Second, it is an official statement that the collectivity of productive factors—enterprises—is itself a commodity to be sold.[12]

Under the old system, a wasteful enterprise could be closed, repossessed, taken over, or transformed to perform new tasks. Whatever planners chose to do, they were obliged to find new homes for the workers, managers, and machinery, which was tantamount to "forcing together the rich and the poor" or simply to "having the poor live on the rich."[13] The thrust of reform is to make enterprises responsible for their own profits and losses, and one mechanism to accomplish this is to adopt the practice of bankruptcy. There is understandably significant resistance to the concept of bankruptcy; in addition to social cost, it is also argued that bankruptcy would make it nearly impossible to utilize a closed factory's productive capacity in a holistic way. The assembly line and machinery would be sold part by part, losing its structural strength and real value.[14] As an alternative, corporate purchase would be able to keep the original structures intact and avoid complex problems associated with relocating workers.

The difficulty with corporate purchase is that even if an enterprise could have its way with the planning system, why would it bother to purchase other money-losing corporations instead of making new investments from the state bank account? In practice, indeed, many corporate purchases were made because the purchasing enterprise was so directed by its superiors. If the purchase is not purely a market decision, the purchased enterprise is able to make a bargain through its own administrative superior. One problem here is the arrangement of cadres in the purchased enterprise: At what level will they serve the new boss? The second problem arises as administrative interference obscures the supposedly predominant position of the purchasing enterprise in the bargaining process—deals struck often fail to reflect the relative strength of the negotiating parties.[15]

The Baoding municipal authorities learned the role of administrative interference from experience. Selected to experiment with corporate purchase, the city found it was essential to broaden the perspective of enterprise managers in the city. The city played an active role not to hinder marketization but to promote market consciousness. The city government encouraged profitable enterprises to expand and promoted the idea of corporate purchase. The government arranged various tax breaks for corporate purchase while lowering support to money-losing enterprises. Additionally, the government considered idle machinery in the money-losing enterprises as a source of capital goods for other enterprises and accordingly rejected applications from profitable firms for further investment in machinery that would otherwise be available through corporate purchase. For profitable firms to expand their productive scale, the most immediate channel available was corporate purchase. Equally important was the government's continuous propaganda campaign aimed at preparing workers and managers for the coming age of corporate purchases.[16]

The Baoding experience suggests that profitable enterprises do not have a strong motivation to purchase money-losing concerns. This explains why the city had to interfere actively in the corporate market.[17] Most Baoding enterprises are nonetheless small compared to those that have practiced corporate purchase for years. For an experienced company like Capital Steel Corporation (CSC), resistance to corporate purchase comes primarily from the purchased enterprise and its administrative superiors in both *tiaotiao* and *kuaikuai* because their complex vested interests would be lost. The CSC has promoted the idea of corporate purchase without reservation for years and believes that corporate purchase is the quickest shortcut to move the Chinese economy from small-scale production to massive socialized production: "It is essential today to form a group of cross-area, cross-sector, and cross-border superenterprises with solid strength. They will be the support of the national economy and make it grow steadily. Based on the existing large enterprise structures, [China] can expedite . . . the formation of international superenterprises through corporate purchase in order to speed up the pace of modernization."[18]

In addition to being a conceptual breakthrough, the practice of corporate purchase requires an objective set of market standards with which to estimate the value of a target enterprise. As it stands today, a target enterprise is owned by the state, represented by both the *tiaotiao* and *kuaikuai*. In other words, it is often unclear specifically who controls what and how much. Calls for establishing stock markets in order to solve the problem of value assessment in corporate purchase have recently been articulated.[19] Once a stock market is established, an enterprise may decide to purchase only a part of the target enterprise. More important is that the purchasing enterprise would be able to initiate the deal directly in the market without going through its own administrative superior, if management so decided.

The operation of a stock market could also break the state monopoly on the flow of raw materials and capital by opening up multiple channels. Theoretically, stockholders of a socialist state-owned enterprise could be other state-owned enterprises, collective enterprises, and private enterprises, as well as individual investors. What is unique about socialism is the creation of workers' stock, which is arbitrarily assigned and guaranteed. This guarantees workers the right to a voice in an enterprise's decisionmaking process. Some thus argue that the successful development of a stock market can contribute to the formation of large enterprises through corporate purchase without being detrimental to the socialist cause.[20] In addition, whenever negotiation of corporate purchase fails, a sunset enterprise can still collect rescue funds in the form of stock sale, hence bringing together (or closer) the two previously separate enterprises and facilitating the formation of financial groups on the Japanese model. In fact, the Communist Party encourages the formation of financial groups more than it does corporate purchase.

Like the rationale behind the promotion of corporate purchase, the reasons to foster the financial group concept consist largely in the perceived urgency of breaking down the rigid *tiao-kuai* system. According to textbook definitions, a financial group is composed of a number of independent enterprises and occasionally research institutes whose activities may or may not be closely related to those particular industries. These participants have similar and compatible business goals and decide to organize into an entity with multiple functions. The financial group is considered the advanced form of "horizontal coordination."[21] In 1988 the National Commission on Institutional Reform together with other government offices wrote "Views on Organizing and Developing Financial Groups." The report concluded that the rise of financial groups would be a structural phenomenon and that companies should issue stock within each financial group.[22]

Once the financial group becomes a legal entity, it will be able to receive raw materials and even capital from the state planner without going through *tiao-kuai* channels. Among the 1,630 financial groups established before the end of 1988, fifteen currently have direct access to planned raw materials.[23] State planners have already created a few so-called center cities and begun distributing raw materials directly to them without passing through their provincial superiors. The idea behind this maneuvering is to break the provincial monopoly on resources. In 1987, planners stipulated that a group of companies could be an eligible entity (like ministries, provinces, and centrally administered cities) to receive raw materials directly from the state. The companies in the group must be closely related, and the group itself must have an independent account, the capacity to bear losses, autonomy in distributing dividends, decisionmaking power, and so on. If this is strictly enforced, financial groups are likely to become new profit-loss centers in the annual national budget.

My concern in this chapter is criticism of this design, though I am interested in legitimacy implications for socialist planners facing the rise of financial groups. Critics in China raise the similar concern that such groups will become another example of rigid planning, as they are identical to *tiaotiao* and *kuaikuai* in everything but name. To further complicate the case, each financial group embodies several enterprises, each having at least one *tiaotiao* and one *kuaikuai* boss. All these interested parties may struggle to control the new conglomerate or simply try to block anyone else from achieving domination.[24] Accordingly, financial groups themselves may fall prey to the regionalism and departmentalism the planner intends to curb.

The legitimacy implication is more serious if financial groups actually succeed in establishing their independent status. The well-known Jialing group combined several enterprises and successfully settled the battle for control by issuing stock to all interested parties. Some have claimed that all signs of administrative interference disappeared overnight.[25] Financial group enterprises, however, still have to listen to their *tiao-kuai* bosses in company operations. Yet they become involved in the operation of the larger financial group, which is not administratively constrained. As a result, all enterprise participants in financial groups have two identities: as executors of the central plan and as supporters of extraplan development of the financial group. In the Chinese context, the puzzle of dual identities is said to resemble a married woman fruitlessly trying to satisfy her mother and mother-in-law at the same time:

A joint enterprise entity [i.e., financial group] is unique compared to an enterprise under the traditional plan system because it is cross-area, cross-sector, cross-industry, and cross-ownership. However, the old system that blocks the formation of the "four crosses" has not yet been brought down. In the case of joint entities that bring together enterprises originally under different authorities, the coordination is extremely difficult, and this is especially true as the current tax policy encourages local authorities to protect and enlarge their own tax bases. Getting together the core enterprises that make up the Jialing group was lucky. It was due to the fact that the National Commission on Machinery decided to transfer Jialing Machinery Co. to the city of Chongqing, and all the other core enterprises were already under Chongqing's jurisdiction. Suddenly JMC became a family member and everything could be handled without animosity. This was coincidence. An opportunity like Chongqing's receiving JMC cannot usually happen to others who are interested in grouping. On the contrary, to force this kind of transfer would sometimes provide the new mother-in-law the opportunity to penalize those whom she has disliked for a long time.[26]

In short, either the new financial group performs the function of the "four crosses" and becomes a sovereign actor in the market, or it will have to suffer similar, if not more serious, intervention from local planners. Whatever the result, the traditional planning system is regarded as a constraint, a negative element, and an imperfect design. In this sense the Japanese model appears attractive. As the Jialing case suggests, once the new conglomeration issues stock, the conglomeration's own financial health and development become everyone's concern. Further development would possibly include exchange of staff between the conglomeration and participating companies and, later on, among participating companies. When the new sovereign financial group or joint entity can be so established, local *tiao-kuai* bureaucracy would necessarily be lured to and attend to the interests of the new entity more than the plan's execution. Planners' design to break rigidity thus undermines their own legitimacy in resource allocation.

When corporate purchase and financial grouping are difficult to facilitate, an alternative way to break the *tiao-kuai* system is to promote the notion of a "dragon-head enterprise" (also known as a "fist enterprise"). A dragon-head enterprise is a dominant player in the local market. It has advanced technology, large output value, greater economy of scale, modern management know-how, and abundant information. In its locality a dragon-head enterprise is the key to development, for a great number of smaller enterprises make a living by supplying the dragon-head enterprise. Furthermore, service industries spring up in the wake of growth at the dragon-head enterprise and its contractors. To further the concept of dragon-head enterprises, scholars have also raised the idea of a "dragon-head industry." Under the precepts of this latter notion, even if there is no such enterprise, each locality can develop a dragon-head industry, with most smaller enterprises in the region producing one major product in concert.

The dragon-head concept actually implies local sovereignty in utilizing the market for the sake of local economic growth. Planners believe that a dragon-head enterprise could expedite the flow of production factors and better their utility. A dragon-head entity can direct the reallocation of raw materials and attract capital from outside the region. In typical discussions of the economics of raw material allocation, a point repeatedly raised is that each locality must try to utilize idle machinery stowed away in the region before investing in new machinery. All new funds available must first be used to compensate for depreciation.[27]

This discussion is especially important as the responsibility system, initiated in the villages in 1978, has emancipated a spectacular volume of excess labor and materials, in turn generating significant momentum for village-level production. Without a dragon-head, these low-level productive activities are consistently the least efficient elements in the Chinese economy; a good proportion of investment has thus been wasted. Their support, however, is indispensable to the growth of the dragon-head enterprise, which in turn can improve efficiency in village factories.[28] Interactions between larger enterprises and village factories are therefore crucial to the establishment of a sound capital goods market.

Village factories vary from locality to locality, depending on differences in historical and geographical characteristics. They often compete with larger urban enterprises for acquisition of raw materials. Village enterprises are small and flexible; they develop a variety of personal connections through which they gain access to raw materials on the market and even in the plan system. Since village enterprises absorb tremendous amounts of surplus labor that would otherwise head for the cities, the state fully supports their development, even though they squander enormous amounts of energy and raw materials. As a result, many large, urban-based enterprises reluctantly idle their machinery for lack of manufacturing inputs.[29]

The best way to accommodate these smaller, nonurban factories in an orderly market structure is to encourage large enterprises to contract out parts production. This would allow larger enterprises to direct the investment of smaller ones and keep them in line.[30] Since many village factories also manufacture consumer goods, it becomes useful to upgrade their facilities so that they can broaden their perspectives and be willing to compete in the urban marketplace. Unfortunately, many are satisfied with smaller volumes of sales in the periodic gatherings of the local market. Under such circumstances it is hoped that association with larger enterprises in the cities can impact upon the quality of low-level consumer goods production in villages, even though these factories receive no actual technological aid from larger enterprises. The positive effect in this instance is to be achieved simply through the eye-opening experience.

Village enterprises can be categorized into six models, two of the most noted being the southern Jiangsu model and the Wenzhou model. Village factories in southern Jiangsu include those around the cities of Shanghai, Wuxi, Suzhou, and Changzhou—areas where industrial development has traditionally taken the lead in China. Interactions between villages and cities in southern Jiangsu are intense and mutually beneficial. The gross product of these village factories accounts for one-third of that for the total area.[31]

Southern Jiangsu also witnessed the creation of some of the first financial groups in the nation composed purely of village enterprises. On the whole, though, village enterprises in the area still specialize in the supply of parts; only their excellent reputation wins them contracts from other areas of the country.

Despite such a reputation, southern Jiangsu village enterprises are dissatisfied with their situations. In a self-evaluation village enterprises in the area expressed their belief that further upgrading and growth are possible only if they are allowed to develop by themselves, without interference from the Communist Party, implying the withdrawal of party cadres from the factory. In reality many village enterprises are continuously staffed by division secretaries of the Communist Party. What is surprising is that party interference is fairly minor in this area, and party cadres here are some of the most business-oriented in the country. These qualities, however, fail to win them much respect:

> Policy mistakes made by village cadres who lack economic common sense often lead to serious waste. Cadre infighting, especially between party cadres and village authorities, has also seriously impacted the development of village business in the entire community. Occasional cadre changes by personnel at higher levels may lead to vicissitudes in the community's factory development. Villagers, who are the real owners of village enterprises, do not have the opportunity to express their opinion on important decisionmaking in village enterprises nor the power to supervise cadres, although these villagers are emotionally strongly attached to these enterprises.[32]

Authorities in southern Jiangsu claim that they would like to deepen local reform in the following three directions: enforce the general-manager responsibility system, extend the application of the product responsibility system, and establish workers' assemblies. The overall goal is allegedly the separation of politics and business.

The Wenzhou model differs in that there is no urban industry to stimulate development around the Wenzhou area. The Wenzhou village enterprises are, without exception, small and technologically primitive. The main force behind Wenzhou enterprises are individual households and, in some cases, joint household shops. Nonetheless, there are complex connections between these households and national and collective enterprises. Many of those who run household contracting concerns work in those national enterprises from which they acquire their contracts.[33] The primary local products are consumer goods, and most households contribute to some aspect of their production. This requires rapid flow of information regarding location of production factors and, above all, labor. Consequently, enterprises that assemble the final products have to move to heavily populated areas with convenient transportation. Longgang County, known as the Peasant Castle, thus thrives.[34]

The Wenzhou model is encouraged because surplus labor can be organized with greater flexibility to reflect market demands. In many cases retired technicians from national enterprises are recruited to work in the area. For example, the Liucheng District of Leqing County alone has recruited at least 700 retired technicians. During peak periods immigrant workers have reached 6,000 or more.[35] Sometimes a whole area is organized into a pseudo–assembly-line network.[36] In the Yishan District, for example, there are roughly 380 households responsible for raw material purchasing, 6,430 households for spinning, 600 for raw material sifting, 1,200 for lace work, 6,490 for weaving, 2,900 for sewing, 2,300 for marketing, and 400 for transportation of one finished product.

The problem with the Wenzhou model is that peasants leave the fields to engage in craftsmanship; hence fields lie fallow, covered with weeds, not crops. And the technological level of production is so low that not only is long-term development grimly finite but the state plan cannot even meaningfully upgrade currently popular, profit-driven productive activities. Planners have two solutions. First, the government may impose taxes on idle fields, set a roof on personal income, and charge an agricultural development fee on each nonagricultural enterprise. Second, the government can actively organize household enterprises into joint enterprises and even into financial groups by participating in larger economic activities in other, more-developed areas.[37]

It is too early to judge whether smaller enterprises and larger national enterprises will develop the relationship based on caring and loyalty that characterizes the Japanese system. Obviously, the spontaneous development of village factories undermines the planners' ability to allocate resources efficiently. Although village enterprises have succeeded in flexibly utilizing numerous idle resources, notably surplus labor, they curtail the planners' degree of freedom. This explains why planners may promote the notion of dragon-head enterprises and dragon-head industries, as they hope that small, localized factories can become a part of the national economy.[38]

Toward the end of 1988, only 5 percent of the products made by village factories were purchased and later sold by the planners according to the plan; 35 percent were parts for national enterprises. On the supply side, 80 percent of their raw material supply came directly from the market.[39] It would appear that village enterprises contribute little to the state plan. Instead, they make the market less predictable and raw materials somewhat inaccessible during times of need. Nonetheless, they supply a fair share of the parts to national enterprises so that the latter will not have to depend too heavily on central planners.

## POLITICAL IMPLICATIONS

The premises of the traditional regime are twofold: symbiosis of political and moral authority and compliant local leadership that converts the rank and file into appreciative followers. China's reform since the late 1970s has been grounded in a completely different mode of political economy. The state planner, who held supreme political command for decades, initiated reform that triggered the breach of the plan system. The planner now encourages corporate purchase, the establishment of financial groups, and the development of dragon-head enterprises all for the purpose of disintegrating the traditional administrative sectors (*tiaotiao*) and blocs (*kuaikuai*) so that the flow (holistic as well as partial) of such production factors as labor, land, capital, and raw materials will reflect market demand.

Sectors and blocs have become snags in the plan system because local leaders have departmental concerns. It is undeniable, however, that local leaders can still legitimately protect ministerial or regional interests because the plan system has always been the symbol of socialism. They may present themselves either as sincere executors of the plan or simply manipulators of interests. In either case sector and bloc interests are dependent upon the integrity of the plan system—without it there would be no *tiao* and *kuai* as unitary receivers of raw materials and capital. And yet the operation of the planning system must also rely on lower-level administrative units like sectors and blocs. Reformers' determination to strike at vested interests residing in sectors and blocs amounts to chopping off the two hands of the plan system.

Since the central planner traditionally tended to represent ministerial interests, reform seems to favor bloc over sectoral interests. Decentralization as designed by reformers constrains ministerial officials much more than it does regional officials. This reinforces the impression that reform targets central planning. In this sense reform in the 1980s and 1990s is somewhat reminiscent of the Great Leap Forward.

The battle (though perhaps most participants are unaware of it and unwilling to fight) centers on the locus of leadership in future political economic development. If planners continue to boost the status and capacity of large state-owned enterprises whose policy would in turn become the single most important determinant of profitability for localized small firms, contractors, and other supporting businesses, these state-owned enterprises would become alternative authorities for those who live in the region and thus render the central regime's appeal to socialist selflessness irrelevant. Reform-minded scholars note the political implications of this contradiction:

> Socialist calls for relatively socialized production to a great extent require the state to adopt relatively centralized management through planning, and this would mean a relatively centralized political system to manage the superstructures. At the same time, socialist calls for relatively socialized production require the application of democratic economic management, and this would mean widespread political democracy as the [norm of] the superstructure. Consequently, relatively centralized, unitary management necessarily collides with widespread political democracy. In addition . . . fundamental contradictions in the commodity economy exist between relatively socialized production and publicly owned but relatively autonomous economic entities of different levels.[40]

The ideological implications are equally serious:

> In . . . the primary stage of socialism, the issue of right or wrong . . . continues to coincide with hostilities among people. If we do not handle this well, these issues of right or wrong, tinged with the feeling of antagonism, will be transformed into ideological conflicts between enemies. At the same time, these issues. . . are all the more complex because party thinking reflects both socialist philosophy and the ideological legacy of the old society. . . . Therefore, resolution of the right-or-wrong contradiction at the primary stage of socialism requires resolving the conflicts among socialist thought, corrupt capitalist thought, and remnant feudalist thought and the contradiction between socialist thought and petty bourgeois views.[41]

The policy to encourage large state-owned enterprise to rise up in order to cut across traditional sector and bloc interests would inevitably create new economic entities at the highest levels and embody the conflict among different theoretical approaches. This type of new economic entity is different from *tiao* and *kuai* in the traditional sense because the former gains momentum to expand from within these entities; the past planning system created vested interests only in protecting the integrity of the system passively, while the new entities strive to augment it. Although the new entities may not have the slightest intention to challenge the legitimacy of central planners, their rise unavoidably constrains the planners' capacity. Fundamentally, planners lose credit as socialist designers since initiative suddenly comes from localized enterprises. These multiple channels for productive goods and services clearly negate the traditional premise of unitary authority: The planner is no longer the sole provider of socialist authority.

The impact on moral authority is subtle and indirect yet significant. The productions-factor market facilitates the separation of political and moral authority. First, large localized state-owned enterprises and local political forces work together on local economic development. This makes local inhabitants more dependent on local leadership for improved standards of living, sometimes even leading to the resistance of extractive pressures from the center. This is particularly true for areas that develop more successfully and are expected to contribute more to assist underdeveloped areas.

Enterprises must satisfy their workers' expectations. Together with local political leaders and the local constituency, they are likely to stand against the state planner at the center. Although this has happened before, reform philosophy simply exacerbates and publicizes the dispute by giving local interests justification they previously lacked. This inner contradiction forces the state planners to depend increasingly on administrative coercion to persuade local leaders to follow the plan. As this occurs more frequently, the state planners can rely less and less on their appeal to selflessness.

Equally if not more profound challenges come from village-based small enterprises, which absorb tremendous volumes of surplus labor. Planners encourage them to thrive in the market in order to lower the state's burden. These workers' brigades used to deal with a stable, albeit rigid, state system of purchase and sale; now they are striking out on their own in a world of autonomous buying and selling called the market. The contrast between the two systems is dramatic: Village enterprises can no longer depend on the state planner for their survival. As mentioned earlier, more successful village enterprises regard party and state cadres as a burden, unless of course they can prove themselves to be truly market-oriented. In the long run, the peasants will nevertheless pay even less attention to cadres as political campaigners, for these roles do not contribute to a living standard now measured not by stability but by growth. Cadres have to choose between being alienated from society and joining the market. In either case the central socialist code would lack a local presenter who can at least familiarize people with the moral jargon of the regime.

There is no prediction that large state-owned enterprises or village enterprises will turn power-hungry and challenge the regime. Nor is there the political economic necessity that they must give up collective socialism or work unit socialism in order to survive in the market. The contention here is that the symbiosis of moral and political authority will become separated at the local level, and the image of selflessness is no longer effective in convincing people of the regime's legitimacy. As a result, the regime's capacity to mobilize social resources will gradually diminish.

For one thing, the regime will not be able to launch political campaigns to achieve certain state goals in the name of socialism or any other utopia. Cadres may feel awkward campaigning for the state and will do so only reluctantly; the rank and file will of course respond with little enthusiasm. For another—and an extremely important factor in understanding the change of political culture—factions in the regime may not be able to resort to mass campaigns in order to rescue themselves from a losing political battle at the center. Since monolithic moral authority has only weak appeal, its fall would not incite significant concern. Political crisis therefore would not come from a direct challenge to the regime but from the lack of legitimating rhetoric that can attract people's attention. This would create pressure to further depend on reform and decentralization for legitimation and in turn make the pretense of a selfless regime increasingly irrelevant. Ironically, those who benefit most from the regime would likely move furthest away from it administratively as well as morally.

State planners must feel ambivalent toward the village enterprise. It resolves a potential political crisis by keeping surplus labor from migrating to the cities and in a sense gainfully utilizes this labor force in production. Since the rise of such enterprises does not completely rely on state support, though, it becomes difficult to discipline them through plan sanctions. With regard to illegal practices or economic waste, the state can intervene only through administrative penalty. This undeniably tarnishes the image of the state as a supreme leader. Financial penalty, taxation, and fees all suggest that state and enterprise are competitors, an image that Confucius and his disciples dreaded and repeatedly warned against.

## CONCLUSION

The Japanese model would now appear remote to Chinese society. There is no such purely symbolic emperor in China as in Japan; political and moral symbols are combined in Chinese politics. Symbols create power; conversely, loss of power tarnishes symbols. Subjection to a high political authority believing in public ownership would always mean some degree of economic sacrifice in China. Since the early days of reform, Chinese socialism has witnessed *legitimate* disputes of interest among individuals, enterprises, and the state. The decline in the state's economic capacity thus (unlike in Japan) inescapably undermines its moral authority.

Yet relationships based on caring and loyalty between large and small enterprises as seen in Japan are not totally beyond reach in China. Obviously,

China's central planners want some close connections between large and small enterprises in the hope that the more efficient dragon-head enterprises can enhance the production efficiency of the smaller ones. The difficulty in China lies in that respect and caring are not characteristic of the current competitive style of reform. Whether the Japanese business model is applicable in China is therefore an uncertain but significant issue. Since political interference has been so endemic in China, reformers have to struggle in order to drag the moral state out of the enterprise. This only reinforces the process of amoralization in politics.

It would almost appear that there is a cultural revolution going on in China's economic system. Planners, on their own initiative, invite small, extraplan players to destroy vested interests in the planning system. This dramatically parallels the style of politics during the Cultural Revolution, when Maoist leaders struggled to bring in students in order to overthrow the state and party system. Mao in the 1960s also encouraged cross-regional union; planners today stress the importance of the "four crosses" (cross-area, cross-sector, cross-industry, and cross-ownership). The Cultural Revolutionaries turned out to be primarily a group of power manipulators; the small enterprise has proved to be the least efficient energy consumer in its productive tasks. The Cultural Revolutionary to some extent succeeded in sharing power with the establishment; decentralization during reform has also allowed newcomers to share economic profit. Most important, the Cultural Revolution completely destroyed the credit of political leaders; reform seemingly has the same function of destroying the moral appeal of central planners.

# 5

# ACQUISITIVE SOCIALISM: THE CONSUMERS' MARKET CULTURE

In traditional China the market for consumer goods was extremely limited. Craftsmen who lived on the market were small in number; even smaller was the population of cross-region merchants. In fact, these merchants were so few that once established in the market, their names would almost be guaranteed a niche in official annals. The underdevelopment of a consumer market resulted both from China's vast subsistence economy and the Confucian disfavor of commercial activities. The subsistence economy disallowed the expansion of consumption capacity in society, and Confucian deliberation justified the official suppression of consumption of non-necessity goods.[1]

Political legitimacy had nothing to do with providing a stable market of high-quality consumer goods nor with improving the commoners' purchasing power. On the contrary, the legitimacy to rule over the Middle Kingdom lay in the pretension that the regime ensured harmonious relations between heaven and humans, forging official compliance with the natural economy. The regime was ideally the political rectifier.[2] In this sense official attempts to promote the consumer goods market would have hurt political legitimacy, for the government would had seemed more interested in material rather than spiritual values.

The proponents of a consumer goods market are consumers and suppliers. The rise of the consumer goods market would encourage citizen consumers to review the government's performance in terms of abundance and flow of consumer goods. The significance of harmonious order would decline and the foundation of political legitimacy would be dispersed. Likewise, an expanding consumer goods market would inevitably witness the growth of a merchant class, whose mundane life-style would likely become the new social model for emulation. Furthermore, the local gentry class would openly engage in commercial activities and forgo their role of moral leader. This would break the ethical link between court and commoner. Finally, the government would unavoidably involve itself or its officials in business operations. The regime would thus lose its lofty pretension of selfless neutrality.

This chapter concerns the political implications of China's economic reform, especially its efforts to introduce a consumer-oriented market in order to provide public enterprises with strong profit incentives to improve their efficiency.[3] The subject is intriguing because there is no equivalent to a Western bourgeois class in China; the establishment of the consumer goods market thus will have to rely upon the socialist regime. The regime must enlighten its socialist citizens about market norms developed by allegedly antagonistic bourgeois classes. However, the ensuing discussion suggests that the rise of the market is not necessarily an issue of transforming socialism into capitalism, since there is no logical argument that socialist enterprises cannot survive in the market. In other words, the market approach does not imply capitalism. The issue is therefore presented here as one of transforming a traditional regime into its more mundane counterpart.

From a logical rather than an empirical point of view, in the first section I maintain that neither Max Weber's argument that Confucianism lacks market motivation nor the neo-Confucianist obsession with the sense of predicament sufficiently explains the subdued performance of the market in China. The suppression of the market was a result of political-psychological necessity. In the second section I look at the supply side, expounding on why Confucianism does not impede the evolution of a commodity economy in its most modern form. Shifting to the demand side, I go on in the third section to study the mechanisms that help bypass socialism in the ascent of consumerism. Finally, I address the political implications of the emergence of the consumer goods market in China.

## THE MARKET AND POLITICAL AUTHORITY

Since the time of Adam Smith, liberal economists, classic as well as neo-classic, have held that the logic of the market and the application of political authority are two incongruent forces. They consider it unwise for political authorities to intervene in market operations.[4] More recently, though, a group of scholars has raised the possibility that political authority may actually contribute to the more effective use of resources in the stage of economic takeoff.[5] Another possible argument is that the market hinders the formation of a long-term strategy or a sectorally comprehensive viewpoint. These proauthoritarian perspectives do not apply to China, since its socialist regime possesses the exclusive authority to engage in planning, yet this has led to enormous waste and inefficiency. For a liberal economist, the prescription for the Chinese economy is thus marketization (which is not capitalism per se).[6]

There are at least three distinct rebuttals. Many Western and Chinese political scientists, including Samuel Huntington, point out the crucial role a leading authoritarian party can play in facilitating economic development.[7] Second, classical writers like Weber held that one must be psychoculturally prepared to overcome the "hurdles" that stand in the way of developing entrepreneurship, and that Chinese culture lacked the kind of inner motivation found in Christian civilization.[8] Third, Lucian Pye asserts that Chinese culture is so imbued with authoritarianism that it is unlikely that individual Chinese could coordinate on their own, without a superior political authority.[9]

Although both Huntington and Pye emphasize the function of political authority in economic development, the former is concerned with political stability, whereas the latter focuses on the psychologically comforting effects of authority. Weber, in contrast, believed the existence of authority alone was definitely not enough; in Christian society, individuals need, look for, and take on the challenge under market uncertainty. Contemporary neo-Confucianists are very critical of Weber's point. These scholars, including Tu Wei-ming, Yu Ying-shih, and Thomas Metzger, call attention to the sense of predicament that philosophical Chinese would challenge themselves to overcome. This, as they believe, motivates typical Chinese to transcend the difficulties they encounter.[10] Scholarship on Japan seems to prove that the inner drive Weber highlighted is indeed exhibited in certain non-Christian societies.[11]

Whether or not the market can grow steadily would appear to be a function of political authority. If political authority is necessary in providing market order and stability, it should be conducive to market operation to some degree. This view obviously has disciples among contemporary Chinese leaders.[12] For Huntington, political stability is the precondition of development, while for Pye it is something much more fundamental. Pye observes that Chinese authority is patriarchal. His notion of moralized authority raises a bold hypothesis about economic development in Taiwan.[13] He thinks that the Nationalist government had a psychological need to prove that its loss of China had little to do with corruption and thus consciously avoided direct involvement in allocating social resources on its own behalf. Nationalist political elites and native Taiwanese economic elites are therefore segregated.

Pye argues that this is probably the first time in Chinese history that political authority does not intend to monopolize economic benefits. Not only did stability contribute to market development, but the growth of the market consolidated political stability as well (an observation open to dispute by the 1990s). Political authority deliberately restrained itself from becoming an exploiting seller in the market but at the same time monopolized political resources so as to protect economic development. Stability thus provided the moral basis of the market: Citizens could work for material gain without negatively alluding to political legitimacy.

The most serious challenge Pye fails to tackle directly is of course the Hong Kong experience. In Hong Kong there has virtually been no patriarchal authority in Pye's sense. John Fei thus contends that whether or not there is a moralized authority is irrelevant to the maintenance of stability in Chinese society.[14] Fei thinks that the people of Hong Kong are motivated by what he calls rational utilitarianism. Individuals work hard in order to promote the collective welfare of those who belong to the same familial group, thus obtaining social status. This is Fei's evidence that what maintains stability in Chinese society is not moralized authority but family-oriented sociocultural awareness. This awareness does not rise or fall with authoritarianism and hence impacts upon the market independently.

Fei's assertion implicitly contradicts a long-standing myth about Chinese tradition concerning market development. Unlike the classic writers, Fei believes that Confucianism has not only been harmless to market operation but has even contributed to the development of the market in modern times. That market forces appeared weak in traditional China must not be attributed to Chinese cultural traits. Nor can China's strong tradition of authoritarianism be guilty of retarding the market, for Pye has demonstrated how authoritarianism may assist economic development in regions including Taiwan. China's past economic problems are therefore not an issue of psychoculture.

An alternative explanation looks to the mode and content of regime legitimation. For more than 1,000 years, the Chinese regime grounded its legitimacy in the pretension that the regime was the rectifier of society. The government consciously suppressed the growth of commercial interests to avoid the impression of spiritual decay or the emergence of alternate power centers. People chose not to develop careers in the market not because they were incapable of doing so or because they were stoical but because this was considered politically threatening. Authority itself was neutral in economic terms, but it excluded the market option from its list of legitimating mechanisms. That the market was limited in traditional China is therefore not a result of national character but one of political legitimation.

With this cultural background in mind, one would expect that there is little justification to argue that socialism necessarily thwarts the growth of the market economy. As with Confucian tradition, although socialism may not necessarily impede the development of the market, the notion of socialism may nonetheless be endangered if the market develops on its own. The issue that the Chinese socialist regime faces is precisely that in its past practices the regime deliberately combined the notion of socialism (like Confucianism in traditional China) with the promise of a withering market. As it realizes that the combination is artificial and strives to revoke this conceptual linkage today, it unavoidably hurts its own legitimacy. The problem is not with socialism (or Confucianism) but with the growing irrelevance of socialism in the regime's mode of legitimation.

## THE SUPPLIER

While the Taiwanese government was the first Chinese regime to consciously and systematically develop a market economy, today's Beijing can be seen as the first Chinese regime that struggles to create a competitive market for nationalized enterprises. The socialist market is obviously much more comprehensive than the court-monopolized market of the dynastic periods. In the socialist market, almost every item of consumption can theoretically continue to be regulated under central planning, for the key to market operation is in allowing profit incentives to impact upon decision in the enterprises, not necessarily to exclude administrative incentives provided by the state planner.

However, there must be other market features in China so that the regime can claim that a socialist market is not just another version of the developmentalism reflected in the market practices of the newly industrialized countries. This is precisely the reason the state planner in China also stresses the importance of preference management (see Chapter 3). Some Chinese scholars assert that enterprises should "self-consciously" and "actively" cooperate with the state plan.[15] At least two implications follow. First, the enterprise will supposedly adopt the state preference as its own and therefore have to modify profit-driven investment decisions accordingly. Second, since socialism requires that "all be enriched," highly profitable enterprises or areas should at times slow down so that others may keep abreast.[16] For example, the regime holds that Shanghai must be "the whole country's Shanghai," not just the Shanghai of its residents, since the city, like all other municipalities, has a unique "obligation in the development of the whole country."[17]

Would such socialist norms that distinguish a socialist market from its capitalist counterpart hinder productive incentives of suppliers in the market? Preliminary research suggests not. One field study in Taiwan finds that cultural factors constrain nonprofit behavior more clearly than do profit-oriented activities; this is called Chinese "cultural bipolarity."[18] The finding is echoed in Lucian Pye's study of Chinese pragmatism. He contends that the Chinese are equipped with a highly accommodating cognitive capacity that allows seemingly irreconcilable values to coexist.[19] The significance is that individual profit-driven behavior may not have to be considered incompatible with the requirement of socialist civilization.

The Beijing regime realizes its citizens' ability to tolerate cognitive dissonance and therefore displays slogans in public places to remind people of collective interests. The more direct interference is done through political campaigns carried out by party organs in enterprises. This way, two separate sets of norms—profit and socialism—inescapably meet along the assembly line. Can they together influence workers' thinking so that workers will always keep collective interests in mind and willingly donate what would have been exclusively their own in order to benefit the collective? With the ensuing discussion I suggest that the effects of these political campaigns have to be limited for four different reasons.

## Shield of Cooperativism

The market economy is often regarded as the symbol of capitalism. Many a textbook in the 1980s portrayed the market as opposed to the plan in terms of the exploitative relationship involved.[20] Market and socialism appear to be two irreconcilable concepts. In fact, since the early 1950s the Chinese Communist Party has debated the nature of the rural cooperative system. The cooperatives performed the function of collecting arts and crafts, foodstuffs, and daily necessities made by individual households and selling the goods to the community to improve the participants' income.

Formal criticism of the cooperative system was registered prior to the start of the Cultural Revolution. In 1964 all village cooperative boards were dissolved for their alleged bourgeois inclinations. The next year witnessed the termination of all inventory shops run by cooperatives, and their business was effectively halted. At the end of 1965, cooperatives at all levels were ordered to transfer all funds except stockholders' principal into state accounts as a type of state investment, at least on the books. Since cooperatives provided a large variety of consumer goods and services, the party condemned the cooperative economy as a "capitalist value-collecting bowl and money-dropping tree" that destroyed "the unity of the socialist market."[21]

The official position on the cooperative economy began to turn around during reform. Since the late 1970s, the party has become more tolerant of the rise of cooperativism. Cooperatives and craft markets have obviously become active again. Cooperatives are one of the most important suppliers of consumer goods on the market. While the goods displayed at a cooperative shop are sold in the name of the cooperative, such an institution successfully brings together products made by individual households, small collective enterprises, and even more advanced village factories. Bonuses and dividends are distributed according to one's monetary contribution in the form of stock as well as to one's actual contribution in terms of goods supplied.

Apparently, as long as the cooperative is officially accepted as one "derivative of the socialist economy" (whatever this may mean), it really does not matter if the participants, individual as well as collective, are consciously socialist. Neither the reinforcement of socialist education and political campaigns nor economic retrenchment in the planning system can affect the private profit incentives behind the public cooperative operation. Reformers actually consider reform of the cooperative system a significant step in introducing market mechanisms into consumer goods markets. In fact, the blueprint of cooperative reform was concluded by the Chinese Communist Party's National Cooperative Party Division in 1981.

Before 1981, cooperatives were transformed into collective shops on several occasions. Most of the time, the transformation reflected the political atmosphere of the time and not strategic moves based upon some economic rationale. The 1981 conclusion has finalized the status of cooperative as collective shop, complete with detailed instructions and theoretical foundation:[22]

1. Cooperatives should work closely with production brigades and peasants, fulfilling sale and distribution assignments given by the state, promoting sales of products made by peasants, and investing in the processing industry. Cooperatives should acquire funds from voluntary brigades and peasants and distribute dividends according to product supply and stock share. Cooperatives should also give participating members special discounts on product purchases.

2. Cooperatives at higher levels should serve the interests of cooperatives and their members at lower levels.

3. Cooperatives should follow the state plan in principle yet adapt to market conditions in practice. Cooperatives should represent the state when signing contracts with people and buying goods from them. In addition to supplying the state purchase plan, cooperatives can run their shops in a flexible and diversified manner, establish their own sales agencies, and purchase what they need directly from the market.

4. Cooperatives should write their books independently and bear all profit-loss responsibility incurred by their operation. Profits should be divided into four categories: cooperative development, tax, dividends, and employee welfare. Furthermore, "no government offices may legally control, embezzle, borrow, and take over" their profits.

Although cooperatives are now officially independent actors in the market, this does not necessarily imply capitalism. The issue here is really not socialism versus capitalism. Rather, it is that socialism is becoming increasingly irrelevant in citizens' daily judgment. Participants in cooperatives may or may not believe in socialism. Their purely profit-driven behavior can sneak into this socialist cooperative institution without sabotaging socialism per se; their business practices simply deny socialism as the source of legitimacy for the regime. The regime still possesses the ability to intervene in the market on behalf of socialism, and this alone can prove that the market does not have to clash with socialism. The irony is that peasants now care less about the state's socialist equalizing function than their ability to earn in the market. The state has no excuse to question their intentions at the individual level, since they all operate in the name of socialist cooperatives. Cooperatives provide the ideological shield they need. Consequently, the regime could no longer assume its own legitimacy even if there were still a genuine socialist consciousness among the masses.

## Economy of Scale

Although market reform is not the same as capitalism, the regime still has to remind its citizens of their socialist duty while performing productive work in the market. The market, in this context, is presented deliberately and exclusively as a competitive mechanism:

> Enterprises as productive units in the market are surely different from natural economic units because enterprises do not produce for the sake of self-consumption but for the sake of exchange for value. Value is accumulated through exchange so that the enterprise owes its existence to value accumulation and begins to operate in a cycle of producing and exchanging for value. Within this enterprise organism, there are also competitive mechanisms. Competition exists among productive workers. As a result, the commodity economy necessarily creates strong momentum for further production and therefore generates new energy.[23]

The premise of market competition is that actors in the market work for themselves so that they are willing to compete. Socialist education would certainly help remind these actors who they are, inasmuch as they would at least have to pretend to socialism in order to become legitimate competitors in the market. In spite of the rhetoric, suppliers in the market earn a profit and therefore risk being labeled as exploiters. Even if the current regime does not wish to label suppliers as exploiters, suppliers should be worried that they would appear selfish, an anathema in both Confucianism and socialism. There is a caveat in this logic, however. Exploiters lose face and worry about social rejection only if they themselves have to encounter consumers in the market. In the modern mode of production and marketing, suppliers have no such worry. They are not like the landlords and the wealthy in traditional society, who were easy targets of blame. In the modern market, consumers cannot possibly pinpoint an exploiter:

> First, there is the breakthrough in terms of space, from limited, closed local market to unitary, open, and nationwide market; second, there is the breakthrough in structure, from the single-dimension market of commodity to the multidimension market of commodity, capital, and labor; third, there is the breakthrough of relationships, from the single, horizontal

economic linkage between suppliers and consumers to the complex, over-
lapping economic networks among economic managers, suppliers, and
consumers; fourth, there is the breakthrough of market characteristics,
from essentially one of commodity exchange to primarily one of capital
flow; fifth, there is the breakthrough of function, from coordinating in the
simple, limited scale of exchange to organizing, coordinating, and con-
trolling in the socialized, large scale of exchange.[24]

In this kind of market, consumer and supply company owner never
meet. In other words, the consumer does not see an exploiter's face,
hence the sense of harmony that may have concerned Weber can be kept
intact. In addition, the theory continues, the price in the market is determined by demand, competition, interest rates, employee compensation,
and so forth, and not arbitrarily set by the supplier.[25] To make the supplier's case even stronger, a significant portion of pricing is still controlled by the state planner, so no legitimate reason exists to accuse the
supplier of thriving on the suffering of the consumer under conditions of
unfair pricing. In reality, of course, suppliers have quickly learned to adjust to the policy of reform and have manipulated market prices to the extreme. The National Price Bureau was established in 1978 and announced
in 1984 that "reform of pricing institutions is key to the success of reform
of the entire economic system."[26] If socialist education does not help pin
down the exploiters, education will likely become irrelevant in consoli-
dating regime legitimacy.

The ever-broadening scale of economy activity, however, thwarts the
work of the Price Bureau. If the bureau could distinguish real from artificial price inflation, the market would be redundant in the first place. The
establishment of the Price Bureau is therefore unlikely to force trouble-
makers out of the market. Artificial price inflation plotted by certain large
enterprises is henceforth left unchecked. The scale of economy thus prohibits the socialist regime from making socialism a relevant factor in private decisionmaking, nor is the traditional pursuit of harmony an effective
check on competitive mentality in the faceless market.

## Defense Mechanism in the Responsibility System

The trouble with the responsibility system in the past had to do with its
ambiguity toward socialism. Critics were concerned because once the
quota assigned by the planner was met, all remaining revenue belonged to
the individual and did not have to go through the process of social distribution. This situation seemed to follow the feudal practice of court extraction during the dynastic periods rather than the tenets of Marxism. Reformers today reevaluate the socialist character of the responsibility
system and conclude that the system would assist producers in developing

care over "the entire process of production and distribution," and hence provide a cure to the endemic problem of motivation under classic socialism.[27]

Interestingly enough, the critics of the responsibility system now come from the other side. Some reform-minded scholars believe that the responsibility system is inferior to the stock system, which simply divides the property of an enterprise into stocks. They maintain that the responsibility system was originally aimed at agrarian reform and has been proved effective in liberating productive forces in the villages. Industrial reform, however, which is tantamount to enterprise system reform, must move beyond the style of agrarian reform, for the assembly line cannot be broken down into pieces as land in the village can. Peasants own what they produce without having to share with others, while workers cannot possibly do the same.

Still, there are a great many supporters of the responsibility system in the city. They counter the critics by pointing out that the stock market in China is too primitive to serve the purposes of industrial reform.[28] In addition, there is the fear that the stock system may well undermine public ownership of the means of production in large state-owned enterprises.[29] However, the disciples of the stock system have succeeded in catching both agrarian and industrial responsibility systems at their myopic style of management. The contractors under the plan system often exhaust all possible resources during the contracted period in order to benefit most. As a result, abuse of land in the case of agrarian reform and of machinery in industrial reform precipitates depreciation.

Those who champion the responsibility system offer a completely different diagnosis. The real issue, according to them, is that the contracted period is too short. A good responsibility contract must be long term, with all employees included and all detailed tasks specified. Furthermore, the contract must allow the contractor to keep all revenue above the contracted amount and deliberately design a linkage between an individual worker's compensation and that worker's contribution to total revenue.[30] Long-term contracting is therefore expected to solve the problem of myopic management and property abuse. The model of urban reform for the camp of the responsibility system is Capital Steel Corporation, which installed a new contract system in 1981 and has since generated overwhelming profits for its employees.

CSC carefully justifies the application of the new system with classic socialist texts, making its experiment with the responsibility system *look* conservative, bold though it is. The manager of the CSC Research and Development Department consciously works two of the best-known slogans into his conversation: "adhering to the four cardinal principles" and "adhering to reform and openness." His true intention cannot be clearer, though: He cautions that the state planner's departmentalist tendency to care for particular ministerial interests at the expense of overall interests could actually damage overall interests *much more than* the departmentalist tendency of the enterprise and its workers in pursuing their own interests. He urges the state planner to have faith in enterprises whose employees consistently fulfill their obligation to socialist development by agreeing to submit a set amount of their product to the state before they can legally and legitimately enjoy any of the rest. He believes it is perfectly acceptable for CSC employees to learn how to improve the company's profitability under the responsibility system without contributing increasing amounts to the state:

> "A set responsible quota" should not be understood simply as "a set constraint of state revenue." A set responsible quota should be understood as a constraint on the enterprise, which must take the state's quota contract as a set mission, like a military decree, and complete it. CSC has a contracted quota that is 9 percent higher than CSC ever had in its history, and it is under such severe conditions that CSC enjoys a policy of keeping above that quota. One should not regret having given CSC a set responsible quota after having realized that CSC has been improving its profitability well over its contracted quota under the new incentive system. Some want the state to share the newly gained profit instead of living within a set constraint of state revenue. This would destroy the rationale of the responsibility system. Eventually, the efficiency level of the enterprise would drop back and state revenue would actually decrease in the long run.[31]

The implication of this discussion is rather serious. An enterprise can now tacitly threaten the state to keep its hand out of the enterprise's till. The enterprise would otherwise quit reform and drop efficiency levels back down to their original point. CSC can legitimately afford to be assertive for two reasons. First, it has enhanced state revenue under the responsibility system, although it has been more successful in raising the company's own profits. Second, CSC nonetheless meets the state quota before it can expand its own accounts, hence socialism exists in a concrete sense. What it demands is that the state not dramatically increase its contracted quota after CSC has been induced to reveal its true capacity. This, of course, is presented in the name of socialism, and logically so.

## The Rise of Collective Enterprise

In many cases a collective enterprise faces the market directly, and only a part of its products is purchased under the state plan. Since this type of enterprise does not always have a contractual relationship with the state, it displays to an extent what is called a petty bourgeois tendency. For the sake of reform, in 1983 the state finally promulgated a new set of rules that officially confirm that collective commercial enterprises are considered one basic form of socialist business and, politically, should enjoy a status identical to that of state-owned enterprises.

Legally speaking, it is reasonable to treat collective commercial and productive enterprises as socialist. Collective enterprises are effective channels to distribute state products to households, since their marketing style is flexible and localized. State-owned enterprises consistently have problems reaching the consumers. Not only do they know little about the local market, but they have no reason to develop the market in the first place. Collective enterprises are likewise socialist to the extent that they are subject to plan restrictions regarding purchase and sale of goods and materials on the list of plan regulations.[32] For these reasons, collective commercial enterprises are similar to agrarian or village cooperatives.

Once the regime deemed collective enterprise socialist, many other private businesses began to operate in the guise of collective enterprises in order to receive privileges reserved exclusively for socialist enterprises. This was especially true in cities, where collective enterprises normally do not have contractual relationships with the state: It remains virtually impossible to distinguish a fake collective enterprise from a genuine one. For several reasons, however, the state is unable to throw the collective enterprise back to its former low political and legal status, the primary reason being its somewhat nebulous identity.

First of all, collective enterprises have contributed dramatically to the flow of consumer goods. For example, from 1979 to 1985 sales quadrupled in village collective markets and grew tenfold in urban collective markets.[33] Since all collective enterprises have traditionally been lumped together in one political category, distinction between village and urban collective enterprises has been rather difficult. It is unlikely that the state can demote urban collective enterprises without damaging village collective enterprises. Finally, agrarian cooperatives are also considered collective enterprises, and cooperativism has become indispensable to the growth of agrarian sectors.

Pye's observation that a typical Chinese has the cognitive capacity to accommodate incompatible goals and values is therefore irrelevant here. Although state planners deliberately impose socialist values on the market, the shield of cooperativism, the scale of the modern economy, defense mechanisms in the responsibility system, and the rise of collective enterprises together protect individuals from the profit-socialism symbiosis. Socialism guides collective policymaking, and profitability directs individual market behavior. Hence, an individual's profit-seeking behavior does not normally show up directly in the market, while the profitability of the collective is always conditioned upon prior contribution to socialist goals dictated by state planners. As long as a collective has safely acquired its socialist label, the individual members bear no burden to prove their purity. This may not necessarily negate socialism in effect but nevertheless hurts the legitimacy of the regime, as long as it is based on the claim of the selflessness of the comprehensive and insuperable principle of socialism. People are no longer self-conscious of the duty that fundamentally differentiates socialism from capitalism at the state level. As a result, duty becomes abstract:

> Following the rule of the commodity economy does not amount to abandonment of politics. . . . Under all circumstances, the goal of the socialist commodity economy to meet the expanding needs of society and the material needs of people must be kept in mind. To accumulate development funds for the state has been and will be an important duty of the socialist commodity economy, and this is fundamentally different from capitalist commerce, whose single mission is to seize profit.[34]

## THE BUYERS IN THE MARKET

In 1990 even the defense industry was a major player in the consumer goods market, which accounted for upwards of 65 percent of its total output, a good portion of which was exported.[35] In recent years the consumer goods market has grown dramatically, but who are the buyers supporting such expansion? Obviously, many of these consumers are cadres and workers in state-owned enterprises, themselves suppliers of consumer goods to the market; others are employed in smaller businesses. Collectives, including enterprises, government organizations, and public-run social organizations, are also major purchasers in the market. On the supply side, enterprise managers often worry about accusations that they engage in exploitation in the name of their own departmentalist interests; resourceful consumers have ideological concerns, too.

The first consideration has to do with the investment-consumption dilemma. State planners would like to save more for further investment, especially in those sectors with longer-lasting multiplying repercussions. In contrast, consumers understandably strive to upgrade their immediate standard of living. Consumers do not attend to issues of national capital and stock management and have a proclivity toward what planners denounce as blind and excessive consumption. The second issue regards the egalitarian image of socialism. Since consumption capacity varies enormously across areas and sectors, the emergence of conspicuous consumptive behavior has had a detrimental effect on the social mood. The state once promoted the image of a few "10,000-yuan households" in order to demonstrate the achievements of reform and encourage more followers to strive for the same status. The campaign was soon scaled back, as it led to increased social anxiety among a majority of the population.

The third concern is moral rather than ideological. The rise of power-ful collective consumers has ensured competition among collectives. The ability to consume more and better has become an alternative social desire. The official slogan that encourages people to "look forward" (*xiangqian kan*) has been twisted to imply "look toward money," as both phrases are pronounced the same in Mandarin. The campaign against spiritual pollu-tion was aimed at this bruisingly competitive atmosphere of consumption. The first two concerns are ideological in that they pertain to the impact upon the integrity of the plan system and the ideal of egalitarianism. This latter concern is more an ethical one and is therefore indirectly related to the issue of legitimacy.

Reform theorists nevertheless stress that the growth of productive forces, which is the root of historical progress, requires that people's ma-terial needs be met first. Accordingly, an active consumer goods market ought to be encouraged during reform:

> The rise of consumptive needs reflects the achievement of socialist eco-nomic law in the area of consumption. . . . In socialist society achieve-ments in observing the law of rising consumptive needs reflect the growth of productive forces, the unremitting development of the socialist commodity economy, and the continuous satisfaction of people's mater-ial needs. All this points to consumption as the locus of basic socialist economic law. One must realize the usefulness of consumption.[36]

In essence, the purpose of consumption is both to generate labor and facilitate people's "comprehensive development." Consumptive activities are considered an essential way to "release people's full potentials" so as to "re-create complete human beings."[37] The issue then becomes what level of consumption would facilitate comprehensive human development and what degree of productive force would achieve that level of consump-tion. It is on these issues that some scholars question the drive for higher consumption.

Many consider the drive for consumption premature because the rise of consumerism reflects neither higher development of productive forces nor improved earning ability on the part of consumers. Rather, con-sumerism is a result of financial decentralization. Funding available to managers of lower-level collectivities, either through higher shares of rev-enue deliberately allowed to promote reform or through manipulation of price differentials in goods between market and plan must first meet work-ers' demands for better living standards. In addition, the responsibility sys-tem in the villages has increased household incomes dramatically. The so-called three new households (*xinxing san hu*) (agrarian professional manufacturers, individual commercial shops, and privatized enterprises) display a predilection for squandering, hence exaggerating and stimulating a local "consumption fever."

Consequently, people begin to buy goods normally consumed only by those in higher income brackets in other societies. Consumption fever then spreads to the cities. As they watch rural peasants enrich themselves, urban workers begin to feel relatively deprived. Enterprises must satisfy rising worker income expectations by issuing bonuses, which are not bonuses per se most of the time. A total of 80 percent of the increase in workers' income can be attributed to reallocation policies within the enterprise, not to higher profitability. Resources originally designed to support enterprise-initiated investment now subsidize worker consumption.[38]

Literature on premature consumption (*xiaofei zaoshou*) in China offers a variety of observations. Some regard premature consumption as the phenomenon of consumption exceeding productive force[39] or, in economic terms, demand exceeding supply.[40] Others echo the Chicago school and contend that premature consumption is simply a monetary phenomenon.[41] Still others see it as a psychological phenomenon and argue that consumers themselves must be responsible for their own premature pursuit of luxury goods.[42] There are nonetheless those who believe that consumers are not to be blamed and the ultimate solution to the contradiction between investment and consumption is to enhance productive efficiency.[43]

Most agree that consumption has to be governed through some form of planning. Reform scholars contend that consumption in the past was excessively suppressed for the sake of capital accumulation. While the lesson that accumulation should not be blindly pursued is still being learned today, the slowdown in accumulation should not damage the ability to satisfy increasing consumptive demands over time. It should be made clear in the annual plan that minimum consumption in the current fiscal year must be at least identical with, if not slightly higher than, that of the previous year; the maximum consumption should be kept at such a level to assure that the increase in this year's investment is no less than the increase in the previous year.[44] In other words, consumption guides investment, and the level of investment is determined by the long-term need to satisfy consumption. This awareness of the role of consumption is considered essential in contemporary consumer education:

> We must strengthen the indoctrination of the basic characteristics and purposes of socialist consumption and, through such indoctrination, provide direction to laborers in planning consumption in their individual lives. The value of this direction lies in the improved effect of consumption. A socialist country should, through the indoctrination of basic characteristics and purposes of socialist consumption, make the masses, especially young people, aware of the great function of consumption in the process of overall human development and, by showing laborers how to plan for consumption in their lives, generate maximium satisfaction of the laborers' material and spiritual needs according to the current levels of social production and personal income. All this is to facilitate the overall development of laborers.[45]

To activate the consumer goods market requires improvement of consumption capacity. Once consumption capacity is increased, however, planners would not be able to continue directing actual consumptive behavior and may choose to use administrative means (i.e., the plan) and education to direct such behavior.[46] However, even the plan cannot be detailed enough to allow continuous regulation of the loose bonus and welfare policies of each enterprise; education cannot effectively transform people such as those in the "three new households," who are typically the least schooled. Neither can the plan influence consumers' perception of how and why consumption is a value. If citizens can go out and consume without appreciating the effect of consumption on the overall development of people, the official explanation concerning the legitimacy of boosting consumer culture would be irrelevant. Likewise, the legitimacy of the planner is likely to be left in oblivion.

## POLITICS OF THE CONSUMER GOODS MARKET

The integrity of a socialist regime is contingent upon the image of selfless political authority. Moral learning occurs as local leaders willingly cultivate the moral sense of the masses and make themselves political role models. Equally important is the regime's seeming neutrality in distributing social resources so that regime and society are not seen as competitors. The socialist regime does not base its legitimacy on its ability directly to provide for the material well-being of the working class, although this factor is certainly relevant.

The immediate counter role model is present in the new "three households." Many of these newly wealthy Chinese are illiterate, some having quit jobs in state-owned enterprises to succeed in the market; some work two jobs because they are unwilling to forgo benefits available only in a state-owned enterprise. The simple existence of these cases provides concrete examples of gross distortion of the collective economy. In contrast, cadres in state-owned enterprises hold enormous resources and have plenty of opportunities to embezzle. Sometimes smaller enterprises use kickbacks to acquire contracts from a state-owned enterprise. At other times a kickback is provided in the form of a gift to the collective as a whole. Today state-owned enterprises are also able to enrich themselves, legally and illegally. None of this, however, seems unusual compared to traditional practices in the dynastic periods, although today's state ideology incorporates entirely different principles.

Socialism as a state ideology prescribes how state and society should behave. Traditional theory states that the legitimacy of the emperor does not depend on his subjects' spiritual purity. In contrast, the socialist regime cannot claim legitimacy if the proletarian class does not take socialist norms seriously. Rank-and-file market behavior did not allude to the integrity of the emperor, who understood that, by definition, commoners could not help but pursue their own interests. In comparison, pursuit of profit and happiness has to be first justified under socialism as compatible with the collective interests of the proletarian class as a whole. This implies that those in the market know their socialist identity, if planners decide that they are the ones who should act upon their own initiatives. Once their own initiatives establish momentum, however, socialist identity becomes irrelevant. Cadres must partially give up their roles as local educators before they can represent the collective in protecting the enterprises' as opposed to the planners' interests.

Many observers believe that socialism has made the regime lose credit and eroded its base of legitimacy. The argument I present here is slightly more sophisticated. Socialism was still the official ideology of the state, and there was little attempt to jettison the notion of collective interests in favor of individual interests throughout the reform decade of the 1980s. This adherence to socialism cost the regime its own legitimacy because the regime was unable to prove why socialism was relevant to citizens' daily life. On the contrary, the reiteration of socialist goals and enforcement of the state plan often led to counteraction from lower echelons, further suggesting that the regime was losing credit. Socialism appears to have declined in China not because socialism is false but because the regime that upholds it has lost the appearance of selflessness. One solution—albeit an unlikely one—is to rebuild the regime's altruistic image. A stock answer is for the Chinese regime to strengthen its propaganda on the viability of socialism:

> [We must not] encourage egalitarianism and spread "red eye disease" [envy], nor should we promote the idea of despising the poor and embracing the rich. We must handle the interaction between demands for letting a proportion of the people get rich first and those for making everyone rich by establishing a new atmosphere of sharing and unity.
> . . . [We must] instill in people the concept of civilized commerce; of making cooperative members emphasize business credit, ethics, quality, and service; of serving the people and self-consciously protecting the interests of the consumer. Petty commercial producer thinking hurts, as witnessed in all kinds of misconduct and false advertisements that hoodwink the consumer. Here, we must use legal instruments to strengthen management of the commodity economy and engage in indoctrination for purposes of civilized commerce . . . so as to satisfy the people's needs.[47]

The state's political campaign causes inner conflict because state employees under socialism, who are supposed to carry out state commands, are also suppliers and consumers who are precisely the target of state regulation. State-owned enterprises, which must theoretically constrain the expansion of consumption funds, must cheat the state planner if they want to assert their alternate role as consumers in the market. Obviously, it is wishful thinking when the state attempts to have cadres and workers as state employees control premature consumption and, simultaneously, cadres and workers as consumers and citizens respond to profit incentives in the market and work hard on the job. For those who experience such role conflict, the solution is easy: They will naturally pursue profit and avoid regulation.[48] This choice would not affect the market, enterprises as resource allocators, or individuals as consumers or workers. It only makes the planners' job awkward, limiting the formulation of future plans.

The regime's efforts to satisfy people's material needs through the promotion of productive forces, achieved by introducing profit incentives in the market, undermine its public image, as such action is incompatible with the existing mode of political legitimation. The stress on productive forces draws individuals' attention away from collective interests and toward material satisfaction—and therefore alienates people from socialism. The planner's deliberate enlistment of profit incentives contradicts the previous mode of legitimation that rested purely on terms of selfless virtue. Literacy and professionalism appear to be penalized, as the least educated thrive in the market, causing confusion in terms of role modeling. Cadres cease to be models of socialist principles and seek to enrich themselves (or at least their collectives) at the expense of the state; they do this right in front of the rank and file, making socialism seem irrelevant in daily life. Those who have succeeded in the market are praised by the state and thus pose a better role model than do those who are versed in classic socialism. Finally, more people working two jobs inevitably encourages opportunism.[49]

The traditional mode of political legitimation allowed the regime to pretend lofty neutrality in times of recession. It also gave people a weapon to keep the state from interfering too much in their private lives. Under socialism the regime's legitimacy as a proletarian representative actually sanctions its intervention in people's private lives and hence its attempts to regulate people's thought. To gain freedom, the revolutionaries could historically gain support from the regime's own pretension to selflessness, pointing out that its own tenets forbade the regime's involvement in the allocation of interests. Socialist citizens cannot do the same, for their regime's superiority lies precisely in the pretension that it is the ultimate owner of all resources.

## CONCLUSION

China's traditional politics does not hinder the establishment of a modern market as some classical writers seem to believe. As a matter of fact, both the collective nature of the enterprise in China, big or small, and the scale of the modern market protect actual participants in market operation from exposing themselves to accusations of selfishness or undermining harmony. In other words, the traditional stress on the virtue of harmony does not hinder the evolution of a competitive market. Government intervention lacks influence because those who are supposed to carry out regulation are exactly those who should be regulated. The comprehensive nature of socialism in China ironically makes socialist norms irrelevant to market operation.

Nevertheless, the operation of the market has yet to challenge the authoritarian rule of the Communist Party. What is hurt is the mode of legitimation, not necessarily legitimacy per se, which likely has more to do with economics. The regime has tremendous difficulties in demonstrating why its collectivistic committment is still relevant to people. If it cannot succeed, the regime will not be able to base its legitimacy on socialist collectivism as it tries to do today. In reality, the legitimacy of the regime depends more and more on continuous economic growth and appropriate distribution of resources between investment and consumption. This does not mean that the regime has to jettison socialism. Socialism can continue to guide state planners in pursuing overall balance among sectors. Whether people can continue to tolerate a seemingly irrelevant ideology's guiding state actions depends on whether increasing consumptive demands can be steadily satisfied and whether the regime can restrain itself from intervening excessively in private business operations in the name of socialism.

# 6

# UNIT SOCIALISM:
# THE ROLE OF THE ENTERPRISE

In the 1980s the general-manager system was introduced into Chinese enterprises. Unlike the old system, in which the party-state controlled an enterprise's investment policy as well as its internal operating procedures, the general-manager system proposes to place the manager under the pressures of the market in the hope of generating cost-benefit consciousness in the business world. As a result, party-state activities in the enterprise must also adapt to a more reflective management style. Theoretically, the manager under the new system acquires enormous power vis-à-vis the party-state. In reality, such a normative redistribution of power among the central planner, the party secretary, and the general manager nevertheless requires adjustments by all parties, not only to dismantle past cognitive orders but also to maintain an equilibrium among their changing role expectations. In this chapter I discuss evidence of an emerging corporate culture and its political implications.

The research for this chapter is based upon field research I conducted in China in summer 1991. The factory in my case study belongs to the category of secondary socialist enterprise (*guojia erji qiye*) with the potential of becoming the primary enterprise in the near future. The enterprise is a model in its locality, and high-ranking party officials from Beijing have toured the factory more than once. I interviewed the general manager, the general secretary of the factory party, one associate general manager, cadres, and workers without (as far as I could detect) any monitoring or advance setup. The city planning board arranged for two of its researchers to meet with me twice, and each time the interview was unsupervised. I also interviewed two other general managers and visited their factories in the countryside, which were participating in joint ventures with the enterprise under study. Interviews lasted from thirty minutes to four hours. The remaining sections of this chapter present the ideal party-state-enterprise relationship as outlined in standard textbooks and the perceptions of real actors as revealed in my interviews.

## THE IDEAL

### Political Work and Entrepreneurship

Although official documents continue to portray an intimate party-state-enterprise relationship, the enterprise is no longer viewed as the receiving end of all policy initiatives as was formerly the case. In contrast, many party leaders advise that the political work of the party-state serves the economic tasks of the enterprise. Accordingly, a standard textbook comes up with four major missions of current political work in the enterprise.

Primarily, political work should assist the enterprise in combating any suspicions in the factory toward the policy of openness and reform. In concrete terms the workers must be made to "appreciate the force of the market and enjoy shouldering the responsibility of passing the test of market competition." The enterprise depends on the supporting party-state to "overcome the rigidities and barricades" created by past misreading of Marxism and Leninism. Since the workers cannot comprehend "new advanced ideological work" on Marxism by themselves, the state will have to inspire them by "the instillation of positivism through political ideological work in the enterprise."[1]

Second, political ideological work should ensure that the enterprise executes the state's reform policy willingly and completely. The enterprise thus produces goods and services mainly to satisfy the social demands for the "upgrading of material and spiritual civilization." The overall purpose of the party-state's assisting enterprise cadres in "breaking old barriers" and "dashing in new directions" is to enable the enterprise to execute party-state policy realistically by "reconciling policy requirements and factory realities." Therefore, one important dimension of political ideological work in the enterprise is moral education. The workers must be made to love the collective and rectify "relationships between individual and collective interests, short-term and long-term interests, and departmentalistic and holistic interests."[2] When this is successfully accomplished, an autonomous enterprise led by an independent general manager is still a highly reliable ally for constantly and self-consciously keeping the policy of reform in mind.

In addition, political ideological work should target individual workers in order to foster activism in the workplace. Since the life of the enterprise centers on production, its ideological work "must also center on production."[3] In recent years a great number of young workers have joined the ranks of China's productive forces. No wonder education is today considered key to building a solid factory identity. With a strong identity, young workers are expected to treat factory work as their own. In this regard the party-state has allowed much more room for the general manager to use material incentives under the reform system. However, there is an equal emphasis on the merit of self-discipline. The Chinese believe that a self-disciplined work force contributes to political stability as well as productive efficiency.

Finally, political ideological work should guarantee the integrity and advancement of "socialist spiritual civilization." It is stated in a Chinese textbook that the enterprise must improvise its unique "enterprise spirit" to prepare its workers, enhance their level of ideology, and resist "rotten ideologies." One essential element in this process of searching for spirit is patriotic education, as patriotism endows the workers both with ideals and a sense of mission. Socialist patriotic education begins with "the history of China under imperialist invasion" and proceeds with the determination to purge China of "imperialist, bourgeois ideology." In order to accommodate the multiple levels (i.e., individual, collective, state, and national) of spiritual civilization, one must integrate enterprise spirit, patriotism, and a sense of national pride.[4]

In short, ideological work in the enterprise has four dimensions: market competition, reform policy, enterprise production, and socialist civilization. Clearly, ideological work under reform does not seek to interfere with the work of production. On the contrary, it is supposed to provide a good ideological foundation for reform. The party-state actually encourages workers to break from past practices but still reminds workers of their indebtedness to the state. This is China's unique style of ideological management: The enterprise is given resources of its own but stands threatened with moral condemnation for abusing its power. The hope is that the enterprise will improve its efficiency in investment decisions and internal resource allocation under market pressures and at the same time demonstrate its loyalty to socialism through occasional services to the state. This is the doctrine of "political work as the lifeline of economic work."[5] Without political work, one cannot legitimately and forcefully carry out modernization, nor can one evaluate reform in lofty, rational terms.

## The Party and Entrepreneurship

Those party members subject to disciplinary action during the first ten years of reform had by and large committed economic, moral, or legal mistakes.[6] Consequently, consolidation of political leadership is no longer the priority of current party work in the enterprise. Party rectification since 1983 has aimed chiefly at strengthening the model effects of partisan workers' performance, so partisan workers are the prime targets of current party work. The ideological work of partisan workers begins with an understanding that party members enjoy no privileges in the productive process and receive no advantages in bonus distribution. However, too much emphasis on the separation of party and enterprise may distract party members from their socialist ideological work. The party cadres in the enterprise thus have the special mission of bringing the state-enterprise-party relationship to the party members' consciousness so that party members can resist materialistic tendencies on their own. To achieve this, party cadres must take the lead in preventing "the exchange of power for money" (*quanqian jiaoyi*) in party life:

> Those party members who grew up under the past practice of the planned economy are not ideologically prepared for the commodity economy. It will take time for them to appreciate the rules of the commodity economy, hence they are unable to grasp the principle of incorruptibility at the present time. In practice, one must separate the guidelines of party life (comradeship) from the rules of exchange under the commodity economy (anonymity). They should constantly be alert to negative elements making inroads into the party organism. . . . Since the use of power by leading enterprise party cadres often touches upon the sensitive issue of resource allocation, they must apply very high-level ideological reflection and a sense of careerism to guarantee self-rectification, and they must ground their position in the party's guidelines and policy knowledge. Then they can conform to the commodity economy and promote the development of the enterprise.[7]

In other words, although most factory cadres are party members, they should orient their policymaking toward the market. The assumption is of course that those party members are less prone to nepotism than non–party members, so that market forces will have a healthy influence if party ideological work continues to succeed. Some believe that opportunism would arise if the party loosened its ideological control over the enterprise. In short, partisanship makes the model worker. It is not political leverage against the enterprise. Instead, partisanship is utilized to guarantee the operation of the commodity economy and modernization of enterprise management.

In the Jilin Chemical Industrial Company, whose party-enterprise relationship is lauded as a model, special attention is paid to the image of the party in the enterprise. Party members are encouraged to help establish a new image for the party:

> Galloping breakthroughs and innovative reforms are the epochal features . . . of the new image of party members under the conditions of openness, reform, and the socialist commodity economy. In challenging the old system and traditional concepts, however, reform has been an extremely complex and difficult task. It therefore requires not only determination and courage but a kind of inspiration to meet all resistance as well. Whether or not a Communist Party member has strong partisanship and epochal self-consciousness is to a large extent indicated by his daring to

ride the tide and to become a trailblazer and creator. The Jilin Chemical Industrial Company has shifted the focus of its party work to economic development. The party organization at all levels persists in reform-oriented education, strengthening the sense of reform and encouraging self-conscious participation in reform among party members.[8]

Because the party controlled virtually all economic resources before reform, it is likely that some party members may undermine reform for the sake of their own vested interests. However, if party members are the first to break from the old system, they can actually become the first beneficiaries of reform. In this sense, party members are encouraged to enrich themselves not because they are party members but because they bravely fulfill the party's call for innovation. Of course, the party does not want to focus attention on getting rich; it would like to promote the image of breakthrough. But the party nevertheless believes that under reform party members would have a stronger incentive "to open a rich and kaleidoscopic field of activities to achieve [personal] success . . . and bring [the enterprise] into a whole new world."[9]

## The State and Entrepreneurship

Since the early days of reform, the state and the enterprise have established a contractual relationship. Through contracting, the enterprise is legally responsible for providing the state with an agreed-upon volume of goods and services. This is how the state ensures its central plan. More important, however, is that the enterprise will be able to keep surplus products, a right legally guaranteed in the contract. The enterprise thus has an incentive to produce more so that it can possess more. Socialism is nonetheless intact since the enterprise must first serve the state as well as directly meet the demand for goods and services in society. In contrast, the enterprise under capitalism pays taxes only after the enterprise collects its own share.

In addition, since the state is the largest buyer and seller, the relationship between the state and the enterprise is asymmetrical. The state can enforce certain rules and assign productive tasks arbitrarily. However, no sooner is the contract signed than the relationship moves toward balance. Postcontractual interaction between the state and the enterprise still involves a dual relationship. The state can tax the enterprise if a surplus in year-end accounts exists after the contracted assignment has been fulfilled. To the extent that the state is the sole actor in determining the tax rate, the relationship is asymmetrical. But the state as the investor shares after-tax profits with the enterprise. The extent of the state's share is often the subject of negotiation. On this account, then, the relationship is symmetrical.

The duality reflects the state planner's ambiguity toward the enterprise. On the one hand the planner understands that the enterprise is willing to "improve its own potential through renovation, save energy, control waste, and provide quality, inexpensive, and marketable goods to society" only because it is entitled to profit sharing. On the other hand, the state planner hopes that the enterprise can assist the state control inflation, enlarge the tax base and revenues, and maintain market order.[10] To just what extent the state should try to intervene in the market has been as large a headache for Chinese economists as for economists in the capitalist world.

The same ambiguity is found in the enterprise. The enterprise would dearly love to have state investment and privileged access to resources, and this requires state intervention. The enterprise would also hope that the state comes to its rescue if and when it finds itself in a financial quagmire. And yet the enterprise wishes the state would fade away through tax reductions, market deregulation, and lower profit sharing. The reality is that before the enterprise can start production, it must acquire funding approval from one division of the state and production approval from another. It is unlikely that the enterprise can leave the state and survive. The irony is that through all possible channels the state propagates the myth that the enterprise is being freed. As a result, the enterprise is convinced that all regulations, and hence the state itself, are negative elements in the productive process.

To alleviate tensions between state and enterprise, those who have dual status, namely, the general manager and the enterprise party secretary, become the center of focus. For quite some time, the secretary was the boss in the enterprise and the manager was the administrator. Reformers thus designed the general-manager system to resolve two kinds of historical role conflict—party versus state and state versus enterprise. In theory, the party secretary is supposed to be "the core" (*hexin*) of the enterprise while the manager is "the center" (*zhongxin*), and the two should be as one (*liangxin he yixin*). Accordingly, the general manager is the boss while the secretary consolidates overall leadership of the leadership group (*lingdao banzi*) under the general manager. With the secretary in charge of cultural and political work, the freed enterprise is expected to stay on the socialist track. Both the secretary and the manager are representatives of the state in the enterprise and the enterprise in the state.

The paradox is that if the state trusts the party organization in the enterprise to enhance socialist consciousness, the state may allow the manager even wider room to maneuver in the market, with socialism falling into oblivion. It is therefore reasonable to question the widely held assumption about the function of enterprise party organs. Now that the simple presence of the party in the enterprise is sufficient to win the minimum trust of the state, it is doubtful that the party secretary would necessarily be more interested in reinforcing socialist consciousness than improving productive efficiency (since all party workers share bonuses). On any account, with the manager's help the secretary can easily muddle through (*zouguochang*) all political assignments. Obviously, whether or not this collusion would occur depends much upon the personalities involved. If the manager and the secretary cooperate as the state designs, the state's leverage in the enterprise might shrink rather than expand. This is especially true if the profit margin is so high that the manager and the secretary would have a material incentive to collude. This is, after all, why the state maintains its ultimate power to reshuffle the leadership in the enterprise.

## Discussion

Dual leadership is not inherent in Chinese political thinking. The Chinese cherish a clear hierarchy with a single superior being at the top, consistently resulting in a clear ideological system that highlights a single value (i.e., Confucianism) and provides legitimacy. A single ruler cannot represent a dual value system since the inconsistency thereof would destroy the credibility of his leadership; dual leadership cannot glorify a single value because duality hurts the credibility of the archetypal order. Under the general-manager system, however, each enterprise has a dual leadership as well as a dual value system. Both the general manager and the party secretary are responsible for both material and spiritual civilization, the so-called two civilizations. The design does not fit in China's long tradition and confuses value priorities in public life.

Furthermore, the general-manager system draws a cognitive demarcation between enterprise and state. It gives the impression that the manager rather than the state is responsible for the economic welfare of the people, and this responsibility can be properly shouldered only if the manager does not work for the state. Not only does the relationship between state and people become more remote, the two sides may eventually develop incongruent interests as well. (This is the focus of the next section.)

Other practices also contribute to the process of alienation of the enterprise from the state. The party's mission among the workers accordingly has five distinct components: to know the enterprise, understand the political economic situation in which the enterprise finds itself, learn the rules and regulations of the factory, comprehend workers' job requirements, and clarify any confusion that lowers work morale. None of the components necessarily includes socialist education, yet all are conducive to the establishment of an enterprise identity. With regard to socialist education, the party secretary must promote as well as defend the party's stated point of view. However, he or she should note that "workers who have different understandings and different views regarding concrete matters in the process of reform should be allowed to express their opinions. As to the issues they fail to comprehend, one must promote discussion, guide with patience, and engage in active ideological education."[11] What are those concrete matters in need of ideological clarification?

> At the present time, the major issues that must be dealt with in a worker's life in the enterprise include housing, employment for his children, day care, dining halls, the young worker's love life and marriage, the retirement life of the senior worker, the engineer's low salary, etc. In our efforts to solve these problems, we must educate the worker to shoulder a heavy duty for the party and the state, continue his style of hard work, and strive for better-quality production to improve the profit margin of the enterprise. [This is the right way of] using one's own labor to ameliorate one's own and society's material living conditions.[12]

It is clearly believed that the best way to have workers identify with the enterprise is to link their personal material interests with those of the enterprise. The lofty slogans of socialist civilization are nearly completely secularized once they reach the level of the enterprise. On the one hand, the constant vision of socialist slogans reminds the rank and file of the rhetorical relevance of socialism. On the other hand, the process of secularization makes such political principles of Marxism-Leninism and Mao Zedong Thought irrelevant to daily life. If political principles of socialism are taken seriously, the enterprise would have to consider the opportunity cost thus incurred. For example, socialist education would take away productive time, rational decisionmaking might be distracted, and so on. Cognitively, if not administratively or politically, the enterprise and the state become two separate entities. The general-manager system, in this sense, strengthens enterprise identity at the expense of state identity.

## THE GENERAL MANAGER VIEWS THE STATE

Both collective and state enterprises have adopted the general-manager system. For the collective enterprise, the linkage with the state is indirect. A general manager of a rural collective enterprise (*xiangzheng jitiqiye*) complains that his factory and the state have "minimal relations" because it has consistently been state policy to "hold the countryside accountable for its own food and clothing." If there is indeed a relationship, it is often conceived of in the negative sense. For example, his factory "has to turn in its profits," there are often new projects that "take land away from the village" on very short notice, and so on. It is "impossible for the village to formulate its own long-term use of the land" under such circumstances.[13] Another general manager in a different village finds himself in a "gray area" where no one cares. His factory is the creation of a joint venture of a county office and a state enterprise and hence has "no direct relationship with any government" planning agency. The county government adopts "a hands-off policy" except for "occasional cost-sharing requests" to help local finances.[14] The only steady contact with a government institution is with the tax bureau. For the rural collective enterprise, the state may be more a constraint than a resource.

The general manager in the state-owned enterprise is usually appointed by the state. In the enterprise under study, the general manager and one associate manager raise many interesting points, revealing a changing concept of the state-enterprise relationship. For example, once loosened up under reform, the current central planning system is thought to have fundamentally transformed the state-enterprise relationship. A successful general manager must also be able to find his or her own resources in the market instead of simply waiting for planned allocation:

> The enterprise has to develop in the market, not in the planning system. Based upon market information, the factory has to fight for [the permission to produce] specific items for the central planner. Many factories wait for the planner to make investment decisions for them—this won't work. It has to be the other way around. The small factories should come together and organize themselves into corporations. Some enterprises start a new product without assignment from the planner simply because they realize that that specific product is profitable. If the planner would like to include the same item in the plan but assign others to do the production, these enterprises would go ahead anyway and produce from their own assembly lines [without permission]. In our factory, for example, the third-stage project was of our own initiative and the state approved funding for the project only afterwards.[15]

This quote shows that the central planning system has undergone revolutionary change. In all central planning systems, the planners are the initiator, and the enterprise carries out the mission assigned. In the point of view just expressed, the enterprise has become the initiator. The whole idea of reform is to create market pressure that can force the enterprise to be cost-conscious in executing its assignments. In reality, the general manager learns more than that and begins to be more flexible and profit-conscious in influencing investment decisions. Nowadays it is legitimate for the enterprise to engage in its own market research and lobby for support by the planners. Moreover, several enterprises can even organize themselves into a financial group on behalf of their business interests. For the enterprise, the plan is no longer the sole guide of production. Rather, it is another instrument, sometimes an essential one, to run its business. Instead of being sandwiched between the plan and the market, as the planners wish, the enterprise manages to channel market pressure back to the planners. Hence, central planning is unexpectedly exposed to the market.

On the issue of profit sharing, both planners and enterprise show enormous departmentalism. For the general manager of the factory in my case study, the relationship between those two involves dialectics of unity and struggle (*jilianhe youdouzheng*). This is not necessarily a new paradox for the central planning system except that reform has opened a virtual Pandora's box of interest expressed from below:

> The center and the locality always fight; the locality and the enterprise always fight, too. The notion that they are entangled in competitive relations is overdrawn, though. When we face the tax or finance agents, we must reason forcefully yet carefully cater to them at the same time. We must maintain a good relationship with them to squeeze out maximum benefits for the factory. Occasionally, we prepare small gifts for them, but of course they dare not take too much.[16]

The small gifts refer to cost sharing. In China it is "corrupt for an individual to receive gifts, but not so for the collective."[17] In fact, the general manager just bought some medical equipment from abroad for the hospital affiliated with his superior bureau. As he is well aware, only a fool would offend the planners.

Another point the managers raise concerns worker benefits. They believe that workers "know only money, and they support us simply because we make money."[18] However, the planners have set a ceiling for annual bonuses. In order to bypass the law, managers look for loopholes. The enterprise I researched started a joint venture with a government bureau in a neighboring county two years ago. Each side contributed 50 percent of the funding, but on the books the enterprise's contribution was only 30 percent. So the bureau would get 70 percent of bonuses, but their arrangement calls for the bureau to use 20 percent to purchase gifts for the enterprise. Since the ceiling does not apply to the bureau, the arrangement does not hurt its interests but helps the enterprise go beyond the same ceiling. Since that 20 percent is a gift to the enterprise instead of a bonus, the ceiling rule likewise does not apply. What is significant about this case is that the general manager's position between state and enterprise has shifted in favor of the enterprise. The general manager is supposed to be the link between the two under the general-manager system. That he sees himself more on the side of the workers than the state may have serious political-cultural implications.

The fourth point worth discussing is that the managers' attitude toward the workers also connotes a type of identity shift. The general manager, for instance, would like to see the workers improve themselves. He conceived of a strategy to help the workers avoid wasting time. He drew up an internal rule that says that a worker without a high school diploma cannot be promoted above the level of sergeant general. This has encouraged many a young worker to attend night school, an accomplishment the general manager is quite proud of. What the associate manager wants most is to project the image of "a good leader," and he hopes that "the workers would treat me like a leader." What frustrates him most is that "my subordinates resist my good ideas and raise a lot of excuses if I push them."[19] This is the speaker quoted earlier who was ready to do battle with the planners on behalf of the enterprise. Obviously, he would not be frustrated but rather filled with a spirit of struggle if the planners failed to appreciate his ideas. He is frustrated, though, if the workers do not embrace those same ideas. The associate manager has begun to identify emotionally with the workers and the enterprise as part of his self-image, leaving the state and the planners outside that emotional ring.

Finally, I queried the associate manager about requesting support from his superior bureaus. His indirect remarks reflect the belief of a true disciple of the general-manager system:

> The Chinese management style is hierarchical, and this is an important thing to keep in mind. When reform started, we used to have the party secretary take the position of associate manager. Management was his full-time job and party work only part-time. The practice is changing today. The general manager must now take the position of associate party secretary. Management is the center of his job and party work is the core; theoretically, the center and the core must be in congruence. However, our general manager is not a party member, and I myself applied to join the party only after I had been promoted to the position of associate manager. We are fortunate, however, to have an open-minded party secretary, although he still needs to meet many requirements set by his superiors. I heard that in a neighboring factory they have a problem of disharmony [between the general manager and the party secretary]. . . . In our factory if we have problems we solve them by ourselves. In many other factories, cadres avoid responsibility and ask superiors to make decisions for them but take all the credit themselves. . . . We do everything by ourselves. Only after we have the solution to a problem do we talk with our superiors and lobby for support.[20]

In other words, a manager does not have to be a party member for "the center" and "the core" to come together. The open-mindedness of the party secretary alone should suffice. In addition, when the center and the core indeed come together, they work things out for themselves. The implication is that if party and state cannot be separated (*dangzheng fenli*), state and enterprise cannot be separated (*zhengqi fenkai*) as the general-manager system has designed. This is because the party in the state can interfere in the enterprise via the party in the enterprise. This manager believes that Chinese management should be hierarchical; in order to separate the party from the state-owned enterprise, the party has to be subordinate, not equal, to the state-owned enterprise. Ironically, the whole purpose of this separation, as he sees it, is to allow the enterprise to develop its own management and leave the state behind. In contrast, those who support the center-core theory worry precisely that the party will lose control over the enterprise as it separates from the state. The interviewee's perception of party-state and state-enterprise relationships is dramatically different from that of either the state planners or the party leader.

The general manager of a county factory acknowledges that he would look to the government only if he experienced "financial difficulties."[21] A former general manager of a school factory who serves as agent in charge of all school factories in his county has an interesting observation (which may have a universal application in other societies): The better the financial situation of a school factory, the more independent it is in running its business and the less it welcomes government intervention.[22] The general-manager system is meant to separate the enterprise from the state so that the enterprise can operate on its own. In fact, though, quite the opposite happens: Those who operate their businesses well request further separation and those in trouble pull back to the state. This process of negative selection would leave the state stuck with enterprises in financial disarray.

It is obviously too early to talk about enterprise independence since the banking sector is still under state control. One should note, though, the cognitive breakthrough in the more successful enterprises. As discussed in this section, those managers interviewed are concerned chiefly about intraenterprise matters, for example, worker benefits, leadership image, profit margin, market research, and, most important, room for independent maneuver. The general-manager system creates a niche (psychologically, perhaps) that would allow and even encourage the enterprise to establish its own identity. In this sense, development of a new management system will eventually collide with vested interests in the party and the state above the enterprise. Successful managers would then no longer be simply state employees but would move closer to being career businesspeople.

## THE PARTY SECRETARY VIEWS THE ENTERPRISE

The party secretary belongs to the party system, and his status parallels the general manager's in the state system. The general-manager system highlights the importance of professional knowledge and necessarily hurts the secretary's leadership. In this sense, one would expect the secretary's dependency on the party at the next higher level to grow. Indeed, one hears endless stories of conflict between the secretary and the general manager. However, this type of disharmony is not always the case. The general secretary of the enterprise in my study, who retired from the military as a colonel only a few years ago, made the following analysis of the manager-secretary relationship:

> Generally speaking, two factors explain why a factory cannot run well: The leading cadre group lacks a high level of cultivation, and there is

disunity. Disunity may exist between the general manager and the party secretary and, consequently, even among workers in the same department. Rumors about who is under whose wing fly. All good things are taken with a certain cynicism. I was once a soldier belonging to the administration side [as opposed to the party side], so I am sympathetic to the way the general manager thinks. Whenever there are problems, we simply consult each other and then go ahead and do it. I am unlike the typical, reluctant secretary who always worries too much. If there is a problem, we think together.[23]

The many workers I interviewed agreed that their secretary is exceptionally open-minded. Basically, the secretary's job description includes the two most commonly mentioned elements: assisting the general manager in ideologically preparing the workers to face the market and guaranteeing the healthy development of the enterprise on the socialist track and according to the planner's policy instructions. If the secretary pays a great deal of attention to the former task (ideological preparation), there is a tradeoff with other valuable activities. Thus he will have to identify with the enterprise much more than with the party in order to concentrate exclusively on such ideological work, which would undoubtedly contribute to his identity in the enterprise. How, then, does the secretary see his job? With regard to job description, he mentions recruitment of party members, cultivation of the workers' sense of belonging, and spiritual civilization in the enterprise. All of these are about productive efficiency in the factory as far as he is concerned. For example, he talks about recruitment in this way:

When we recruit new party members, our criteria have nothing to do with political ideology. We want to know . . . if the target person is self-disciplined on the job, industrious, and self-restrained. Our factory has high standards regarding cultivation, so we require that workers complete at least junior high school. We observe the target person for three years, examine his performance in school, and ensure he was not a troublemaker before.

On the workers' sense of belonging, he emphasizes participation, though the real focus is nonetheless productive efficiency: "We hold discussion sessions or call a workers' assembly. I recall when we started a new product a few years ago, many people opposed the move. We wanted to acquire new technology; more resisted. Old cadres in particular were against the idea of renovating the dining hall and the dormitory. We held a series of sessions to explain the policy again and again. All this was done by the party." As to spiritual civilization, the most important thing is to educate young workers at the time they enter the factory about proper commitment to work quality: "Spiritual civilization can guarantee the core [productive force]. Young workers who just left vocational school are used to an undisciplined life-style. Many squander their parents' money. We set up an unprecedented meeting with parents. We let the parents tour the factory, tell them how much their children actually earn so that they would know if the children spend too much, and suggest ways to help our workers deal with all kinds of problems."[24] The secretary in this case study thus represents the archetype of a reformer. He is rarely worried about the political loyalty of his workers; his major concern is obviously productive efficiency in the factory.

Other secretaries also demonstrate a preoccupation with economic work. One county secretary who is responsible for party work in three rural enterprises remarks:

> The most important job for the party is economic construction in the village; other administrative works come next and partisanship building still further down the line. With respect to so-called spiritual civilization, we are frankly weak; the most we do is resolve conflicts in the village in order to maintain harmony. Most workers staying in the village are older workers, thirty years old or so. The younger ones do not stay because they want to work in a state-owned enterprise. Some go to college and will later be assigned to a state-owned enterprise. Those who stay cannot be very young. Occasionally, I have to meet requirements of the government that the village supply labor force to support some national projects. *But I appreciate departmentalism. That's why I always try to keep the better workers for the village.* You know, this is the place where I grew up.[25]

It is clear that he has no hesitation in revealing his dissatisfaction with the state. His partisanship cannot convince him of the legitimacy of national economic development at the expense of local development.

The party secretary in China thus begins to stand on the side of the enterprise instead of the state. This is more than a matter of cognition. At times an enterprise secretary does not wish to be promoted to a superior government agency. On the contrary, secretaries in a government agency sometimes fight for opportunities to be demoted to a lower-level enterprise simply because "there they can share the bonus." Consequently, the enterprise secretary, who does not want to lose his job, is understandably worried that dissatisfied workers might report to his superiors about his weaknesses, real or fabricated.[26] In a worst-case scenario, he would be forced to placate the workers. Under such conditions, it is hard to imagine that the secretary can be a good representative of the party. Regarding the recent decision to purchase another near-bankrupt factory, the secretary describes overwhelming departmentalism:

> For example, the government agency ordered us to purchase Factory X. I disagreed and the general manager disagreed as well. But our superior

insisted that we make the purchase. We all resisted. Finally, I told the
general manager we could not resist any longer. They would remove both
of us, I told him. In that case we would have nothing. All right. I had to
do all the ideological preparation for the workers to face this purchase.
The general manager was unwilling and unprepared to do things like . . .
the ideological preparation for the purchase. The party had to do it.[27]

This explains why he does not like the reputation the enterprise enjoys. He
complains that the government always "wants us to make donations" or
buy useless items.

In such a profitable enterprise, the secretary receives a bonus second
only to that of the general manager. As long as the secretary has such an
incentive, he is more than willing to assist the manager in upping the profit
margin. His contribution would simply be winning his superior's political
trust. A trustworthy political image always pays off. If he succeeds, his
factory can gain tremendous advantage in its maneuvers in the market. The
state manager and planner naturally feel safe with a good party secretary
at the helm of the enterprise. In this sense, the secretary is the protector
of neither socialism nor central planning. Rather, under the flag of the
party, he protects the enterprise by bargaining away state intervention.

## THE WORKER VIEWS THE GENERAL MANAGER

Under the general-manager system, workers may have to deal with a totally different type of manager who demands strict discipline and strives
for more. Many believe that for the benefit of the workers a good manager
makes a profit for the enterprise and a bonus for the workers. Both the
workers and the general manager agree that an enterprise can easily handle
its worker-manager relationship as long as the enterprise has a high profit
margin. Among the workers interviewed for this project, few expressed
any significant degree of dissatisfaction. The high bonus capacity is the
key to management success according to the general manager himself. Yet
the workers I interviewed seemed to view a capable, disciplined manager
as moving in a separate sphere. For example, one young worker thinks she
hasn't the slightest chance of seeing the general manager pass by because
"he has a limousine."[28] She receives work instructions from the sergeant
and might see the general manager only when he comes in on a routine
Monday-morning inspection, but such contact is remote and brief. Another
said that she would never talk with the general manager because "he must
be very busy and one cannot bother him with one's own trifles."[29] The
workers do not expect to see the manager often because they "trust that he
is buried by his work."[30]

Interestingly, although the general manager appears to be a remote
figure, the workers do not necessarily regard him as a fixture of a state

now perceived as an entity distinct from the enterprise. Some, cadres especially, nonetheless appreciate the dual role of the manager position. One sergeant keenly analyzes the paradox built into this duality: "On the one hand, the general manager should stand on the state's side. He should help the state make up supply shortages [as the planners see it] by completing productive assignments. On the other hand, he must also stand on the enterprise's side. He has to struggle to multiply the revenue of the enterprise. But if the general manager receives no support from his superiors, he definitely won't succeed."[31]

A department head fully agrees with this line of analysis. For him, the general manager "cannot assume leadership in the factory without state support." However, he thinks that "under the general-manager system, we have a hierarchy of worker, sergeant, and department head, and most of them have little interaction with the government."[32] Another department head argues from a different perspective:

> I think I can and should influence the general manager in his decision-making, for the whole enterprise should be considered one unit. However, one can trace hierarchy in the factory back to the government as one would trace an artery stretching from the government through the general manager to the department head. *Everyone is a part of the government.* Equally true, however, is that everyone must also have his own place. When you move to another factory, for example, you know that you will have to find a new place specifically for yourself.[33]

The difference between the two department heads does not involve the duality of the manager's roles but whether the notion of duality also applies to roles in the lower echelons.

This subtle difference is not an issue at all for real role players at lower levels. Generally, they do not see the general manager as part of the state, although they realize he is constrained by the state. A sergeant remarks on the above-mentioned purchase of another factory forced by the city government: "When it comes to that purchase, the government had to do a good ideological job on the general manager because he wholeheartedly resisted. In turn, he had to do a good ideological job on the workers. The workers generally realized that the factory could thrive as it does today because the state was willing to invest in our projects. On the whole, [people know] that the general manager stands on the factory's side."[34] In fact the workers do not think of the state-enterprise relation as an investor-manager relation. One office worker with a college degree thinks that "ordinary people have no relationship with the government" and that they "depend on the general manager to make decisions for them." Accordingly, the future of the factory "to a large extent relies upon the general manager's vision and wisdom." In her eyes the government comes to the factory at most for "inspection purposes."[35]

Another worker argues that the government and the enterprise belong to "two totally separate fields so that decisions in the factory do not require state approval."[36] One college graduate explains this indirectly: "The second stage of the current project was exclusively a task inspired and led by the general manager himself, who searched throughout the world for the most advanced assembly line. . . . Now we are moving into the third stage, in which the factory develops all the products for itself. You know what I mean if you just want to ask about the relationship between the enterprise and the state."[37] In the workplace, therefore, the view of the state is by no means positive. A former high school teacher who had severely criticized the general manager in the rest of his interview expresses one bold opinion:

> Our general manager is very good at controlling the direction of long-term development. . . . The reform [he leads] is good in this sense. . . . Of course external as well as internal factors have contributed to the success of the factory, but we cannot deny that the general manager indeed made a contribution. . . . For example, if you are the government and inferior, the general manager can resist you. This makes the factory better off. I cannot say that the factory shielded by the general manager is necessarily an extralegal Eden. But the shield has its function to the extent that it protects the factory [from the state].[38]

The way in which workers perceive the state has apparently undergone fundamental change. An interviewee quoted earlier is unique in seeing everyone as a part of the government. Nonetheless, both the notion of duality and the myth of separation of state and enterprise reflect a cognitive restructuring. The implication is that the enterprise develops a separate identity for the workers. Above all, it is viewed as an independently operating enterprise constrained externally by the state. Even the interviewee who believes everyone is part of the state agrees that everyone must also find his or her own place in the factory. This changing perception is consistent with the aforementioned shifts in the views held by the general manager and the secretary, though probably for different reasons. This consistency may motivate the workers and strengthen their position in making their own judgments about the propriety of government policy, policy that affects them and policy that comes from a separate and remote entity.

## THE GOVERNMENT VIEWS THE GENERAL MANAGER

The local planners understand the paradox of duality precisely as it is. According to a research fellow working for the local planning board, however, the board is divided as to how to conceptualize the manager's role properly. One group holds the traditional view and maintains that the general manager is "99 percent representative of the government." Others contend that the manager must be allowed to be creative for the sake of enterprise development. Still others argue that the manager under reform represents neither the government nor the enterprise but "himself"; he should be a career-oriented entrepreneur.[39] Nonetheless, the research fellow finds that the trend favors the second view. He struggles to integrate the latter two perspectives:

> It is hard on him. Some general managers are elected by the workers so they must cater to them. But he has to face pressure from the government at the same time. His salary is not really that high, but with bonuses and awards, he is quite all right. That's why he persists even though his job is tough. A small group of entrepreneurs has emerged in China. They work out of careerism and target the world market. They aim high on economic scale and efficiency.[40]

What makes the planners cautious and sometimes frustrated is that many general managers have good personal connections in the government, and this undermines the government's attempt to regulate the market. The planners may set a ceiling and floor for worker benefits, bonuses, awards, depreciation, reinvestment, and so forth, but there is always "room for maneuvering and manipulation." Well-connected general managers never fail to take advantage of this room.[41] If the manager is obsessed with profit making, planning suffers. For fear of losing control, the government occasionally intervenes arbitrarily with rigid regulation: "Funding outside the budget system is available mostly through depreciation, reinvestment, and other profit-sharing mechanisms. The only way to prevent the enterprise from abusing its own funds is to arbitrarily set an amount, and all investments above that amount have to be reviewed and approved by the planning board. No one is pardoned for stealing through investment."[42]

The problem, of course, is that the board's perspective often differs dramatically from the enterprise's. The former is concerned with balanced overall development, while the latter is more concerned with its own. The perceptual gap may create friction. One research fellow on the board recalls the unpleasant purchase of Factory X made by the enterprise in my case study:

> The purchase decision was made together by the planning board, the bureau of finance, the bureau of tax, and the bureau of industry. The major concern was the low efficiency of the purchased factory. The purchase, however, hurt the vested interests of its cadres and was resisted. The purchasing enterprise also appeared reluctant. That's why a purchase is usually initiated by the government. The planning board is quite influential on this type of issue. For this reason, it is normally headed by officials at the governor's or mayor's level. If a purchase affects the whole area, the initiator is often the bureau of industry. The planning board will have

to approve the case before the bureau begins to arrange it. We do have a few cases where the board turned down the proposal. Sometimes the board will listen to the factories involved in the proposed purchase.[43]

In short, the board worries about unbalanced development. This straightforwardly violates the departmentalistic concern of the enterprise and also defeats market considerations that the board itself would like to see prevail.

It is not in any sense unusual in a capitalist country for businesspeople and government officials to fight. In China, however, the position of general manager in the state-owned enterprise is a government job. Since state-owned enterprises are unambiguously the leading force in the economy, the significance of state-owned enterprises and their general managers as a collectivity is much more dramatic than in the capitalist state. Thus the meaning of state-enterprise incongruence in socialist China is that the government gradually loses control over managers as lower government officials, and, moreover, these managers develop a unique identity in the enterprise separate from the state. No wonder the planner is worried and the party may feel threatened even if there is no sign of intended political challenge.

## CONCLUSION

The separation of the state and the enterprise was originally conceived of as the best mechanism to bring market pressure to bear on lethargic state enterprises. With renovations to enterprise party structure, the enterprise is believed to be able to keep the state and the planner in mind and self-consciously utilize market forces to streamline enterprise structure while, with the state's backing, containing the influence of the market. In my case study, however, the enterprise party organ appears preoccupied with ideological work related only to productive efficiency. The concern of the party is trifling; abstract propaganda no longer finds a place inside the enterprise. In the enterprise I studied, the managers and the secretary alike have developed their special enterprise identity. Most important, all see the state as a constraint that comes from a source outside the enterprise. The trend seems to suggest that in the people's perception the enterprise in China has moved away from the state.

The emergence of an enterprise identity has two implications for the changing political culture of China. First, the emerging enterprise identity is based upon departmentalistic and individualistic considerations. These considerations are necessarily materialistic and, some would add, achievement oriented. The Chinese traditionally identified with a hierarchical order, an omniscient leader, and the collective. The separation of state and enterprise has been instrumental in fostering a trend to amoralization. When the separation becomes irrevocable, the process of amoralization undermines the traditional source of legitimacy based upon moral superiority (or the pretension thereof).

Second, there emerges a group of entrepreneurs who are capable of winning people's trust without first passing some sort of state test or gaining the omniscient leader's direct or indirect approval. If the grassroots leader arises outside the current political system, the current regime cannot expect to have followers who uphold socialist doctrine by emulating local leaders, traditionally selected and recruited only by the government in the center. If the government cannot prove its integrity or stimulate selfless empathy among the rank and file, citizens may criticize it for failing to lead and teach. The general-manager system may thus profoundly impact China's political-cultural mode.

The general-manager system emerged in the 1980s partially as a design to save the regime from a legitimacy crisis in the aftermath of the Great Leap Forward and the Cultural Revolution. That solution created its own momentum and established its own unique identity, a side effect few could have anticipated just a decade ago.

# 7

## MANAGERS' SOCIALISM: INVESTMENT MOTIVATION

Chinese reformers have struggled for close to a decade in their attempts to reconcile market mechanisms and central planning, this being perhaps the most difficult task since the reform movement was initiated in the late 1970s.[1] In the tradition of liberal economic theory, government intervention and market are contradictory notions. In socialist conceptualization, however, the central planners can and should regulate the market, which in turn should guide the productive decisions of each enterprise. Many Chinese economists believe that the socialist central planners do not have to command enterprises directly through administrative channels to make them follow the plan. Ideally, the planners can regulate the market to such an extent that the enterprise would move in the planned direction without losing profit incentive. Since the early 1980s these economists have enthusiastically discussed the implementation of such economic levers as interest rates, discount rates, tax rates, and money printing—all familiar to the liberal economist.[2] In practice, though, the Chinese central planners continue to exert direct influence over thousands of national enterprises through the administrative system.

Local planners engages in detailed planning just like the central planners, with investment in any planned field subject to their review. This practice of itemized review can become a tedious process for planners at any level. In addition, the policy of financial decentralization in the early years of reform has encouraged a rapid money flow and as a result overburdened the financial system with a substantial volume of unregulated credit. Double-digit inflation was one consequence, and this in turn has prompted planners to intervene in any investment proposal over an arbitrarily set amount. Some economists who dislike the rigidity of this type of review or intervention have nicknamed planning under reform as "one stroke of chopping" (*yidaoqie*),[3] otherwise referred to as indiscriminate policy barricades.

On the other hand, the general-manager system presents the manager with more intraenterprise management levers and more room in marketing goods and services. This aims precisely at having the manager share the profit of the enterprise as well as making up the loss. The planners put the manager directly under market pressure while at the same time requiring of the manager a prenegotiated amount of goods and services. Under these conditions, the use of the general-manager system indeed creates sufficient profit incentives for some microlevel actors to utilize the market as fully as possible. In theory, general managers can develop new products, start a joint venture with overseas business, and open their own bank credit accounts. They are also encouraged to make their own decisions on promotion and demotion inside their enterprises and to simply replace administrative sanctions with financial disincentives. All this is in line with the slogans of economic reform, especially those that downplay the administrative system because of its lack of efficiency.

Generally speaking, as the planners are reluctant to give the market total freedom, so the planners are naturally suspicious of the manager's willingness to fulfill the plan. There is always the tendency for local as well as central planners to intervene, paradoxically protecting the enterprise from the market. Most important, there is the lack of sanctions against enterprises that fail to meet the market requirements and incur large losses on the state's balance sheet. In other words, although a hardworking manager may earn a good material reward from the market, there is no guarantee that everyone else who could get by without testing themselves in the market would do the same.

If the material incentives alone are not sufficient, the planner arranges administrative incentives. Managers who perform well by proving themselves in the market may get promoted. Furthermore, the state may offer moral incentives by publicly praising managers' contributions to socialism, insinuating that lethargic managers lack socialist virtue. Both administrative and moral incentives fall short in pushing the majority of the general managers to face the market. If, as the planner would always assert, managers are responsible for providing a steady supply of goods and services to the state at low prices, why would they also feel responsible for profit loss? The more resourceful enterprises, above all, have this grievance: Inasmuch as they have the mission of regulating the market, their job is not to beat others according to the logic of the market; rather, many are supposed to operate against the logic of the market so as, for example, to reverse inflation and hence help the state regulate the market.

These enterprises do acquire their raw materials mostly through the planning system. Few have complete control over the quality and price of those raw materials. Why would anyone try to beat the system just to face the risk in the market? General managers can indeed become socialist heroes if they work hard and are lucky, and in the process they may enrich their workers as well as themselves. But only a very few have opted to do that. In this sense, this minority who strive to become the kind of entrepreneurs that the planner anticipated in the early stages of reform are the ones who deserve attention. In this chapter I examine what motivates a manager to look for investment opportunities in the market despite all the above-mentioned disincentives. I also analyze how highly motivated managers maneuver to enlarge their own living space by undermining the rationale of the planning system.

As for the previous chapter, the field research for this chapter was done primarily in a Chinese factory in summer 1991. I mention neither names nor places in order to protect those involved in the research from political investigation. This project contains thirty-two interviews. For the purpose of this particular chapter, I include only interviews with four general managers. These general managers or associate managers work for either national enterprises or collective enterprises; one enterprise is large and three are small. The interviews with these managers were unsupervised and lasted anywhere from one to three hours.

## INVESTMENT MOTIVATION

### Mr. G

From a technical point of view, the primary aim of an investment is a return on that investment. Without such a return, an investment is no longer such. A good investor aims high, but a high return may have a different meaning for different investors. For Mr. G, for example, a high return confirms his sense of professionalism. Mr. G is the general manager at Factory F in City A. He was assigned in 1985 as an associate manager roughly four years before his scheduled retirement. Shortly thereafter, he was promoted to general manager with responsibility for manufacturing a certain item City A wanted to develop. Amid the political cries for infusion of young blood in the 1980s, his retainment was by any standard an exceptional case. The new assignment at the age of fifty-six was truly a confirmation of his leadership. At the time of my interview with him, Mr. G was sixty-two, and his contract with City A was not due to expire until the following year. Finally, that he is not a Communist Party member makes his case all the more unusual, since most general managers in national enterprises are also party cadres.

Mr. G is an engineer whose family fell into the bourgeois category at the time of the revolution; its property was therefore liquidated. He was among those purged in the antirightist campaign of 1957. His work unit recognized his professional background and solid training in engineering and decided to keep him; his wife was less lucky and became a menial laborer. He nonetheless despised those who had saved him from a rectification campaign. Mr. G admits that he is a very serious person, so serious that he rarely smiles. Workers in Factory F often complain of this in their interviews. Mr. G thinks that the appearance of seriousness contributes to his reputation as a professional engineer, believing that only people who care about work quality can afford not to smile and still win respect.

During almost every family interview, Mrs. G complained to me that her husband intentionally as well as unintentionally offends people in the factory administration because "he positions himself too high and refuses to speak to party cadres with respect." Mr. G argues that his pride rests on his professional knowledge, and for this reason alone, he must ignore etiquette to build his professional reputation. He worries about the young workers in his factory today, who he thinks know only money. If he were to relax even a little, the young workers would soon lag behind in quality requirements.

For decades, Factory F produced items that gave it above-average profits, and the workers were apparently satisfied with the status quo when Mr. G first arrived six years ago.[4] When the planners of City A assigned the production of a new item, workers vehemently resisted. Mr. G thus faced multiple challenges: He had to persuade the workers that the new item was a mission to be carried out "like it or not"; he had to find ways to keep the bonus level at least as high as it had been; under the pressure of reform, he could no longer depend on the planners to provide unconditional funding, meaning he had to arrange credits with banks and pay interest in the subsequent stringent years critical to the survival of the new assembly lines; and, finally, the technical requirements for producing this new item greatly exceeded the existing technical level.

Mr. G was not thinking of these critical problems at the time—he was aiming high. He began to envision the world's most advanced assembly line in his factory. He thought he had only a four-year time frame in which to fulfill his dream, since he was originally scheduled to retire at the age of sixty. Technology to produce the assigned item had in fact already been developed in China, and the city planners expected Factory F simply to import the technology from neighboring provinces. Mr. G, however, turned down the domestic source, believing the most advanced technology in question existed in Japan. Mr. G spent months convincing the city planners that it was imperative for Factory F to start at the most advanced level. He succeeded in acquiring loans from national banks and signed a contract with a Japanese corporate group that had for years been trying unsuccessfully to break into the Chinese market.

The final round of negotiations took three days and two nights, with only short intervals between each session. Even six years later, the Japanese side still remembers Mr. G as a true Chinese nationalist for protecting the Chinese side's profit sharing and a shrewd businessman for cutting the Japanese share to the minimum.[5] Other factory cadres agree with this analysis since they had a rather easy time dealing with the Japanese side in subsequent contacts. They found that the Japanese seemed "afraid of" (*hen pa*) Mr. G, and Mr. G thought so, too. On the whole, nevertheless, Mr. G agreed to allow the Japanese firm a good share of profit under the condition that the technology be transferred in its entirety to Factory F in the first two years of the contract. In the factory's terminology, production during this period is called the first-stage program.

The joint venture proved to be a great success and fostered confidence in Mr. G's leadership. Factory F not only cleared its debt much earlier than scheduled but also increased bonus sharing for each worker to one of the highest levels in China. Mr. G, however, was soon unsatisfied with the assembly line. He did not like that the whole assembly line came from Japan, and he did not wish to send all his technicians to Japan for training because of his personal anti-Japanese sentiment. Although he knew that the Japanese assembly line was by far the most advanced of its kind in the world, he wanted better. He divided the Japanese assembly line into several parts and looked for the world's best technology for each part. When the first-stage development started operations, Mr. G was already traveling the globe (avoiding Japan) in search of better technology. (In 1992 he began plans for a new plant with technological assistance from another Japanese *zaibatsu;* it started operation in 1994. He said that this was to pit one oriental barbarian [*dongyi*] against another.)

He ran an extremely high risk in putting together an assembly line composed of machines from all over the world, as it would fail if there was even the slightest incompatibility among the parts. He could not know anything for sure until he put the pieces together—in other words, after having spent all the money on them. Going on Factory F's incredible first-stage program record, City A quickly approved the entire plan. Only Mr. G's very close colleagues understood the risk, and they "were in a cold sweat for him." This was the beginning of the so-called second-stage program in the factory's history. By this time Mr. G was sixty but was willing to stay on to complete preparation for the second-stage program, knowing he had the city planners' trust and the workers' support.

The second-stage development likewise proved to be a great success. The new assembly line is truly international, with a majority of parts imported from the United States and Italy. It runs 40 percent faster than the Japanese line, and the quality is even better, according to the Japanese technicians themselves. American as well as Italian experts were present at the factory when I conducted the interview, and technicians from Factory F are currently trained in Maine. Mr. G has proudly announced that he has the best assembly line in the world, but he did not stop there: The third-stage program is already in progress. Mr. G easily persuaded the city planners to support Factory F in developing a new item using technology similar to that used to produce the item assigned five years ago. The city decided to keep him on until his sixty-third birthday. (In fact the city turned down his retirement application again in 1994.)

The first-stage program not only successfully completed the assigned mission but far exceeded the specified targets. The second-stage program gained the initiative from within Factory F (or, more precisely, from Mr. G) and developed the world's most advanced assembly line. The second-stage program nonetheless produced an item assigned earlier by the city planner. The third-stage program continued to ride the momentum of the second-stage program. But the planners did not select the item; Mr. G did. Since Factory F contributes a substantial amount of tax revenue each year, the planners enthusiastically approved the recommendation that was supported by Mr. G's own market research.

According to Mr. G's self-evaluation, he ran such a high risk in the second-stage program primarily because he wanted to surpass the Japanese. Although this chapter is not concerned with the issue of personality, Mr. G's investment behavior has to be understood against his political and engineering background. The political purge he experienced certainly reinforced his dedication to work quality. It is in this arena that he has defeated those who purged him and denounced the criteria that questioned his integrity. Mrs. G confirms that he feels disgust toward the party.

Since he became the general manager, he has put the factory's party under firm control. He prohibits political education from infringing upon work time and on several occasions has cut the budget allocated for party work in the factory. The general secretary is effectively denied any role in managerial decisionmaking. One can see the force of reaction here: Mr. G is almost obsessed with the continuous improvement of technology and work quality. Signs of relaxation would probably give rise to the fear that the party and politics he so despises may once again thrive. This partially explains why he felt unsatisfied soon after the triumph of the first-stage development. There was no rational reason for him to carry a heavy debt to start the high-risk second-stage program after he had successfully fulfilled his mission. With reform in progress, he finally has the opportunity to assert himself and to play by his own rules. He acquired this opportunity exactly because his reputation for professionalism won him trust. Proving his ultimate concern for quality can be conceived of as the final act of his career.

In the above sense, then, it becomes an insult to evaluate his performance in material terms, as he himself once stated: "Of course all general managers have personal gains and benefits. For example, our salary is a bit higher, our apartment is more spacious, and the opportunity for promotion is there if you try. But none of this is a big benefit. Why, then, would a general manager struggle to death on the job? For reputation. The Chinese always must save face. [I] would like to do something useful before I retire. I would look better." In other words, by "doing something useful," he looks to contribute, not to take. To what, then, does he contribute?

> Why did I run such a high risk in designing the second-stage program? You seem puzzled, right? This is not strange at all. Let me tell you, this is why it is good to have socialism. Socialism means that everyone eats from the same big bowl and no one pays. How can I possibly come up with money to invest? I used the state's money to invest. If I lose money, actually it is the state that loses money. If I had to use my own money to invest, I guarantee you that I would not have done what I did. So you see, sometimes socialism can be a good thing to have.

A cynical listener would conclude that what Mr. G did was to use the state's money to make up for his professional loss during the years of the revolution. His case involves both a personal debt and a social debt: a personal debt because the idea of socialism curbed his career in earlier years, a social debt because the loss of quality in socialism as it was practiced retarded economic development. The risk he ran appears relatively insignificant in comparison to the debt incurred in the past.

A manager like Mr. G is the exception rather than the rule in the sense that he puts quality far and away above profit. However, he is not entirely unique. For example, he works neither for promotion nor for personal material gains nor yet for socialism. This is not necessarily different from an entrepreneur under capitalism, for material gains are, after all, lesser sources of motivation. Once people meet the basic living standards according to their society's own criteria, they have their own sources of motivation based on their personal lives. Two other cases deserve discussion.

## Mr. N

Mr. N is an associate manager at Factory F. Mr. G has been grooming Mr. N as his possible replacement since Mr. N was promoted to the level of senior engineer. Mr. N has an interesting perspective on investment:

> An investment decision depends both on market demand and on the central plan. The factory must evaluate the market. Once one spots a trend in the market, one can grasp the opportunities in the market. Then the factory must go back to the central plan to look for the items that are closest to the opportunities in the market and ask the planner to assign those items to the factory. This should be how the market and the plan are combined in the future. The planner should not be the one initiating a productive assignment. Rather, the factory should look for what it wants to produce in the plan. Unlike our first-stage program, which was assigned by the planner, our second-stage and third-stage programs were initiated by the factory. We fought to get the parts of the plan that were closest to our programs.

These remarks are part of a new outlook on the central planning system that I discuss later in the chapter. The question here is, Why would a socialist enterprise be willing to develop its own products?

Mr. N believes that different people have different needs. Managers are prepared to take certain risks in the market for two reasons: First, they cannot deny the "social tide" (Mr. N's term for the market), and, second, a person with a certain level of "cultivation" (as Mr. N refers to education) needs a higher level of satisfaction. He analyzes the success of Factory F:

> A man must wait for the opportunity to come. There is a social tide, and no one can move against it. One would definitely fail otherwise. Our factory adapts to the tide correctly. Like myself, I got the promotion and became an associate manager, but it wasn't me who created everything for myself in the social tide; it was the superior who brought me up. I can't make things happen for myself, although sometimes I dream of moving in order to work at some other place.

Although one cannot create the tide, one can at least help the factory adjust to the tide. As an investor, Mr. N takes the planning system for granted. He even identifies with the planning system. According to Mr. N, Factory F's investment decisions will not be "blind" (meaning directionless), for there is always the plan constraining market alternatives. Factory F is conscious of the plan and wants to fit into the plan. Against the popular impression that a socialist enterprise can succeed only through backdoor manipulation, which usually undermines the central plan, Factory F starts with the premises set up by the planners. However, the plan can work only if it is consistent with the social tide, and the job of the manager is to coordinate the two. So an investor must consider three parameters at the same time: the market, the plan, and the capacity of the factory. Mr. N argues that a factory is professionally obliged to persuade the planner that the factory can fulfill a certain part of the plan better than other factories can, just as Factory F did in its second- and third-stage programs.

Mr. N acknowledges, though, that whether or not managers are persuasive depends on their personal connection with the city's planning board in addition to their past record. Nonetheless, the arguments managers present cannot stray too far from the plan, since the city planning board has its own concerns and is accountable for the larger plan of the central planner. Negotiation thus guarantees that both elements—the plan and the market—are seriously considered.

The second point Mr. N makes about investment motivation has to do with the nature of people's needs. He finds that those who appear more motivated in Factory F tend to be those with less education. These are the people with the greatest prospects for the future. They can move along the promotion ladder from sergeant, to sergeant general, to department head.

Finally, they can expect to move into the leading group in the factory before retirement. A technician with a college degree, by contrast, lacks this sense of upward mobility. Unlike lower-level workers ("who can be satisfied with X-rated movies" if they don't get a promotion), a technician has few chances for promotion. Mr. N believes that this lack of mobility explains why many college graduates want to move overseas.

With this understanding, Mr. N stresses his own need to be "a good leader." He wishes that workers would treat him like a leader. In his own words, he would like to "cultivate the workers so that they can enjoy a higher level of civilization. . . . Eventually, they would know their own values and what contributions they can make to the factory. This would help them develop a sense of self-confidence. . . . They would then feel an intimate relationship with the factory." Like Mr. G, Mr. N seems concerned neither with material gain nor with promotion. Unlike Mr. G, Mr. N has no obsession with work quality but is more preoccupied with fostering a sense of belonging among the workers. For him, the ultimate source of motivation must come from his dedication to Factory F. In essence, this is an identity issue. This type of motivation is again consistent with the character of entrepreneurship under capitalism or in any other economic institution. In its ultimate form, investment motivation under reformed socialism does not depend on socialism, promotion, or material gain.

## Mr. H

In 1988 Factory F started a joint venture with a small rural factory in a neighboring village. The factory is a collective enterprise supported by the village government. Mr. H, who is the village chief, also heads the factory. He understands the limited technological capacity of his factory and has decided that his factory can, at best, serve as a subcontractor for other, larger factories in the city. He does not believe that there would be any chance of success for his village to manufacture final products for the market. Asked about the rationale for a village government to invest in manufacturing, Mr. H acknowledges that there are risks involved, especially as funding for this village enterprise comes directly from villagers' savings from the past decades. Mr. H analyzes the situation:

> We simply want to serve the village better. We only hope to reach a certain profit level so that everyone in the village can get rich simultaneously. We are able to start our own manufacturing because the whole nation is enthusiastic about getting rich under the reform and because the changing family structure in the village forces us to. That's why we must start our own factory. Otherwise, villagers in the neighboring counties would wear better clothes and eat better food than you do. Everybody has to save face, so our village must develop. However, we can at best be the subcontractor for larger enterprises. It is too risky for us to produce final

goods for the market. I can't do this. What if we lose money? In that case the common fund in the village would be gone.

He explains that he is not simply repeating the widely circulated reform slogan "everyone can get rich simultaneously" for the visiting interviewer:

It is quite natural for people to long for more money. In fact, I am definitely able to acquire contracts from the market for myself and hire my own employees. But if I did this, this would incur the red eye disease [envy] in the village. So I must help everybody, not just myself. This is a tradition, just like men's salary must be higher than women's. We have to invest with the common fund and share the profits with everybody. Personally, I earn roughly 6,000 yuan a year and my workers 3,000 yuan or so. Our own business is done in the village and has little relationship with the state.

For Mr. H, the development of the village is apparently a matter of saving face, in part because in order to start the business in the village as a collective enterprise, he has to use common funds. This constrains him from taking any risk in the market because he cannot afford to lose money that belongs to the village brigades. Two of the three projects his factory handles have absolutely no risk since the productive process is purely manual. Only the one with Factory F involves a discernible risk: The village has invested in machinery, maintenance, and raw material knowing all along that Mr. G may decide at any time that Factory F no longer needs the subcontractor and will produce the parts on Factory F's own assembly line. Mr. H realizes that the greatest risk to a small factory is that the contractual relationship with a patron is inherently unstable. Mr. H believes that in order to survive he has to depend on both the quality of his work and the right connections—and "the connections are extremely important." In his case the contract with Factory F was acquired through the introduction of a relative's relative. Investment was undertaken only after the contract was secured. This practice unavoidably imposes a time constraint on the scale of production and serves to illustrate why scale in small rural factories tends to be limited.

For Mr. H, earning money is an important motive but not the only motive. He needs to consider how much he personally can earn with respect to an average villager in order to maintain social harmony in the village. He also needs to make sure that his village does not lag too far behind the development of neighboring villages in order to avoid the sense of relative deprivation. Mr. H thinks these considerations reflect the influence of socialist ideas. Another constraint he must keep in mind is that he must succeed. Mr. L, the party secretary of the village, has the most keen observation: "We all grew up in this village. If we fail, how can we face the villagers?" This unique notion of socialism is consistent with the traditional emphasis on egalitarianism and harmony. Regarding investment, villagers' socialism thus appears to be a negative element in the village enterprise's decision whether or not to take a risk in the market. This is the opposite of Mr. G's case, where workers' socialism seems to have allowed him to make risky investments for Factory F.

Watching household enterprises thrive in the village, Mr. H and Mr. L take a cynical view. Mr. L argues that household businesspeople "have nothing special. They depend on little tricks like tax evasion." He emphasizes, though, that "the problem in our village is less severe than in others." In other words, for Mr. H and Mr. L, personal wealth is not praiseworthy; collective wealth is the key, and that is because "one should compare oneself with people in other villages." Many Chinese observers worry about this type of competition among villages and people, but this is exactly what village leaders are most concerned with. The implication is that investment reflects a social-psychological drive in addition to the profit-oriented rationale.

## Discussion

Investment behavior in socialist China under reform has moved closer to a Western model. In more successful enterprises, one finds the same kind of entrepreneurship as under capitalism. The general managers begin to identify with either the factory (Mr. N) or the product (Mr. G). The immediate concern is invariably the development of the enterprise. Personalities and social backgrounds may vary and lead to different attitudes toward the factory and the productive processes, but the difference blurs as the factory identity develops. The rise of a clearer factory identity is obviously not the result of socialist education nor a direct result of material reward. Reform cannot guarantee the emergence of a strong factory identity in every factory, but the process of reform nevertheless allow its emergence to reflect the more aggressive personalities as well as social backgrounds of the managers in some factories. Each entrepreneur has his own reason to work hard—Mr. G is a heroic leader, rebounding against the trauma of the past; Mr. N combines his personal goal with the factory goal and therefore moves closer to his Western counterparts who are disciples of the theory of humanitarian management; Mr. H, in contrast, is the typical oriental entrepreneur who feels responsible for every worker's benefits. They rise up because of reform and in order to alter reform.

### SOCIALIST CONSCIOUSNESS

Although the personalities involved in an investment decision may be more concerned with self-actualization, sense of belonging, saving face, and egalitarianism than with the socialist development of the country, it is still possible to argue that the process of making a specific investment decision may still involve socialist elements. I thus turn now to the process of how a specific investment decision is made in Factory F to examine the socialistic nature of the review process.

In Factory F there are three key elements in the process of investment review. The first is pricing. The pricing of parts affects the choice among producing in-house, purchasing from the market, or investing in a separate plant to produce the parts. Since Mr. G is the manager of a second-ranked enterprise (with over 1,500 employees), in his negotiation with Mr. H, Mr. G simply dominated. Mr. G determined the purchasing price of parts Mr. H supplied. In a neighboring village, Factory F has a joint project with a prefectural enterprise. Pricing is also an internal decision made solely by Factory F. In this case study, the asymmetrical relationship determines the locus of pricing decision. Therefore, the question is really how Factory F reaches a decision on price. As the interviewees revealed, Factory F does not give any privileges to its partners in their purchasing contract. The price of parts is determined solely by the market, which means "the lowest available price known at the time of contracting."

At the same time, however, Factory F must calculate the opportunity cost thus incurred and the opportunity benefit thus forgone. Generally, the manager must compare the cost of producing on an internal assembly line with the cost of contract. In addition, he must know how much the contractor (partially funded by Factory F) could lose by not dealing with Factory F and how much additional profit Factory F could indeed accrue by contracting out the needed parts and producing other goods. The market price Factory F detects guides the investment decisions of its contractors.

The second issue is how to choose subcontractors and joint venturers. As mentioned earlier, both subcontracting and joint ventures require personal connections. A joint venturer is easier to control than a contractor, for Mr. G can personally make sure that the work quality meets his strict standards. However, it is a daunting task to start a joint venture. That is why many national enterprises prefer subcontracting. In Factory F the office of design is responsible for specifying the standard of the parts contracted out. The office of arts (*gongyi*) draws the diagram to help the potential contractor make the sample product. The sample goes back to the office of design, and, together with the relevant department heads, the office tests the product. Finally, the sample reaches the department of quality for inspection. Mr. G personally set up the procedure, which he believes is more professional than that of many first-ranked enterprises.

The other issue concerns the rate of return. Mr. H and the aforementioned joint venture both decided that the anticipated rate of return must be above 10 percent for them to make an investment; however, neither explained the figure. Factory F faces a far more complex situation. Since Factory F adopts a high bonus policy, Mr. G must set the rate of return higher to satisfy expectations. In fact, there must be a slight increase in bonus each year to make the workers happy. In addition to this bonus pressure, a factory as famous as Factory F must deal with various contribution requests from superior agencies. For example, during the few weeks of the interview period, Factory F made at least three donations: one to the city basketball team, another to a village theater, and the other to the city bureau of industry's hospital. Finally, Factory F has a larger than average debt ratio, so Mr. G would like to pay the debt as much in advance as possible. This certainly requires a higher than normal rate of return. For all these reasons, Mr. G said that in Factory F's case an investment review would require that the rate of return of a proposal should be above 35 percent. Some sources suggest that the estimates before the second- and the third-stage programs were indeed well above 35 percent.

What these interviews suggest is that the investment review in a successful socialist enterprise like Factory F is by all means market-oriented: Prices are set by the market; contracts must be based upon work quality (though personal connections are equally critical); investment reviews are evaluated against the estimated rate of return. None of these logically implies the demise of socialism in China. The significance is that none of these can prove that China is socialist. An expert on China from Taiwan somewhat sympathetic to socialist ideals regrets to see that under reform socialist consciousness among workers has received the least attention. Even though socialism can accommodate commodity economy in theory, socialism cannot survive without socialist consciousness.[6]

## PLANNING AND THE GENERAL MANAGER

Central planning is the identity of socialism. The supposed comprehensive dominance of the central planner dramatizes the paramount power of the proletarian class. The integrity and power of the planners symbolize the legitimacy of the political regime inasmuch as it has not yet withered away as predicted in Marxist theory. If the central planning system weakens or its range shrinks, one of two possible connotations is unavoidable: Either the political regime is no longer the monopolistic representative of the proletarian class, or the Communist Party is no longer the monopolistic representative of the regime.

In all this argumentation, the degree of proletarian representation of the Communist Party declines. Either way, the local planners will share in proletarian representation. The same logic can apply to a local planning system, so that the local proletarian representation is shared by the real planners in each enterprise. The more successful real planners are concerned mostly with the development of their enterprises, not with socialism. In this sense, there is really little if any difference between those successful socialist entrepreneurs and those successful capitalist entrepreneurs in terms of their first target of identity. The difference lies in their approaches to investment, management, and social connection.

To the extent that entrepreneurs can substantiate, revise, or design parts of the plan, they share in proletarian representation. Within this ideological context, the significance of Mr. N's remarks about the role of his enterprise in the planning system is dramatic. In Mr. N's opinion the planners, central as well as local, are hindered by a lag between the time they receive market information and the time they make a decision. More aggressive enterprises cannot help but allocate resources upon their own initiatives and therefore step on the planners' toes. Enterprises thus may become the initiators rather than the receivers of a subplan. For example, a model enterprise like Capital Steel Corporation of Beijing repeatedly urges that the planner respect its autonomy and allow independent capital accumulation within the CSC without attempting interference. The CSC would certainly enjoy more room for investment decision as more resources are under its exclusive control.

Factory F has moved even further. According to Mr. N, both the second- and the third-stage programs were first envisioned by Mr. G. The proposals submitted to the city were based upon the market information that Factory F had collected through its own research. Factory F had decided for itself the main item in its proposal before trying to match its proposal with the central plan. What Mr. G did with the city planner later was simply to identify specific spots in the central plan that looked similar to his proposals and to argue that those spots in the central plan should be assigned to Factory F. In reality, then, it is Factory F's own plan that brings life to central planning. Mr. N believes that this is clearly the trend of future entrepreneurship. If an enterprise has two eyes, he contends, it must use one eye to follow the market, the other to study the plan. When the two eyes focus on the same spot, that spot belongs to the enterprise.

What if the planner refuses to assign that particular spot to the eager enterprise? Mr. N thinks this will not happen in the future. If the planner insists that the other enterprise get the assignment, that latecomer (late in terms of technology, market information, and motivation) would not be able to compete with Factory F, which would execute its own proposal even without the assignment. The planner would thus face the embarrassing situation in which the selected factory is defeated by the autonomous one in the market. More important, the whole idea of planning would be undermined if two enterprises are engaging in similar projects. An overlap would suggest lack of efficiency.

A rational city planner would therefore have to succumb to tacit pressure from Factory F. Factory F would gain tax breaks and loan privileges and in return would provide an enlarged tax base, occasional donations, and handsome statistical achievements that the city planners would be able to brag about in front of the central planners. In other words, once an enterprise earns itself a good professional reputation, it can act much more freely than an outsider can imagine, sometimes substantiating, revising, and refusing the plan without appearing to do so.

To the extent that Factory F can affect the actual contents of the plan, it is similar to a private enterprise. Mr. J, the owner and general manager of a private enterprise in a neighboring prefecture, is a good case for comparison here. Mr. J was the head of the textile division at the prefectural bureau of countryside enterprise. He decided to quit two years ago. He now has a textile factory with over 100 employees. He knows the textile industry so well that most of his contractors are large national enterprises. Factory F depends partially on state investment, whereas Mr. J looks exclusively to banks for loans. (Although Factory F depends more and more on bank loans rather than state investment.) Mr. J can accumulate personal funds for future development through profit making, whereas Factory F has to share profits (with the state) before it can apply them toward its own growth. So in terms of source of funding, Mr. J and Mr. G are much closer than they previously were.

The flat corporate tax rate is 35 percent of factory profit for a private enterprise. The profit does not include Mr. J's personal salary (as high as 2,400 yuan a month!), which is a part of expense. He has to pay an additional personal income tax with a flat rate of 40 percent. For Factory F, the normal corporate rate is 55 percent, and the personal tax rate is progressive over 420 yuan a month. On both corporate and personal accounts, Mr. J seems to have received better treatment. When Mr. G fought for the planner's support, what he wanted was precisely those tax breaks and other privileges that would allow him and his workers to evade taxes. So in terms of tax obligation, Mr. G's thinking pattern moves closer to Mr. J's.

No one could guarantee that the general-manager system would always create managers like Mr. G or Mr. N. In fact, the system often fails to stimulate the large socialist enterprises. That is why Chinese economists are still struggling with their approach to the market.[7] Nonetheless, for natural-born entrepreneurs, the general-manager system has certainly opened up a whole new world. Their aggressiveness signals the emergence of a new entrepreneurial stratum, even though they may operate from different motives. They create the plan through practice in the way judges make law through cases, though to a lesser extent. The original idea of reform was to use the market to guide the enterprise and to use the plan to regulate the market. It may turn out to be a different loop, with the market guiding the enterprise and the enterprise completing the plan accordingly.

This is an innovative interpretation of the meaning of central planning. Instead of designing a plan-oriented market, those successful enterprises begin to force the system to center on a market-oriented plan. Since the plan cannot possibly reflect the immediate market situation, the rational planners may gradually realize that the plan can and should only touch upon the country's overall needs. The enterprises must be coaxed to substantiate the state plan with a detailed production plan, which in turn is based upon solid market research. If this happens as reform progresses, the nature of socialist planning will be very similar to the well-studied state planning in many developing capitalist countries.

## CONCLUSION

Central planning is the essence of socialism. The drama of legitimacy of a socialist regime lies in its maneuvering resources to achieve the government's national goal of growth and distribution. Since the intended decentralization and subsequent economic disaster during the Great Leap Forward, the credibility of central planning has been brought into question. Not only did Mao's call for self-reliance and egalitarianism hurt the pretension of central planning, but the continued operation of this ideologically reluctant central planning system has proved to be a stimulus to development.[8] During the Cultural Revolution, all past planners were seen as "capitalist roaders." The tight control during the post-1970 Cultural Revolution itself was later denounced as "holding everything in one palm" (*yibazhua*).

It seems that nothing the state initiates has enjoyed credibility since the start of the reform movement. The general-manager system thus shifts the responsibility of development to microlevel actors. The process of reform creates another paradox for the regime. The regime wishes to save itself from a political legitimacy crisis by decentralizing the economic system, but its legitimacy as planner actually weakens as a result of the emergence of a new entrepreneurial stratum.

The rise of entrepreneurship is in part a direct product of the general-manager system. The reform policy contributes equally to this new social phenomenon. The reform policy allows the enterprises to accumulate their own funds, activates countryside factories to support the more advanced enterprises, and opens all kinds of professional banks to overcome bottlenecks in capital flow. All this inflates the monetary pressure outside the planning system and forces enterprises to adjust to the market. Money flowing outside the plan has amounted to about 50 percent of the total

paper money. Under these circumstances, enterprises naturally tend to regard the privileges available in the plan system as instruments to gain
leverage in the market, not guidance.

Lethargic enterprises that depend on the state for support to survive
will eventually face market pressure as the planner realizes the power of
the market. In fact, the planner began to apply greater pressure to those enterprises under protection in the latter part of 1991. Many enterprises on
the brink of bankruptcy according to market criteria were shut down. The
essence of socialism is undergoing a dramatic change. The political implication is unavoidable: In the future the central planner—or, more precisely, the Chinese Communist Party—will no longer be able to follow the
traditional practice of placing symbols of political and ideological virtue
above everything else and still claim legitimacy. The expanding capacity
of the rising entrepreneurial stratum cannot be easily explained away in a
system whose legitimacy comes from the integrity of central planning.

# 8

# INDIVIDUALIZED SOCIALISM:
# THE WORKERS' CULTURE

This chapter continues my report on field research I conducted in a Chinese factory during summer 1991. The focus of this chapter is workers' culture, the shared cognitive processes whereby the meaning of belonging to the factory is related to the meaning of the individual worker's life. In short, workers' culture is composed of collective sense-making processes. Scholarly investigations of workers' culture so defined are limited. Andrew Walder studied the subject among Chinese immigrants in Hong Kong.[1] Although I concentrated on a Chinese factory, my thesis in part supports Walder's notion of neotraditionalism. I found, however, that the two types of worker Walder named are most likely spurious categories.

I interviewed twenty-two workers and cadres (I did not include general managers and party secretaries in this particular area of research). Interviews lasted from thirty minutes to four hours and were conducted without the direct supervision of management; a twenty-five-year-old assistant (a third-year worker) accompanied me on most interviews. I selected workers in five of the factory's seven plants. Most interviewees worked along the assembly lines, and none was from the logistical department, whose staff made up approximately one-third of the overall staff. My assistant helped in identifying cadres, as they tended to dress like the workers. Because of the high number of cadres at each level, I had no control over which cadres I interviewed. Nonetheless, there was no sign of manipulation in the interview arrangements. As for white-collar workers, sampling depended on who happened to be nearby, whether my assistant knew the person, and if the person was willing to provide an interview.

## BACKGROUND NOTES

Literature on Japanese corporate culture consistently notes the prevalence of lifetime employment in big corporations. Some hold that the lifetime employment system is the modern version of Japanese feudalism, the company serving as the modern domain and the worker as serf.[2] The institution of lifetime employment may therefore help satisfy the Japanese search for

psychological dependence on the one hand but block the Japanese workers' class consciousness on the other.[3] One leading scholar on Japanese
economy goes as far as suggesting that lifetime employment can readily
explain the group orientation of Japanese workers, which contributes to
productive efficiency (as opposed to the allocative efficiency stressed in
the West) through enhanced devotion and self-sacrifice.[4] It is widely held
that lifetime employment is consistent with the Japanese character and
conducive to the reconciliation of collective and individual interests.

Traditional wisdom about China also confirms that the Chinese have
an equally strong need for stability and dependent relationships. Forty
years of communist indoctrination have done little to change this tendency, as one career China expert asserts.[5] Additionally, since the early
1950s Chinese authorities have consistently reiterated the point that the individual and the collective interests must be reconciled.[6] All this closely
parallels the Japanese character. Lifetime employment under Chinese socialism, however, has become a frequent target for attack during economic
reform of the 1980s and 1990s. Indeed, the Chinese experience is dramatically different from its Japanese counterpart. Chinese scholars repeatedly
assert that lifetime employment is responsible for "the bad habit of the
great rice pot" (*daguofan*), that is, that everyone eats from the same bowl.
Cadres as well as workers are accused of using state resources for individual gain, preventing the establishment of a genuine collective identity.[7]

There is no feudalistic tradition in China as in Japan; Chinese culture
does not cherish comprehensive loyalty toward authority. Confucianism
actually encourages emeritism if state authority deviates from the spirit of
dao, the essence of which can be sensed only by the individual.[8] In other
words, the freedom from overall obligation to people holding office may
have given the Chinese a higher degree of liberty in making judgments independent of their social status. In fact, the ideal Chinese emperor is one
who is only remotely relevant to the citizen's actual life and in public performs primarily ceremonial functions (and those functions automatically
win loyalty and thus power for him). If the emperor does not compete with
the rank and file to enlarge his own interest base, there is only a weak material tie between state and society to accompany the spiritual tie. This is
especially true in a society where pursuing interests is regarded as socially
undesirable. The Chinese identify themselves with a spiritual leader only
if his kingdom rests on a spiritual rather than a material image. Lifetime
employment does not mean as much to the Chinese probably because the
Chinese did not have the same hierarchy of close material relationships the
Japanese had under feudalism.

Consequently, the results of lifetime employment in socialist China
are far removed from the productive efficiency witnessed under capitalist
Japan's lifetime employment system. Chinese socialism allows little room

for maneuvering in financial treatment among individual workers, for if the workers fail to identify with the collective, maximizing minimum wages only retards the incentive to work. Since there is no serious penalty for failing to promote collective interests, one can probably get by comfortably without doing so. The Chinese case is further complicated because the individual is socially disallowed from pursuing collective interests for the sake of enhancing individual interests, and the collective is not supposed to have material concerns. Lifetime employment can therefore create two opposite types of motivation, with the collective identity being the intervening variable. When the collective identity is strong, as in Japan, workers do not have to worry about self-interests while satisfying collective interests, about which they are also highly concerned. When the collective identity is obscure, as in China, workers do not have to worry about collective interests while enjoying an acceptable standard of living under egalitarianism.

The general-manager system, which is only a recent addition to the Chinese political economy, purports to create some institutionalized incentive mechanism that can motivate the general manager as well as the workers. Under the new system, general managers enjoy rather loosely defined power concerning internal personnel decisions including promotion, demotion, and, above all, membership in the leading cadre group (*lingdao banzi*). This way, or so the intention is, the profit or loss of enterprises becomes the direct responsibility of the general managers, not the supervising government agency. General managers may have stronger incentives to supervise the performance of the workers, and they are supposedly the best people to do so in light of their expertise and proximity.[9]

General managers can also reform the internal salary structure. They are encouraged to break the salary package into three parts: basic salary (following state stipulations), seniority salary, and position salary. The leading cadre group decides how much difference is allowed on the scale of seniority. Senior, nonprofessional workers can be discriminated against in a young and expertise-oriented plant; similarly, younger workers can suffer in a lethargic, sunset factory. The opening up of position salary has enormously increased the power of the general managers. With the leading cadre group, the general managers decide what type of work should incur how much reward. They are therefore equipped with a financial instrument to bring material incentives to their lowest levels. Normally, managers will reward the most laborious job nearly as well as highly innovative technical tasks. The formal reward confirms socialism; the latter guarantees the new profit orientation.[10]

The iron rule of general managers is most felt in the area of bonuses. Unlike the salary scale, which general managers cannot remove once settled, the bonus scale must meet whatever criteria the managers set. They may penalize those who fail to meet their sometimes peculiar standards (regarding sick leave, dress code, even daydreaming) by taking away the bonus on an ad hoc basis. In a highly profitable plant, the general manager would have much stronger leverage, with more resources ready to apply to bonuses. However, in a factory that is behind schedule and hence short on profits, the general manager would be reluctant to act. The combination of the general-manager system and the bonus system therefore produces positive feedback to a profit-generating plant to earn more and negative feedback for a loss-generating plant to stay behind.

## SENSE OF FUTURE AND COLLECTIVE IDENTITY

### A Field Report

An important question during the interviews was what the interviewees expected of their own lives in five to ten years. Their answers in turn have a significant bearing on larger questions: Can the economic reform rebuild the socialist appeal of the regime through consolidation of lower-level factory identity? Can the collective identity be created in such a way so that belonging to it becomes as much of a work incentive as bonuses? And would workers seek to satisfy their sense of belonging within a factory system that is a branch (albeit sometimes a weak one) of political and administrative authority? Since most interviews were conducted at a highly profitable factory that has been a model enterprise for quite some time, the identity issue in that particular factory alludes to the identity issue of economic reform as a whole, assuming the final success of such reform. The task of this section is to discover any systematic influence of the factory image on the workers' sense of future.

*Workers.* As expected, most interviewees appreciate the factory's determining role in their daily lives. However, few expressed a sense of self-actualization in their work lives, nor did they consciously utilize the factory connection in achieving their life goals. One college graduate acknowledges her previous ignorance about "the complexity of society" and hence feels "very uncomfortable" with her recent assignment in the factory. But she does not believe she can do anything about her position:

> [I] cannot think about the future. I simply have to stay. I don't want to study abroad. You know, if people think you are going abroad to study, there will be no end of it, and the manager will not take you seriously. It would be horrible if this should happen and if you should eventually fail to acquire the grant to leave the country. It is difficult to go abroad. I don't have money nor any relatives in Taiwan or overseas who could help. But some of my friends maneuver really hard. I guess they are not

satisfied with their working environment. My factory has good profits and is in good shape. Besides, it is impossible for me to leave my work or ask for permission to move. Basically, I plan to stay in this factory. The chance for me to move is nil.[11]

At best it appears that profitability makes the working environment acceptable—but not necessarily enjoyable. A hoary thirty-one-year-old who recently moved back from extremely poor rural surroundings to replace his father, who retired from the same factory, sounds unemotional about the sudden rise in his salary.[12] He refuses to talk about his past or his future:

The factory has a good profit margin—better than where I was [long sigh]. Future? Hard to say. It's difficult to talk about it. Life in the past was truly bitter. As to what I did [sigh], it is difficult even to talk about it. I have some savings now; perhaps I can get married in one or two years. I left for X Province when I was young and came back as a replacement almost three years ago. Future? Hard to say, hard to say. I am satisfied with my work, fine [looking toward the sky with tears in his eyes].[13]

Though his educational level is quite meager, that alone cannot explain this interviewee's resignation; intellectuals are similarly passive. A junior engineer who graduated from college seven years ago exhibits a negative attitude toward the factory even though he was enthusiastically involved in its modernization six years earlier. Asked about his future, he has no direct answer:

[I] feel depressed [*men*] [long silence]. Why don't you ask some other questions, and you will come around to appreciate why I said I was depressed? You know, people are different by nature; some would like to emphasize spiritual life and some material life. I'm probably in between. I'm emotionally attached to this factory because most of what I know I learned in the factory. If some day I leave, I will be willing to come back and help if the manager calls me, and I will not ask for any reward. China has been losing its traditional morality since the ten-year Cultural Revolution, and gentle Confucianism has gone. But I don't despise those who pursue material interests because I understand them. But I need to be understood, too. My parents always want me to become a dragonlike great man [silence]. Many people struggle to leave the country, but this is not just their personal issue, since everyone wants to leave. Many of my friends are gone already. It is not important if I get the promotion and become a middle-level engineer because the meaning of my life is outside the system of engineering.[14]

A more radical view suggests that a factory, with or without profits, can do its workers little good. One interviewee never considers his career development in the factory as meaningful:

I've never thought about it, and ordinary people have never thought about it either. In fact, if not for your question, I wouldn't even know that I have never thought about it. What can you do, anyway? Maybe I want to be the boss. But you can't just start like this—where are you going to get money? How about the situation in the United States? You have to be the boss in order to make your own money. In this factory, you spare your lifetime. It really doesn't matter if the general manager is a capable person. The policy of opening and reform does not impact the ordinary people very much; the atmosphere is somewhat better, though. Inflation goes faster than pay raises. You know, I was a teacher before; I got into this factory through the backdoor. Teaching is boring because there is no respect shown toward intellectuals. Besides, the salary is embarrassing. What city's youth doesn't want to leave the country? Intellectuals want to go to the United States. If you are not one, you can go to Japan as a laborer and in three years, you will go home rich, with tens of thousands of yuan. Who would come back once gone . . . ? It may look like every household has a color TV and a VCR, but that's overconsumption. Food becomes too expensive so that people eat little and cheap and ironically save some money to buy luxury stuff. In reality, life is not better under reform. Only a few can make money. Most people stay the same.[15]

What makes this interviewee special is not his analysis of reform but his attitude toward the kind of money his factory is making. He earns more than 400 yuan a month (in 1991), which certainly entitles him to a position in China's upper income bracket. He feels unsatisfied because he does not "own the factory." Instead, his "fortune is controlled by the factory."

Even for those who clearly see no future outside the factory, their image of the factory does not seem to provide any strong work motivation. A thirty-nine-year-old former high school teacher has given up on his own future:

It is too late to think about my own future. When I was only twenty-something or even a teenager, I did have some ideals. I tried but failed, and now it is too late. Probably I am not smart enough, but the basic problem is my age and the limit of my learning ability. I have an eleven-year-old son. I don't have too many expectations for him. Well, I do have some hope but will not impose my ideas on him. My only wish now is that my son grows healthy and I can fulfill a father's obligation. As for myself, I am through. I have no way out and will just move on like this. Didn't Deng Xiaoping say that the great atmosphere had been formed? The little atmosphere around myself cannot make too much difference. . . . As a human being, I'm naturally not satisfied with everything, but I won't make any effort to change anything.[16]

Workers with more than fifteen years of experience are numerous in this particular factory, though few are over forty. Their attitude toward the factory is shockingly passive. For one interviewee, age thirty-eight, "the most important thing is to take good care of my child," since "my age has reached such a level that I can't do anything now."[17] Another interviewee, well shy of forty, feels insensitive toward the "younger" generation because he "doesn't care if the younger generation is different from our generation and doesn't give a damn whatever bad things the young may do to the factory."[18]

The "younger" generation obviously has more hope for their future. Nevertheless, this sense of future does not seem to have produced a factory identity. A twenty-year-old worker talks about her own prospects: "I haven't really thought about it. What am I doing now? Well, I spend a lot of time in night school. I think a high school diploma will help me in the future, although I don't know how. I guess I don't want to lag behind. The general manager encourages me to study more, but I don't know if I will try college; I don't know what I could study. . . . I wish the factory could allocate more time for me to study."[19]

Another female worker, only eighteen years old, had exceptional self-confidence. She was enlisted by the factory from an occupational school less than a year ago. Her sense of the future, however, is not clearly linked to the factory either:

> I want to become a singer and sing better and better. I want to go to the singing school in the future, but I don't want to make it a profession. My dad doesn't like it but my mom is pretty supportive. A friend of mine is a professional singer. She makes money. I'm not ready for that yet. I didn't go to night school, but I do study at home, and I can get the high school diploma if I pass the examination. I want to travel in the United States—not stay there, just travel. I like some of the American singers, but I like the Taiwanese and Hong Kongese songs most. Dad said the best songs were in China. Everyone in the factory knows me because I sing well. Cadres don't know me because they all have families, aren't interested in singing. Among the younger generation, they all know me; that's what they tell me.

She brought all conversation back to singing over the entire course of the interview. She apparently enjoyed her reputation among other young workers, but that seemed to be the only link between the factory and her thoughts of the future.

*Cadres.* A few cadres show a notably strong careerism. They are generally over thirty, hopeful of further promotion, and either party members or in the process of becoming party members. For example, a forty-year-old department head who has held that position for ten years and serves as department party division secretary is highly conscious of the career opportunities ahead of him:

> I hope to do a good job in my position and will strive for promotion when opportunities come, perhaps becoming the general manager either in this

factory or in another factory. After that, I can try another promotion to an even higher level. A human being needs to think, and it is all right with me if some people think only of money. My thinking is simply that I must enhance the productive level of the factory. I want to compete, and competition is a good thing. I have a college degree with a good track record. I have been in this position for ten years and am ready to move on, even to a position of a different nature. . . . I've been here for eighteen years. Emotionally, the factory is my place. A human being needs a position . . . and should want to affect the great atmosphere. It is too much to talk about directing the great atmosphere, but I can influence it.[20]

He is truly unique in terms of self-confidence and sense of belonging to the factory. Other seemingly motivated cadres are less aggressive but equally positive toward life in the factory. A thirty-one-year-old sergeant who transferred from another province not too long ago talks about his future:

I wish to have a harmonious family life, and I want my child to grow well and better than his parents. He should go on to college and even study abroad. We will try everything to support him. As for myself, I am in the process of joining the party. I was in the [youth] corps before; the head of my department would like to see me become a party member. Besides, I would like to complete high school. . . . I've never thought about things too far away. . . . My style is that I must do a better job than my predecessor. Now that I am a sergeant, I want to be better than the former sergeant, better than all the other sergeants. . . . The most important thing is to set yourself up as a model. I have good experience so that no one could really compete with me at my job. . . . But I never really thought of becoming the head of the department or the general manager in the future. Never. There is more to be learned about the new machines we just bought. I am not capable of leading a larger division.

At a higher level, a sergeant general who is thirty-eight years old and has spent twenty years in this factory has also developed a high degree of identification with the factory:

I've never thought about promotion, but I do study at night school to prepare for a high school diploma because the general manager is a person who emphasizes a diploma. I became a party member only very recently, and this was after a long period of observation. . . . The general manager will retire in one or two years; I begin to worry about the future of our factory. He made quite a contribution to our factory. The factory has changed a lot in the past twenty years. I can only hope to serve this factory. Even though I have to travel about two hours to get to work, I don't mind. The factory is making good money. That's why I did not ask to move, although I might as well have done that a long time ago. We just had a farewell party for an old comrade. He witnessed the development of our factory in the past thirty years and was really touched by what he saw today. I understand him because I also regard the factory as my family.[21]

Even those who are dissatisfied would agree on this aspect. One older worker expressed concern that their capable general manager would soon be leaving, saying, "We all worry that there are going to be big changes."[22] Nevertheless, her worries focus on the general manager, while the aforementioned cadres' are on the factory. For example, another department head who is now thirty-five obviously identifies with the factory, not the general manager:

> I have been here for fifteen years. I am lucky to have been promoted to the head of the department since I don't have a high school diploma. I've reached the highest point in my career. I'm not interested in a college degree. I just want to do my job. Since I am the secretary of the party division in my department, I'm naturally conscious of my mission in the factory and am highly self-motivated. I don't think too much about my future; I feel fine with what is right now. . . . I work for the factory, not for the general manager. Changing the manager doesn't affect me a bit.[23]

Among those more active, there are those who do not identify with the factory. A forty-six-year-old associate director has shopped around for a better job over the past ten years and exhibits a rarely encountered brand of individuality:

> For seventeen years, I taught English at an international trade company, then I moved to a Shanghai factory for six years as an engineer. I came to this factory three years ago. I don't think moving is that bad, although people generally don't do it at all. Everyone should want to move on. I cannot guarantee that I will not move to another place, although this is not in my plan now. I need to learn more in order to become a senior engineer. I am forty-six now, but I have strong motivation.[24]

For this interviewee the factory is more an instrument of self-actualization than a place to belong to.

## Discussion

Any conclusion drawn from this selected presentation of interview scripts is partial at best. Nonetheless, some general observations can be made. First, Walder's finding that workers' behavior cannot be readily explained by a category breakdown according to worker level or position appears at first glance to be confirmed. Walder argues that workers' behavior can be better categorized by how active they are in seeking protection and promotion from a patron-client type of relationship.[25] In other words, there are two subcultures among Chinese workers: active-aggressive and passive-defensive. Further analysis, however, suggests this categorization is meaningful only with at least three qualifications.

First, attitude toward factory authority is influenced by workers' orientation toward life outside the factory. Although workers may hold a positive attitude toward work and therefore appear agreeable to the consolidation of the political-moral authority of the general manager and the party, they may not really identify with the factory. Some interviewees display this tendency; in addition, of those who identify with the factory, most are not aggressive promotion seekers. Being active or passive, identifying with the factory or not, and having certain personal goals in the factory do not show a clear correlation in the interviews.

Second, Walder's observation that worker level and position do not correlate to attitude toward authority is subject to revision. It is not only difficult to define activism but equally difficult to identify activists with a definition. Regardless, all interviewees who are activists (a commonsense usage) on the job and loyal supporters of the factory authority are above thirty years of age. They are either party members or quasi party members with cadre position and seniority. Two are the heads of their departments, one a sergeant general, and one a sergeant. Their overall orientation toward factory authority appears to be a function of their cadre positions. For example, one department head knows that there is little chance of promotion for him, and the sergeant is worried about his ability to handle his current job well. Are they active-aggressive? Neither strives for promotion yet both are conscious of their missions within the factory. The sergeant general is not an active-aggressive worker who seeks promotion and protection from a patron; he is simply emotionally involved in factory affairs. The question therefore becomes, Which necessarily occurs first—a positive attitude toward the factory or promotion? Does positive attitude contribute to promotion or vice versa? Our examples suggest that promotion to a higher position comes first and an activist attitude follows. Although my analysis is not conclusive, Walder's observation does seem premature.

Third, the causal relation between party loyalty and activism is not at all clear. In the process of promotion, it is often the case that the cadres at the next higher level decide who receives a promotion, while those selected do not always have prior knowledge. In fact, if one shows any interest in promotion, the chance of promotion might drop. The lower the level, the less those selected for promotion might feel they can pull their way up.[26] As a result, workers who *are* promoted may be astounded to see their efforts confirmed and hence develop a sense of appreciation and participation. Likewise, if the cadres believe that promoted workers are worth further investment, they will invite them to apply for party membership. All cadres interviewed said that with regard to the promotion decision, they never felt pressure from below. A type of client-patron relationship develops after people reach certain levels and begin to realize their chances for higher career goals. In fact, two of the three associate managers of the factory I visited were not party members when they were promoted. When promotion did come, both were flattered and soon developed a high sense of obligation to the factory.[27]

In this particular factory it is especially true that the general manager promotes only those who appear able to enhance the level of efficiency in the production process. When the leading cadre group is profit-conscious, it becomes progressively more difficult for subordinates to discern what type of worker the group prefers; they can only try to prove themselves on the job. The success of the Beijing Print and Dye Company, for example, has much to do with the boldness of the general manager to make unexpected but accurate promotions. The secretary of the company party then invited those new cadres to join the party:

> Those who are capable are not those who are perfect. . . . Those who are capable prove themselves in the process of reform but cannot always meet the party criteria. However, for the sake of the Four Modernizations and the needs of reform, the party has the obligation to help them be accepted by the party. . . . [We] let carefully selected cadres shoulder the heavy responsibility [of reform], refine them in the process of reform, and create favorable conditions for them to grow. When they mature, we make further investment [in them].[28]

Other case studies concur, and all seem to point up a similar slogan: To become a party member in the age of reform one needs "more than good ideology and morality."[29] Walder's neotraditionalist workers would fare worse in a reform-oriented factory.

Nevertheless, most interviewees do not seem to have clear ideas about their own futures. Those who have given it substantial consideration usually do not believe that they have real control over their lives. Those who do not identify with the factory can find their life goals only outside the factory system. These workers are generally passive toward their jobs. Except in the case of one interviewee, the acceptance of factory identity accounts for strong work motivation and a positive attitude toward the factory (or lack thereof). Attitude toward factory authority, therefore, seems to have a stronger correlation to factory identity than to neotraditionalism.

## COLLECTIVE BEHAVIOR AND IDENTITY

Theoretically, one can observe workers' collective behavior either in the union or at the factory assembly. However, the union works closely with the factory and the party. Problems the union is enlisted to resolve involve mostly very individualized cases. One worker observes: "The union is supposed to be on the workers' side. It should be that the workers are the plaintiff, the general manager is the defendant, and the union is the attorney for the plaintiff. How can this ever be possible?"[30]

If the union is not a good representative for the workers as a whole, the factory assembly may serve better. Representatives of the workers who attend the assembly are often cadres of varying levels, though this does not imply that the assembly is only for political show. Although assembly operations may not always meet ideal requirements, the function of the assembly depends on many factors: the attitude of the leading cadre group, the scale and profit margin of the factory, and the technical level of the productive process. For example, a large factory with hundreds of representatives in its assembly is often subject to severe criticism during the session because of the variety of grievances. One worker mentions having enjoyed the assembly at his former workplace because there was always criticism and on occasion counterproposals on how to develop the factory.[31] In the factory I visited, the assembly usually ran quite smoothly because the factory makes enough money to silence representatives' criticism. In addition, the technical level of its productive process, and hence the management, is quite sophisticated, and the discussions at the assembly are often beyond the technical grasp of the representatives from the lower echelons, who thus are stymied in their participation.

In the factory in question, the assembly meets twice a year. Since there are few dissenting voices and discussion is often very technical, though, few workers pay attention to it. One worker, for instance, thought the assembly met only once a year.[32] As a result, those who are not satisfied with the work environment have no place to publicize their concerns. An older worker complains that he is always short of work to do and therefore is handicapped in bonus allocation. He wants to work, but the management refuses to assign him more work. He wants to change assignments: "It is not my fault that I don't have enough to do. I told them and they won't help. My mouth aches from talking to them too much. It is impossible for me to move to a new position. The assembly is only a formality [and can't help]. Whatever those above me say counts. We have no influence over policy at all. They say that the assembly has power that is simply not being utilized. That's what they say. [The assembly is] only an intended myth."[33]

Does the assembly have power? Both departments heads interviewed say yes. One acknowledges that "the assembly has yet to run well according to its design" but stresses that "strictly by law the assembly can veto the general manager's decision, although people don't know about this."[34] He does not worry that "people may abuse the power of the assembly." He feels that "even though people understand its power, they still would not use it." The other department head has tried to be a model of how to use the assembly: "The assembly can supervise the general manager. Many people think that representatives just have to raise hands and pass the development plan and go home. In fact, in our assembly many people have this misunderstanding. Since I am elected to represent workers, I must speak for them. I will never go to the assembly simply to raise my hand and go home."

Why is it, then, that the assembly fails to function well? Most cadres believe that this is because over the past few years the general manager has adequately proven his ability to make money. As a matter of fact, when the incumbent general manager arrived six years ago, workers held strong suspicions toward him. One worker recalls the difficulty the general manager had when he initiated a major reshuffling and launched a brand new product six years ago: "Workers resisted strongly, and this voice could be heard clearly at the assembly." Workers do not remember this history and today think "the assembly is a formality."[35] Another interviewee gives a more sophisticated analysis. He finds that workers are concerned with bonuses and only bonuses. The assembly is "indeed a formality on other issues." One could expect to "hear more criticism if you don't make money."[36] Once there is criticism, the pressure is on. The general secretary of the factory party comments:

> Some say that the assembly is a formality. As a matter of fact, this is an issue of one's culture [level of consciousness]. If the decision made proves correct, certainly no one would say anything at the assembly. But on many issues in order to prepare the assembly we must first go through the tedious process of persuasion, otherwise the assembly may veto the general manager. Besides, if we make a bad decision [profit loss], I guarantee you that people will scold us at the assembly.[37]

In any case, the leading cadre group has been hesitant in vitalizing the assembly. The assembly can exercise substantial powers within the factory according to the People's Industrial Enterprise Law (PIEL), passed in 1988 by the Seventh People's National Assembly.[38] Enterprises, however, often attempt to dilute that power with vague language in their internal rule books. For example, the PIEL gives the assembly the power to review the enterprise's overall orientation, long-term development plans, annual plans, investment programs, important technical innovation programs, worker training programs, ratio of reinvestment, dividends and portfolio, and the choice between contract and rental responsibility systems (clause 52, item 1). Beijing Print and Dye Company, for example, lumps everything into one sentence, resulting in a single regulation stating that the assembly can "hear the work report by the general manager." The PIEL gives the assembly the power to "review and then pass or veto" the adjustment to the salary schedule, while at Beijing Print and Dye the assembly "discusses and passes" the adjustment. This suggests that the leading cadre group does not appreciate the assembly's potential role in management.

Neither the union nor the assembly provides the symbol of workers' collective identity. This explains in part why the workers in China's socialist enterprise do not respond to lifetime employment enthusiastically. The workers and the factory are linked though work instructions from the superior and the issuance of bonuses. The assembly meets twice a year and is composed mostly of cadres, so it becomes an extended administrative meeting. The only difference is that in the assembly issues are bonus-related. It is not difficult to envision that the cadres may choose to lower the ratio of reinvestment in order to satisfy the workers at the assembly by issuing more bonuses. Though this might contribute in part to the legitimacy of the leading cadre group whose career goals may fall well outside the factory, the long-term interests of the factory may be sacrificed to a certain extent.

## CONCLUSION

The Chinese factory affects the lives of its workers in all respects. Yet even under such circumstances, factory identity is generally weak among workers. The factory provides board and in most cases housing, and it governs commuting. The leading cadre group, however, has yet to develop a true sense of attachment to the rank and file. On the one hand, a socialist factory recruits its workers through a public (state, provincial, county) system of labor distribution, so there is no pressure on the supply side. On the other hand, the factory has veto power over employees' transfer applications. This is sufficient leverage, for if workers apply and are rejected, they would have problems with their co-workers. Again, this prevents pressure on the supply side. From the workers' point of view, they do not enter a factory upon their own volition, nor do they believe that they have much influence over the factory where they get their first—and likely their last—job assignment.

Accordingly, the workers and the factory do not meet on a voluntary basis, and there is no need for each side to prove its attraction; they don't identify with each other in the first place. Especially since the initiation of reform, it is unpopular to emphasize things like identity, thought, and ideology. The leading cadre group does not believe, right or wrong, that there is anything besides money that can motivate the workers. When I told the general manager that some workers expressed their affection toward the factory, his first response was that they were "bragging." He

believes that "the workers know money and only money. You don't have
to interview them. I can tell you what they think."[39] One worker complains, "The general manager rarely shows up in our plant. If he comes,
everybody hides. He just wants to see if you hang your jacket on the wall
so he can fine you."[40] Some believe that the general manager allows the
unequal distribution of work to disguise the financial penalty to those who
receive low-bonus assignments or no assignment at all.[41]

Although they complain, few would even entertain the idea of opening
up their own shops on the market: "It is impossible to start a shop. The
rent may go as high as 2,000 yuan a month. If the factory loses money, I
may try some night job to make it up. Boy, the day work is exhausting
sometimes; where is the energy to run your own shop? Besides, the price
of raw material for individual shops may be quadruple the price for people's enterprises." Although it is theoretically possible to borrow money,
according to an interviewee, the bank cannot be persuaded that "an individual shopkeeper can compete with collective enterprises." More important, a worker who leaves the factory "cannot use his petty expertise without the assembly line."[42] In a sense, workers consciously choose to stay
where they enjoy little sense of attachment. The Chinese traditionally seek
identity from kinship groups. Under socialism, they are supposed to identify with the workplace. When this sense of identity cannot develop and
there is little chance to replace the factory with another group, anxiety and
frustration simultaneously occur.

What separates China from Japan is that the tight relationship of rights
and obligations between the workers and the factory is not combined with
a sense of belonging and identity. This happens not only in some of the
most successful factories but also in those that suffer a low profit margin—and they are the majority. This is the crux of the problem of China's
workers' culture: Most have no vision and refuse to identify with their factory. The more fortunate are elevated by their superiors and may gradually
develop a sense of future and belonging. Most workers, though, must be
prodded by material reward. Nowadays, in surprising contrast to the days
of the Cultural Revolution, even moral issues are handled with money. In
the factory, violations of socialist civilization (for example, watching X-
rated movies) are punished by fines. The implication for the regime is that
the workers of today's China are no longer available in a large-scale political mobilization to achieve constructive goals. This implication may
need to be proved by further empirical study. Nevertheless, what is already
clear is that the base of the Chinese socialist regime has undergone a
process of materialization. This guarantees that workers will interpret the
meaning of socialism and subscribe to its tenets in idiosyncratic and inconsistent ways.

# 9

# PROFITEERING SOCIALISM: SCHOOL ENTERPRISES

Economic reform in China has fundamentally shaken the tradition of central planning. It is highly unlikely that when reform was initiated in the late 1970s, reformers could have anticipated all the possible effects of such measures. The rigidity of central planning makes it difficult to conceive what the post–central planning system may look like. Reformers are now especially uncomfortable with the loss of control over currency flow in the market, with more and more paper money falling into private hands—or, more precisely, into public hands for private use. This unbudgeted flow of capital has two major sources, according to many Chinese economists. One source is group consumption (*jituan xiaofei*) by state-owned as well as collective enterprises.[1] The consumption capacity of a typical enterprise has improved dramatically in recent years because reformers have deliberately allowed enterprises an increased profit share and easier access to loans. The other source is accelerating group investment, especially investments made by rural collective enterprises.[2] These small enterprises find themselves in a competitive market with plenty of profit opportunities. The potential for inflationary pressure is there at all times.

In this chapter I present an example of the second category of unbudgeted money flow, the case of a school enterprise. Most discussions of unbudgeted money flow, including those in China, rarely touch upon this area. At best, however, I only scratch the surface of a much larger problem. School enterprises are one of the many new productive businesses arising from the reform process that crystallize complicated urban-rural networks and that reformers have repeatedly encouraged state-owned enterprises to organize, mobilize, and utilize. Reformers believe that by breaking with the legacy of central planning, those smaller productive units, which are often more active and profit-oriented, can serve reform well. In prying open the market, these smaller units can establish connections with larger enterprises constrained by the traditional planning system, contributing to the demise of such planning. State-owned enterprises can develop their full potential only after the planning system declines, so in this sense non–state-owned enterprises are the vanguards of the reform movement.

In this chapter I discuss a portion of the effects of reform in Chinese society, especially the rise of school entrepreneurship and its implications for China's political tradition. Literature on reform in China concentrates primarily on policy rationale and factionalism at the upper echelons of power. Few have paid attention to those cadres and managers in the lower echelons, though managers at the enterprise level are the ones who must interpret and actualize reform. These lower-level managers are the opinion leaders to the extent that they translate reform policy, activate the market, and account for and allocate profit. It is difficult for observers to gain access to these managers; even Chinese scholars would be highly suspect if they were to attempt field research in such enterprises. Managers naturally dislike this type of research, as it discloses those secrets of the trade so crucial to the operation of their business.

I conducted research for this chapter through the arrangements of a contact I established while teaching in the United States; the study took over two years to prepare. The original purpose of my trip was to investigate Chinese corporate culture under reform in a state-owned enterprise (see Chapter Ten), but by chance I was introduced to a school factory manager, which opened up a whole new field of research for this chapter. All connections were personal and all the arrangements through personal connections (*guanxi*): No Chinese officials were informed. Only those party secretaries who had privately approved the field trip in its original form might have known that I later extended my study to a neighboring village. My research design aimed simply at discovering how a typical school enterprise operates, what the debates surrounding the rise of school entrepreneurship are, why the government encourages such school-run businesses, and how the enterprise and the government interact.

There are four methodological caveats. Since I had little knowledge about school enterprises before I began my research, the interviewees themselves may (intentionally or not) have shaped the sort of questions I asked. Interviews may have brought up interesting issues that I saw only later and thus had no opportunity to pursue. Second, because I interviewed exclusively the successful managers, my research may show an atypical optimism. Third, I could not tape or take notes during interviews but had to rely solely on memory, so the possibility of inaccuracies is far higher than it would be for recorded sessions. Finally, my data cannot be checked by other researchers because I had to take every measure to conceal the interviewees' identifications in order to protect them from political harassment.

## WHAT IS A SCHOOL ENTERPRISE?

In the early stage of reform, Premier Zhao Ziyang proposed that all government units "generate their own income" (*zixing chuangshou*).[3] Since the whole idea of reform centered on the promotion of productive forces, some material incentives were deemed proper. The reformers realized that individual work incentives were essential to heighten efficiency as well as creativity. The first task of reform was therefore to "bring into play the active nature of all individuals" (*diaodong geti jijixing*). However, precisely because the reformers lacked resources, there was no effective incentive mechanism available to them. *Chuangshou* was therefore the most creative incentive mechanism they could invent. The policy of *chuangshou* was designed to allow any government unit to share profit earned in the market. More important, a government unit was permitted to enjoy a much more privileged profit-sharing ratio than a typical state-owned enterprise. Since it shares profit, it may borrow from the market and initiate its own productive projects that meet market demand. Theoretically, the planning system enlarges its own tax base as all government units thrive in the market.

Now that the rationale of policy is to encourage all potentially productive forces to face the challenge of the market, the nature of the productive business each government unit engages in varies with its market research, not with the nature of its daily administrative business. In fact, the reformers want those who orient themselves toward market forces to get rich faster. The reformers' objective of promoting efficiency and productive forces is therefore compatible with each unit's objective of getting rich (through bonus sharing). If the type of business of each government unit is irrelevant to the policy of *chuangshou*, public schools certainly are legitimate actors in the market. Privileges for schools are even more attractive than for other government units, as many local authorities simply waive schools' tax payments. Everyone seems to agree that salaries for elementary school teachers are embarrassingly meager, so the government would lose face if it took too much profit accruing from the *chuangshou* business in the school, which some nickname "the third kind of business."[4]

The slogan the National Commission of Education uses to legitimize school-run enterprises is "learning in frugality through industrious work" (*qinggong jianxue*), which now has become the title of a commission-sponsored periodical specializing in school entrepreneurship. The concept of school entrepreneurship as an effective tool for teaching industrial ethics and frugality is truly innovative and helps avoid the conservative impression that Confucian scholars are driven by profit.

The slogan encapsulates two missions of a school enterprise in addition to generating a higher income for teachers: The school administration should share the profit and use it for school renovation; teachers should consciously enlist students in extracurricular learning along the assembly lines. School-run enterprises generally use one or two classrooms to place the assembly line so the productive site is nearby and practical learning is thus facilitated. (Because of the safety hazards of allowing children near machines, however, practical learning may mean occasionally watching the machines through windows, as observing alone is thought to be able to build a sense of participation in socialist modernization.)

As mentioned above, school enterprises enjoy tax exemption. Enterprises normally pay a 55 percent flat tax, but the county government in this specific case study stipulates that schools pay a 35 percent flat tax instead. In practice the local government currently forgoes the tax in order to encourage more schools to run businesses.[5] As a result, school businesses do not contribute to the county's educational fund, and this is in part how schools are encouraged to run businesses. Under the creative leadership of its chief, the county's bureau of education has decided to run its own business: If the schools can operate businesses, why can't their superior? As a matter of fact, it is much easier for the bureau to start a business because it maintains a collateral relationship with the bureaus of finance and industry in the county, bringing all sorts of privileges to the education bureau's enterprise. In addition, with its political status the bureau of education would enjoy relatively easier access to borrowing and be more likely to attract reputable joint ventures from the urban sector. If there is a profit, both bureau employees and the county educational fund would benefit.

According to the bureau chief, there has been a serious financial problem concerning the welfare of retired and handicapped faculty and staff. The county also lacks additional funding for faculty training. The chief aims high. He intends to enlarge the service range and improve its quality after the two bureau-run factories start full-scale operation, in a year or so. Because the central government sets rigid requirements for use of educational funds, each county must find its own resources outside the budget system if it wants to improve the quality of life for its faculty and staff. In order to avoid charges of corruption, the bureau under study started its business in the name of school enterprises (which is officially encouraged). In 1990 the bureau chose as investment sites two elementary schools that appeared dormant on the business front. The factories are located outside the schools, and the deal is that the schools and the bureau will share profits once the business begins to make money. This is another type of school enterprise.

## MANAGING SCHOOL ENTERPRISES

The first task of a school principal is to find a general manager. In most cases the principal invites a member of the faculty to assume the responsibility. The general manager normally recruits staff from among colleagues. In a rare case the principal may serve as the general manager at the same time. Once faculty members begin to work for the enterprise, they of course lag behind in their teaching duties; according to the payroll they are still teachers nonetheless. The principal thus is forced to maneuver in order to cover the courses previously taught by those with business assignments. Theoretically, when the enterprise makes money, only those with positions on the payroll share profit. In reality, few would oppose allowing those faculty on the business side to share a bit more.

One problem that may become more serious in the future is the peculiar style of bookkeeping in the school enterprise. Because the enterprise is a part of the school, it need keep just one accounting book. Collective enterprises usually keep two ledgers either for tax evasion or for specialized internal management needs. Since school enterprises do not pay taxes, there is little need to keep two ledgers, though they may do so simply to avoid government regulations concerning the relative ratio among depreciation, reinvestment, bonuses, and educational use. In addition, it is virtually impossible to distinguish whether an expense is allocated for normal school operation or business operation when there is only one ledger for the whole school; for the sake of cost management, school enterprises generally do have at least one separate book. With the personnel and the bookkeeping officially presented as a part of school operation, the education and tax bureaus experience enormous difficulties in auditing. But because the current policy is to encourage as many school enterprises as possible, the trouble is deliberately ignored. The head of the education bureau acknowledges that this may pose problems in the long term.

Another issue is funding. The school cannot possibly expect financial sponsorship from the government, since the rationale of school enterprises is precisely *zixing chuangshou,* as noted above. It is equally unlikely that the schools can come up with investment funds from their annual budget, and the bureau of education would certainly not approve this tactic anyway. Funding must be found somewhere else. Usually there are two sources: borrowing from a bank or investment by a large state-owned enterprise. The latter source is usually arranged in the form of joint venture—the school provides human resources and land, and the other partner comes up with capital and technology. In the case of the two above-mentioned bureau-run enterprises, both sources are present: The bureau obtained 50 percent of initial costs through bank financing, and the joint venture partner provided the other 50 percent. This type of coordination is precisely the model of market socialism that the central planner has touted for years. Under the slogan of cross-sector coordination (*hengxiang lianhe*), the central planner believes that joint ventures by investors across sectors and areas can alleviate the rigidity of the central planning system. The planner would like to have investors act like stockholders without appearing to be stockholders, for political and ideological reasons.

Banks, however, are understandably skeptical about the credibility of school enterprises and are naturally hesitant about extending credit; it is an open secret that most schools are dirt poor. Banks likewise could not resort to legal means if the investment proved to be a failure and the school was unable to honor the repayment schedule. Furthermore, banks may have legitimate doubts about a teacher's ability to run a factory. To acquire funding, therefore, the school must rely on the government to establish workable channels through connections or exchanges of favor. One possible alternative is to attract a reputable joint venture partner whose creditworthiness may be a sufficient guarantee to generally dubious bankers.

The productive scale of a school enterprise is often limited, especially one in a suburban area. A school enterprise is thus similar to a typical collective enterprise in the countryside. The mentality of a school entrepreneur, though, is quite different. In the two factories where I conducted interviews, both general managers dislike the analogy between their factory and a typical rural factory. They feel that rural factories are run by peasants whose style is "myopic, of poor quality, and sometimes illegal." A school enterprise is run by respectful teachers who observe market ethics. Most importantly, teachers feel the inner drive "to expand the scale and improve the technological level step by step." In the two factories under study, one has adopted a semiautomatic assembly line; the other has been struggling with an automatic assembly line. Both school enterprises are capable of maintaining their facilities.

Nevertheless, a school enterprise is still far behind an average urban state-owned enterprise in terms of technology and employee training. An urban state-owned enterprise recruits its new employees from occupational schools. In the countryside a school enterprise sometimes has to negotiate with the county government regarding employment. In one of the factories the bureau of education has invested in, the county government provided the land and nine workers. While the county government tried to keep the best workers for the village and dump the laziest ones on the bureau, the bureau looked to recruit the better educated, and the villagers fought for the opportunity to work in the factory. The general manager recalled that fight as a "personnel hurricane." "Fortunately," the technology requirement was moderate, so the quality of the work force was not a prime issue at the time.

In most cases even a large school enterprise needs no more than five classrooms: one or two for assembly lines or machinery, one for packaging, one for stock, one or two for office use. The number of employees is most often fewer than thirty. In one of the bureau-run enterprises, however, the plant occupies over an acre of land and has more than fifty employees, though this is the exception rather than the rule. In fact, the general manager of that particular factory realizes that the use of space in the factory is quite inefficient and has decided to allocate a part of that space to growing vegetables. He also looks to private enterprises for possible rental arrangements for the remainder of the space. By contrast, a rather small factory that uses only three classrooms with twenty-two employees has achieved an average profit of Rmb50,000 a year.

Most school enterprises do not manufacture finished products for direct consumption. The major purchaser is often a large, urban, state-owned enterprise or a relatively advanced collective enterprise. In establishing the connection with a large enterprise, the majority of the interviewees believe that the right personal network is the key. There can be exceptions, of course. In fact, the general manager of one of the very successful school enterprises under study personally called on each potential buyer when the business was first started. The general manager himself served as the marketing chief; he found that market demand was stronger than expected during his one-on-one marketing trips. Nonetheless, this is a rather unique style of marketing in China. Most factories depend on friends and relatives to locate potential buyers.

Because they produce primarily spare parts, the planner does not regulate their market. As a matter of fact, since school enterprises do not depend on the state for either investment funding or raw material allocation, there is no need to deal with the planners as all state-owned enterprises are required to do. The bright side is that school enterprises maintain the flexibility needed to survive in the market; the dark side is that the state will not come to their rescue when they find themselves caught in a financial crunch. In any case, if the planners happen to categorize its product as an "important item" (*zhongda xiangmu*), the enterprise must submit the productive project for approval before making an investment, such as in the case of a state-owned enterprise but without the parallel privileges enjoyed by a state-owned enterprise. These constraints explain why the safest approach is to produce the essential parts of a final product that has a stable niche in the central plan and to secure connections with a state-owned enterprise manufacturing that product.

Finally, compared to university enterprises, school enterprises appear rudimentary. Most university enterprises not only supply products of a higher technological level but also provide post-sale service. University technicians are also available for consulting. For any school enterprise to reach that level, the county government would have to invest much more than it could possibly imagine. In this sense, school enterprises are no more than typical rural collective enterprises, despite the intellectual capacity of their managers. Figure 9.1 illustrates the school enterprise system.

Since the school principal and the chief of the bureau of education normally are not directly involved directly in the operation of a school or bureau enterprise, the key to the success of the enterprise appears to be the general manager and the director of the county's office of school

Figure 9.1   Regulating School Enterprises

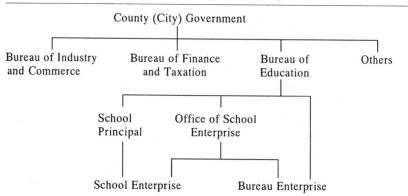

enterprise. But do the general manager, the director, and the chief have the same perceptions of one another's roles?

According to the director of the office of school enterprise in the county I studied, an enterprise is financially independent from the office in theory, except that the enterprise annually submits 2.5 percent of its profit to the office to cover operating expenses. In reality, however, when a school enterprise encounters a financial difficulty or needs short-term operating funds, its general manager usually looks first to the office for help. The director can arrange for the general manager to meet potential supporters (that is, banks). Occasionally, the director, with the help of the bureau chief, can assist in acquiring the approval of the other bureaus in procuring property, raw materials, and credits. This is especially true for the bureau-run enterprise, where the director and the bureau chief have a direct and immediate stake. The director makes the following observation:

> I must help them solve all kinds of financial difficulties. I must help spread the management experiences of those successful enterprises and straighten out other general managers' ways of thinking. The director protects as well as manages the enterprise. When different bureaus send inspectors, I must accompany them on tours of the selected factories. When I evaluate the general managers, I look at their efficiency level. I also review their managerial policy to see if they follow the government's general instructions on, for example, safety regulations and environmental protection. When an enterprise wishes to start a new project, the manager needs to get my approval. . . . My experience suggests that a profitable enterprise always looks for more autonomy, while a money-losing enterprise is usually highly dependent.[6]

The director is obviously most concerned with efficiency. He is also the bureau's frontline representative in managing the enterprises. The interesting thing is that the director himself was previously general manager of a successful school enterprise and was promoted to his current post only a year before I spoke with him. This background is especially useful in relation to the auditing process, since there is no specialized auditing agency in the bureau of education. The chief therefore recruited a former manager who was familiar with all the tricks of bookkeeping. The director believes that there is no objective standard that the chief can use to evaluate his performance. He thinks that the most important criterion has to be the average profit level of the county's school enterprises. This is sufficient disincentive to keep him from interfering in the operation of any profitable enterprise. Still, he feels obliged to provide detailed guidance to enterprises that lose money. As a result, the relationship between government and successful enterprise becomes remote and that between government and struggling enterprise reluctantly close. The director sees the paradox but feels that he can do nothing to change it. He acknowledges that most general school managers simply want to use him.

One general manager describes the relationship between his (bureau-invested) factory and the county government:

> [My factory] has no relationship with the government. The bureau of education adopts a hands-off policy toward us. They don't intervene. Sometimes there may be a few requests for specific apportionments [*tanpai*]. That's all. The bureau will have to deal with the bureau of industry and commerce and the bureau of finance and taxation for us. As a result, since we are basically a school enterprise, we don't pay taxes and we enjoy lots of privileges. . . . The bureau of education and the factory don't relate to each other otherwise. Their major concern is that we make enough money for them, and that's it. . . . I don't need the rigid planning system to constrain me; I am under nobody's jurisdiction.[7]

The general manager of another model enterprise is quite straightforward: "The most important thing is to make money. The party organ in the school carries out spiritual campaigns from time to time, but the factory is intent only on productive efficiency. The principal does not bother with the factory as long as the factory gives him money. The government's policy of tax exemption helps a bit. We have much room to maneuver because the bureau, the school, and the party don't interfere."[8] Indeed, this particular general manager is confident and independent. He does not have to worry about the charge of spiritual pollution since he makes money for the whole school, not for himself. Both the chief and the director praise his contribution to the socialist educational system. When he makes money, the director receives credit in front of the chief, who in turn is relieved not to have to worry about the welfare of the teachers.

The chief understands the government-enterprise relationship in a similar way:

The bureau of education does not take any money from the school enterprise. . . . The bureau, together with some large state-owned enterprise, establishes its own joint venture and a portion of the profits will be deposited in the pool for educational funding. The schools are poor, so we hope to find ways to improve the welfare level of the school faculty. The rule says that a school enterprise should submit 35 percent of its profits to the bureau, but since they are poor we forgo this obligation. They only have to contribute 2.5 percent to cover the office of school enterprise's operating costs. The school is requested to use 45 percent of profits for facility renovation. If the faculty would like to use the money to tour Beijing in the summer, for example, I will approve the trip as long as the money does not come from the original educational budget. On the part of the bureau, I also have to coordinate with large state-owned enterprises in our own business in order to generate funds to enhance the welfare level of the retired faculty.[9]

There have been charges, though, of "fiddling with education" and "fiddling with spiritual civilization." The chief gives two responses: He consults with the bureau of labor to arrange educational programs for non-faculty workers; he makes sure that school enterprises promote the atmosphere of industry and frugality to enlighten the student body. The director takes the charge even more lightly:

Many people oppose the idea of a school running a business. They think that running a business will distract the principal from education. This is insightful. Yes, if the principal has enough to worry about, he will lose his concentration on education if he spends too much time on business. Our job is education and his [the general manager's] job is enterprise; that's why we let him handle everything. . . . All spiritual civilization needs a material base. Remember, in the days right after liberation, we used to have a high level of spiritual civilization. It was the ten-year Cultural Revolution that polarized everyone in politics.[10]

The director notes that, as far as he knows, no successful enterprise faces the dilemma of an interfering principal. On the contrary, the principal gets involved only if there is a problem.

Unfortunately, field research did not permit me the opportunity to interview a principal. From others' remarks, there appears to be a consensus that the principal should have nothing to do with the operation of the school enterprise. Furthermore, the managers welcome the interference of neither the chief nor the director; they want to be left alone. If everyone puts a priority on profit making, people and enterprises are evaluated accordingly, and success implies more for everyone (through profit sharing, bonuses, or the trickle-down effect), who would want to raise the issue of spiritual civilization beyond some feigned gesture in the public arena? In this sense, the party, the regime, and the school have compatible interests.

## POLITICAL IMPLICATIONS

China's political tradition shows a strong proclivity toward moralization. Political legitimacy depends on the pretension of selflessness. The ideal is for leaders to pose as models for the people. In the process of education, the leaders cannot help but rely upon symbols and local leaders—who have internalized the symbols and the associated norms—to spread the sense of legitimacy and nobility of the state-owned leadership. Local leaders, be they the gentry or the cadres, play a critical role in educating the polity.[11]

The rise of school entrepreneurship seems to signal the decline of such a political tradition. Not only has the traditional base of rectification (intellectuals and schools) undergone the process of materialization, but legitimacy has also come to depend more and more on leaders' ability to deliver economic welfare and less and less on rectification of the political and social order. The rise of school enterprises therefore suggests four connotations.

First, relations between the general manager and the director of the office of school enterprise involve almost no sense of social obligation or authentic mutual respect. In theory, the director is a sort of state symbol, while the general manager is the representative of society. The interaction between the two seems to involve pure interest calculation. Between the local collective enterprise (the productive unit representing demand in society) and the large state-owned enterprise (the symbol of the state planning system), a similar trend of amoralization can be detected. The uniqueness of the latter relationship is that state and society are linked here through some variety of personal connection, either friendship or nepotism. Without such connections, state and society have lost an institutional link.

Since the director does not evaluate the general manager by the latter's collectivistic commitment, and the chief does not evaluate the director by the latter's dedication to socialism, the role of ideological judgment is downplayed. It is likely that the material emphasis in the current standard of personnel review may eventually benefit society as a whole through the development of productive forces. But abandoning the collectivist values contributes to the erosion of the moral monopoly the Chinese state has held for more than 1,000 years. The breakdown of that monopoly is indicated by the spread of new, material criteria. One has to wonder what the basis for political legitimacy of such a society would be if neither pluralism nor democracy took root.

For the general manager who cares about the profitability of his own factory, not aggregate national profitability, the legitimacy of the director lies in the latter's ability to help him profit, not to help the county profit.

He must be able to manipulate the banking system for the sake of the manager, not just stick to socialist principles. For the chief who takes an overall view of the whole county, the director must be able to improve the welfare of the whole county as well as facilitate the advancement of particular factories. Again, he considers the most important thing to be profit rather than egalitarianism. The manager and the chief may share a similar expectation of what type of job the director has; the paradox lies in that the manager and the chief agree on the material front yet not on the socialist front. Socialism or not, the image of the state is quite different today in terms of the source of its legitimacy.

Second, cadres are traditionally the educators serving national leaders. At the present time, however, neither the chief nor the director is in any position to rectify order in society. On the contrary, they believe that their job is to liberate productive forces hidden in society from the past planning system, and they must use material incentives to lure people to work. Local cadres begin to associate local interests with their own interests. The state defines interests in the way society defines them, so that the state endeavors to employ the market mechanism to reflect society's view of its true interests. As a result, cadres no longer serve exclusively as educators for the state center.

The implication is significant: Political stability over such a wide landscape has been possible because of the help of local leaders. It would be irrelevant, if not nonsensical, to have the mass media broadcast an ideal life-style and goals dramatically divergent from those of local leaders, as people would become all the more aware that collectivist rhetoric is pure pretension and would thus be further alienated from the traditional type of regime. In fact, the joint venture between a school enterprise and a local state-owned enterprise often involves some kind of exchange: The state-owned enterprise provides capital, and the school enterprise returns with special arrangements whereby the state-owned enterprise can evade taxes. Society and the state's local leadership collude.

Third, just as the chief and the director serve as the representatives of the state vis-à-vis the manager, the manager serves as the state representative vis-à-vis the school workers. As just mentioned, the general manager who worries only about market and profit cannot take on the role of new selfless leadership. For a general manager in a large state-owned enterprise, there are always political and ideological missions to complete. In comparison, the general manager of a school enterprise has no such pressure. He is under the "jurisdiction of nobody." He does not even bother with formal ideological education. His only mission is making money, and this is understood by everyone in the school. Regardless of his personal views, the general manager of the school enterprise serves as a countermodel. This is indeed a rare occurrence in the history of local leadership in China.

Finally, in all school enterprises under study, there is not the slightest evidence of spiritual civilization (in terms of ideological rectification). The school party concentrates its efforts on persuading all to join the productive process. The party secretary, who also shares in profits generated by the school enterprise, seems obliged to clear up any concerns in the school about developing school entrepreneurship; all political education centers on productive work.

## CONCLUSION

In the county under study, the total value in the products made by the school enterprises accounted for only slightly over 1 percent of the county's total productive value in 1990. The profit generated, however, was about 20 percent of the total educational fund for 1990, according to a source inside the bureau of education. If 45 percent of profits was reserved for educational renovation, as stipulated, each school thus had on average an additional 10 percent of its budgeted funding in 1990. This is certainly a significant figure. The school enterprise has become a new trend in China. It does not earn massive sums owing to its limited scale, but precisely because of this, it enjoys flexibility under the "jurisdiction of nobody." There is no effective regulation of its activities, and there is currently no intention to impose regulation.

This is the lesson: Local leaders jettison their post as educators and become profit pursuers; as a result, the Chinese political regime is forced to rely more and more on material incentives over moral incentives to maintain its legitimacy. On the material battlefield, local leaders satisfy society better than the central planner. The myth of one supreme selfless being is gone. To what extent will this transform the Chinese political-cultural landscape? No one has to argue against socialism, nor is anyone interested in championing capitalism, for the ideological banner does not seem to be the issue. And it is this ideological alienation that best represents the style of China's reform.

# 10

## CONCLUSION:
## THE PRINCIPLE OF SELF-CONSCIOUSNESS

Although reform has changed China's political economic style significantly by deliberately enlisting individualistic, materialistic incentives, it retains a rather traditional key element. This is true to the extent that the principle of self-consciousness continues to have an impact upon policy outcomes. In reconciling socialist and collectivist concerns with individualistic profit incentives, this seemingly self-contradictory principle is typical in countries under the double pressures of both market and socialism; it is not necessarily unique to China.

In the previous chapters, I described the symbiosis of collective interests and individual interests throughout Chinese society, the plan guiding and adapting to the market, and the state enterprises negotiating with the planners above and with the workers below. In between, managers also look out for contractors in public as well as private sectors. In addition, workers in state enterprises live under the banner of work unit socialism yet invest their lives with personal meaning. Most, if not all, understand the irony of this dual identity. It would appear that the past problem was not in socialism per se but in the violation of the symbiosis of interests of different levels, either in the form of rigid planning or in the cycle of mass initiative. This lesson may be a useful reminder that a presumably resolute move toward individual interests under reform may cause difficulties in the future.

From the Western point of view, however, China looked very different in 1995, six years after the Beijing massacre. Chinese economic reform stalled in spring 1989, reflecting both economic retrenchment and political realignment. Suddenly, reform was frozen and the so-called conservatives were in control in Beijing. Deng Xiaoping's visit to southern China on the eve of the Chinese New Year in 1992, however, broke new ground for reformers. Within less than three months, the reformist camp regained its lost momentum in the propaganda battle. Indeed, this comeback confirms the typical Western mode of analysis or China's cyclical pattern of using the plan and the masses alternately: There are reformist and conservative antireformist factions, and their prime difference lies in how fast they believe China should carry out its reform. In fact, the dispute in Western academic circles concerns primarily how the Chinese state has succeeded or failed in mobilizing social resources for the sake of growth, sometimes in the name of socialism, at other times in the name of reform.

One focus of Western concern is how much influence the Chinese state exerts over society. Put somewhat differently, the issue is whether the state-society differentiation in China can be held off as the Communist Party deliberately keeps the distinction between the two obscure in the name of socialism.[1] In this sense, analysts are particularly interested in determining if the state has penetrated traditional Chinese society. In contrast, political economic research on industrialized societies often attends to movement in the opposite direction, focusing on how society has penetrated the state.[2]

Many scholars have examined the nature of Chinese state and society. Discussions about the relative strength of the Chinese state appear in research on both the industrial and the agricultural sectors. For example, there is the argument that authority in the Chinese workplace establishes itself through a cliental system.[3] Workers can be broken down into two groups: one tends to be more active, the other more passive. The active group seeks promotion and other personal gains by performing state functions along the assembly line as well as on the political front. Normally, these loyal servants of the state depend on specific superiors to take care of them. Policymaking in the Chinese workplace thus resembles neither Western pluralism, which presupposes interest group formation, nor traditional authoritarianism, which rests entirely on private relationships.

According to this view, Chinese policymaking is organized around state positions. Those in state positions have enormous influence over the allocation of resources in society. Those in the lower echelons who seek more benefits and welfare would have to prove their trainability and loyalty by performing political assignments correctly and aggressively. If this performance in turn assists their superiors in winning popularity among *their* superiors, they are rewarded. This type of relationship naturally reinforces the political myth of the state and consolidates, in the public arena, the state's legitimacy.

In contrast, there is the view that the Chinese workplace can in a sense transform state requirements and even distort them in protecting the interests of an enterprise or factory. This is sometimes termed work unit socialism.[4] Chinese workers depend on their employers not only for their salaries but for other aspects of life as well, including housing, marriage, and retirement allowance, all of which are allocated and arranged through the enterprise system. Once assigned to an enterprise, workers can expect to spend the rest of their lives there. Each enterprise thus develops its own enterprise culture. Workers and cadres regard the collective gain of the enterprise and the distribution of that gain within the enterprise as the most essential issues in their daily lives.

Work unit socialism stresses the importance of the internal pressures of an enterprise. Managers would have tremendous difficulty managing their factories if the general expectations of workers regarding their legitimate share were not met. Not only do general managers themselves have to spend a great deal of their lives in a specific factory, but their chances for promotion are contingent upon their ability to maintain harmony in the factory. General managers cannot expect easily to satisfy workers who have little fear of losing their jobs. As a result, consensus achievement becomes the style of decisionmaking in the work unit. The perspective that work unit socialism portrays is therefore rather different from the picture given by the clientelist view. The work unit is itself a relatively autonomously developed community, and its collective interests must first be met before general managers can successfully perform state-assigned tasks.

As in the industrial sector, researchers of the agricultural sector strive to theorize the state-society relationship. The clientelist perspective finds its counterpart here.[5] Some scholars argue, for example, that village politics that affects rural resource allocation mirrors politics in the industrial workplace. Production team leaders must be on good terms with state managers in order to evade at least some state demands for grain quality and taxes in kind. Since the state arbitrarily decides how much the team needs for survival, villagers are in such a vulnerable position they become subject to state pressures at their own sacrifice. This is why personal connections with the state agent are critical to the interests of the villager.

The state purchases and sells grain according to the state plan. The planning system ensures the position of the state as a controller in the agricultural sector. Reform since the late 1970s, which created the family responsibility system and the grain contracting system, may ironically serve to reduce the state's influence and submit it to a local autocracy. This happens because as villagers are permitted to retain and sell production in excess of the contracted volume, they are able to generate surplus for themselves and remain outside the control of the state plan. As new cliental patterns evolve, the state may gradually fade away and society may reemerge as an autonomous entity operating against the state apparatus just as it had before the communist regime came to power.

In opposition to this view is the "honeycomb" analogy, which describes villages under Chinese communism as rather autonomous components of local communities.[6] On the one hand, Maoism periodically encouraged the local community to depend on itself for all-round development. On the other hand, traditional values and ways of life have survived the advent of a communist regime. As a result, local leaders always find ways to cheat the state and beat the system. It may appear that the state, as the center of power, constantly gives directions to local communities. In reality, those living in the periphery continue to pay loyalty to traditional leaders, some of whom now lead in the name of the state cadre, but the game of local protectionism is the same as before. In short, the communist regime has failed to penetrate traditional society, organized like honeycomb and highly protected against external interference.

As reform brings in the notion and the practice of the market, though, the traditional community faces the threat of disintegration. Some contend that once villagers become free competitors in the market, they will no longer depend on the local gentry for improved living standards. This way the state would gain better access to peripheral communities through policy that influences the operation of the market. While the clientelist perspective is in awe of the state's extensive reach, the honeycomb approach questions the state's capabilities. While the clientelist perspective looks at reform as a mechanism that may allow local autocracy to thrive at the expense of the state's capabilities, the honeycomb theory views reform as a possible tool to enable the state eventually to penetrate and modernize society.

Is it possible that these two perspectives can be reconciled? Is it possible that the Chinese communist state has indeed successfully penetrated society, while at the same time society has successfully protected its integrity in pursuing collective interests? If it appears unlikely that both are correct, let us recall the parable of the two blind men touching an elephant, each trying to determine exactly what the animal looks like by feeling only one part of it. It would be extremely difficult to lead them to believe they had each given a correct account of one aspect of the elephant, yet each would be mistaken if he were to claim that his interpretation represented the sole truth. What perspectives, then, can allow mutual penetration of state and society? It seems that the Chinese mind-set has allowed state and society in China to overlap, thus making possible such mutual penetration. (In Chapters Four and Five I discussed exactly this irony of dual roles in both consumers' and production-factors markets.)

In the Chinese context political campaigns usually mix forces representing state and society. For example, the Cultural Revolution was initiated by a portion of the party-state to enlist the support of students in political battles in the realm of the state. On the one hand, radicals began to take state positions and become parts of the state. On the other hand, the Cultural Revolutionaries could not move beyond the original factional setting and were contaminated by state affairs. Analysis of this type cannot treat political conflict and social cleavage along state-society lines but along factional lines instead. This perception suggests that the state must have penetrated society in order for social forces to split along factional lines. One may also contend, though, that society must first have penetrated the state for the state to define respective positions in the state arena. The challenge to the state-society analysis of Chinese political economy is that a typical Chinese performs both state and societal functions; hence cadres are also mandarins and communists are members of the gentry.

Both the Confucian and socialist themes obscure distinctions between state and society. The Confucian theme fosters a mind-set that enables the Chinese to serve the state as if they were fulfilling social obligations. The socialist theme molds a mind-set that leads the Chinese to recognize that there is no society outside the state. The state obviously penetrates society since all workers must work for the state and accept state ideology. Society also penetrates the state since workers believe it is legitimate to allocate resources in the name of the state to satisfy their personal needs. As state employees, workers by definition perform public functions in supposedly private realms, leaving no room for genuine privacy; as proletarians, workers own (by squandering) whatever the state claims, leaving the state a somewhat spurious organ.

The struggle between state and society becomes a struggle within each mind-set. In Chapters Six through Nine of this book, I portrayed precisely this inner contradiction as it involved the post of general manager, from the general manager's, party secretary's, workers', and planners' perspectives. The Chinese dread the notion of the state-society demarcation because it implies the possibility of disharmony. This cognitive constraint is nevertheless insufficient to thwart state-society interaction in an objective sense, for state officials inescapably develop vested interests and departmental viewpoints as opposed to indigenous peasant perspectives. This conflict between state and society is also consciously condemned in official ideology, which claims that the party represents the proletarian class (society) to lead the government (state). Acts that attempted to empower either state or society at the expense of the other historically led to policy disasters.

It turns out that the state always appears as the representative of collective interests; society, of individual or departmental interests. Where the state-society demarcation lies, however, is not definite. Therefore a state enterprise is a part of society when contrasted with the central planners (who certainly embody the state), but it becomes a symbol of the state as opposed to its workers, who represent society. For effective operation, the state has to depend on society to feed back information regarding the reality in society. This leads reformers to change hard planning into soft planning and to adjust to market information sent back by enterprise managers—who have learned to pick up the particular part of the plan that gives them an edge in the specific market niche where they consider themselves most competitive and their business most profitable. Similar visions apply to the relationship between middle-sized as well as large state enterprises and other actors in the market.

Ideally, state enterprises improve their agility through cooperation with dealers or contractors who maintain close contacts with the consumer goods market and the production-factors market. The state enjoys the privilege of having a big picture of the economy, attuned to what is supposedly most needed and thus most profitable in the long run. This may effectively attract actors at lower echelons to cooperate with the state. If enterprises keep the plan firmly in mind, the state will gain through them useful information across all regions and sectors and ensure the accuracy of the long-term view it in turn provides to these enterprises. This is what ideal market socialism looks like. The short-run interest conflict between the planners and the enterprise or between the enterprises and their workers serves as useful information for both. The seeming liability, when appropriately handled, can be turned into an asset.

The principle of self-consciousness is therefore also a doctrine of self-interests. Enterprises are encouraged to see a larger and longer-term picture to complete their roles as agents of the state, to appreciate the planners' struggle in employing market pressures as well as socialist pressures. Market pressure keeps enterprises from relying exclusively on the state for improved circumstances; socialist pressure prevents them from total obsession with profiteering in the market. In theory enterprises can survive both short- and long-run development imperatives only if they are cognizant of the double edge of the principle of self-consciousness. (The short-run imperative concerns productive efficiency; the long-run, collectivistic growth.) They have to consider both individual and collectivist interests in order to promote both causes and to keep the extremes in check.

Here I enlist some native Chinese perspectives on the state-society analysis in order to appreciate the argument that Chinese state and society could not easily be separated from each other without causing an eventual countermovement. Unfortunately, major policy disputes in China followed this pattern of action and reaction up to the time of the interview I now turn to (and probably up to the time readers read this book). I conducted this seven-hour interview with two mid-level Chinese officials, both in their mid-forties, in spring 1992 (precisely the time Deng Xiaoping launched another round of reform). One is trained in the West and the other a self-educated man who was victimized during the Cultural Revolution. In order to protect their identities, I have kept the location and specific timing of this meeting confidential. There is no way to prove their analysis, but their views are indeed illuminating and, more importantly, differ from both prevailing Western and popular Chinese views. This alternative story is insightful in other aspects as well.

Briefly, the usual contention between red and expert, localities (*kuaikuai*) and sectors (*tiaotiao*), and revolution and rationality is conceived of as reflecting a broader conflict between peasants and technocrats that started right after the People's Republic was founded. The first battle, later known as the Gao-Rao incident, was described as a purge of technocrats by "peasant rascals." The term *peasant rascal (nongmin pizi)* refers to those who do no appreciate any planned act and despise hierarchy, subtlety, and incrementalism. These rascals were primarily cadres who became revolutionary leaders in red districts before 1949, while most technocrats were from the eastern provinces. The representative peasant rascal was Deng Xiaoping and Gao Gang the principal technocrat.

A larger-scale fight broke out in the antirightist campaign of 1957, the final year of the First Five-Year Plan. Grassroots peasant rascals responded to Mao's call and rose up to purge general engineers in national factories. As a result, Soviet advisers lost access to general managers, and local planners who depended on general engineers to communicate with foreign advisers were at a loss. This exacerbated the absurdity of the Great Leap Forward campaign, leading to a number of wasteful practices that should have been prevented if not for the campaign against engineers. The two interviewees estimated that from 1950 to 1957, approximately 2.6 million Chinese were imprisoned and 2.2 million died.

Rascals grabbed more power during the Great Leap Forward and assumed the position of general manager in many a national factory. The more politically active and opportunistic ones won political positions in these factories. Since 1958, social forces in factories thus gained a strong base for the peasantry. The failure of the Great Leap Forward ironically compelled the central planner to allow more profit incentives in local factories. The peasant rascals who had consolidated their hold on industrial resources utilized their privileges to benefit themselves. My interviewees believed that Mao approved of the rascals' actions because it was the peasants Mao wanted to help. Some time in 1961, factory workers were officially categorized as state employees. From then on, their salaries were stabilized, and fringe benefits increased steadily over the years. The peasants' and Mao's obsession with peasant revolution thus seemed to have become part of the vested interests created by the state.

Yet the two interviewees acknowledged that agricultural sectors were the most disadvantaged in the process of development. Peasants in the villages were forced to subsidize industrial development in three different forms: planned price differentials between industrial and agricultural goods, tax in kind (primarily foodstuffs), and forced labor. Peasants as agricultural workers, however, are not the same as peasants as a social class. Policy discrimination against peasants as agricultural workers must be understood, the interviewees stressed, against the background of policy benefiting peasants now working in the industrial sector. Mao's concern for peasant interests was embodied in his policy toward workers in national factories. Peasant workers in industries thus had parallel interests with state employees normally called bureaucrats.

This bewildering rise of peasant workers in industry made the political battle started by the "four cleans" (*siqing*) campaign incredibly confusing. State work teams that were supposed to rid the villages of feudal practices were used by all sides to strike their opponents. On the one side, the peasant rascals attacked local plan officials in the name of the work teams; on the other, state officials led different teams to fight newly emergent peasant rascals. During the Cultural Revolution, it became official that only poor and lower-middle-echelon peasants were eligible for jobs in state factories. State enterprises were staffed by former peasants who thought, acted, and maintained social connections as peasants.

The reform initiated in 1979 indicated another cyclical rise in peasant forces, as it set up the responsibility system in villages and deregulated prices on agricultural products. Peasants benefited significantly from deregulation, and its urban counterpart in 1984 was modeled similarly. The whole idea of reform, headed by Deng Xiaoping, Hu Yaobang, and Zhao Ziyang, centered on decentralization. The key was to deliver resources to lower-level productive units headed by peasant rascals who had risen to power twenty years ago. The problem, however, was that they did not appreciate market operation, so their newly found access to resources only built individual workers' wealth. For Zhao, for example, reform was tantamount to "generating income" (*chuangshou*) for state employees, primarily workers of state-owned factories. Zhao expected peasant rascals in urban industry to use resources to improve living conditions for factory workers.

The economic problems China faces today reflect this historical battle between peasant rascals and state planners. Economic overheating and inflation are caused by overconsumption, which in turn is caused by decentralization. As resources are consumed, the two interviewees worry that factories will fail to upgrade and eventually become a burden on the state. Decentralization is like "drinking poison to deal with thirst." Their statistics show that 80 percent of the parts for color televisions and refrigerators are imported, suggesting a lack of advancement in technology.

Deng's remark that reform concerns the survival of the regime is precise, for reform was designed to enrich peasant workers in the cities—and rapidly, lest the regime lose legitimacy. The so-called conservatives are misunderstood in this sense. They are the ones who really care about technological upgrading. The point in dispute between the reformers and the conservatives is therefore not one of policy nor of political power. It is in the ultimate sense a battle of identity, a battle of mass socialism versus state socialism. The reformers identify the regime with the support of peasants who created the regime in 1949; the conservatives identify the regime with socialism, the key to which is central planning as opposed to decentralization. This explains why the leading reformers are obsessed with decentralization: It shifts responsibility for bettering living standards from the state to the masses and thus may rescue the regime from its legitimacy crisis.

The two officials who spoke to me sympathized with the conservative attack on reform, not because their ideologies are close but because they do not regard decentralization as an economic policy per se. Decentralization creates inflation; a sense of relative deprivation arises as corruption becomes increasingly widespread. My interviewees therefore see the irony in the Beijing massacre: Students gathered to criticize the reform led by Zhao for its obvious corruption and inflationary effects, yet Zhao came out the hero of the student movement. Reform is in trouble to the extent that its executors are mostly peasant rascals in state-owned factories, and they hold the regime's legitimacy hostage in exchange for favors under reform.

The central planner loses control when local authorities negotiate quotas under the tax responsibility system. Guangzhou authorities refuse to thoroughly inspect trucks coming from Hong Kong and deliberately permit smuggling, which helps the area's economy. (In fact, its representatives vehemently opposed a new tax system in the People's Congress in spring 1994 just to protect Guangdong's tax base.) Shandong Province contributes as little as Rmb200 million in annual revenue and still complains about shortages. The two interviewees are not upset that socialism may be gone, but they are less pleased that reform lacking in economic policy may replace it.

The most interesting point revealed in this interview is that the two officials contend that peasant forces have penetrated the state apparatus since 1957. Some leaders in the state, including Mao and Deng, consistently applied policies that benefited this peasant force because they believed that it held the source of regime legitimacy. The dispute over whether the state has penetrated peasant society would appear almost peripheral in this mode of analysis. The state itself is occupied by society.

One lesson to the student of Chinese political economy is this: If there were distinct and separate state-society structures in China, one would not expect to see such oscillations between forces representing state and society; one or the other would consistently dominate. Instead, the relationship can be characterized not as state against society but as a kind of particular contract between the two.[7] In fact, only if one recognizes that state and society overlap can one explain the alternation in power of the seemingly predominant forces. In other words, mass socialism and state socialism do not compete for support from two groups of people between whom the balance of strength would determine which system prevailed. Instead, mass socialism and state socialism compete to invoke social and state roles within each individual. The struggle exists not between two groups of people, although that is how it may appear; the struggle exists between the two selves within every Chinese citizen's consciousness. The resulting balance of strength between state and social selves can be easily adjusted to meet whatever situation is at hand. Such shifting does not create serious psychological tension for the ordinary Chinese.[8]

My analysis calls for further empirical investigation. Researchers need to know the background of most general managers and cadres of state-owned factories, when and how they entered the factories, and how they have adapted in the intervening decades. To appreciate the argument that Deng's reform policy aims primarily at generating regime legitimacy at the expense of efficiency through decentralization is nonetheless against the mainstream. Accordingly, reform would fail if Deng's obsession with legitimacy were not transformed into serious deliberation on economic grounds.

This final observation, as yet unproved, is well in line with my approach throughout this book: For the sake of its own legitimacy as well as long-term balanced development, the state in China cannot simply jettison collectivist goals and moral incentives. The introduction of other incentives, primarily material incentives, becomes essential to emancipating productive potential, which is equally critical to political legitimacy. This unavoidably leads not only to policy cycles in order alternately to satisfy individualist and collectivist ends but also to seemingly inconsistent behavioral patterns as China's people negotiate the inner stuggle between two sets of comflicting interests.

# NOTES

## CHAPTER 1

1. Ronald Dore, *Flexible Rigidities* (Stanford: Stanford University Press, 1986); Ronald Dore, *Taking Japan Seriously* (Stanford: Stanford University Press, 1987); Michio Morishima, *Why Has Japan "Succeeded"?* (New York: Cambridge University Press, 1982); Peter L. Berger and Hsin-huang Michael Hsiao, eds., *In Search of an East Asian Development Model* (New Brunswick: Transaction Books, 1988).

Dore's argument is more *historical* than *cultural*. Nonetheless, the title of his book (*Taking Japan Seriously*) suggests an intimate relationship between cultural and historical factors. In contrast, Hofheinz and Calder contend that political factors are more important than cultural factors. Even so, the political factors they identify, for example, flexibility, predictability, and hierarchy, are in all respects cultural. See Roy Hofheinz Jr. and Kent E. Calder, *The Eastasia Edge* (New York: Basic Books, 1982).

As to the negative impact of culture on development, see Lawrence E. Harrison, *Underdevelopment Is a State of Mind* (Lanham, Md.: Madison Books, 1985).

2. James Rosenau, *Turbulence in World Politics* (Princeton: Princeton University Press, 1990).

3. See chapter 1 of P. J. Pemple, *The Misunderstood Miracle* (Ithaca, N.Y.: Cornell University Press, 1988), pp. 17–24.

4. Richard Wilson, ed., *Value Changes in Chinese Society* (New York: Praeger, 1979).

5. Chih-yu Shih, *The Spirit of Chinese Foreign Policy* (London: Macmillan, 1990).

6. Suzanne Ogden, *China's Unresolved Issues* (Englewood Cliffs, N.J.: Prentice-Hall, 1989).

7. Peter Van Ness and Satish Raichur, "Dilemmas of Socialist Development," in P. Van Ness, ed., *Market Reform in Socialist Societies* (Boulder, Colo.: Lynne Rienner, 1989).

8. Lucian Pye, *The Mandarin and the Cadre* (Ann Arbor: Center for Chinese Studies, University of Michigan, 1988).

9. See Ogden, *China's Unresolved Issues,* pp. 110–111.

10. Ibid., p. 346.

11. On socialism constrained by traditional morality, see the discussion in Richard Madsen, *Morality and Power in a Chinese Village* (Berkeley: University of California Press, 1984), pp. 244–264.

12. Ibid., pp. 72–80.

13. Ibid., pp. 205–219.

14. Kwang-kuo Huang, "Face and Favor: The Chinese Power Game," *American Journal of Sociology* 97, 4 (1987): 944–974.

15. Kwang-kuo Huang, "Modernization of the Chinese Family Business," *International Journal of Psychology* 25 (1990): 593–618.

16. See Max Weber, *The Religion of China,* trans. Hans H. Gerth (New York: Free Press, 1951).

17. Thomas Metzger, *Escape from Predicament* (New York: Columbia University Press, 1977).

18. Hung-chao Tai, "The Oriental Alternative: An Hypothesis on Culture and Economy," in H. Tai, ed., *Confucianism and Economic Development* (Washington, D.C.: Washington Institute Press, 1989), pp. 6–37.

19. Kuo-hui Tai, "Confucianism and Japanese Modernization," in H. Tai, ed., *Confucianism,* pp. 70–91; also see Nakane Chie, *Japanese Society* (Berkeley: University of California Press, 1970).

20. Metzger, *Escape,* pp. 191–193.

21. Koike Kazuo, "Japan's Industrial Relations: Characteristics and Problems," *Japanese Economic Studies* (fall 1978): 42–90.

22. Metzger, *Escape,* pp. 214, 231.

23. On the comparison of corporatism and pluralism, see Harmon Zeigler, *Pluralism, Corporatism, and Confucianism* (Philadelphia: Temple University Press, 1986).

24. Lin Fang, "Chinese Modernization and Social Values," in D. Sinha and H. Kao, eds., *Social Values and Development* (Newbury Park, Calif.: Sage Publications, 1988), pp. 56–64.

25. Ibid., p. 63.

26. This combination of good and bad makes the selection of cultural traits extremely difficult and political for modern Chinese philosophers. See An Lan and Yang Furei, "Review of Confucian Research in the Past Ten Years" ("Shinianlai kongzi yanjiu pinghua"), *Jianghanluntan* 12 (1988); Kuang Yaming, *On Confucius* (*Kongzi pingzhuan*) (Shangdong: Qilu Bookstore, 1985); Liu Zuochang, "The Theory and the Progressive Implications of Mencius' Thoughts of Benevolent Politics" (*"Mengzi de renzheng xueshuo jiqi jinbu yiyi"*), *Shixueyuekan* 1 (1985); Gui Fu, "Comments on Mencius' Thoughts of Benevolent Politics" (*"Mengzi renzheng sixiang pingyi"*), *Neimonggu shidaxuebao* 4 (1988); Liu Weihua, "The Features of Evolution in Confucian Thought" (*"Kongzi sixiang yanbian de tedian"*), *Shehuikexue zhanxian* 3 (1985); Li Qiqian, "On the Value of Confucianism in the Modern Society" (*"Lun kongzi sixiang zai xiandai shehui zhong de jiazhi"*), *Qiluxuekan* 1 (1989); Chen Bohai, "The Constructive Perspective on Chinese Cultural Spirit" (*"Zhongguo wenhua jingshen zhi jiangou guan"*), *Zhongguoshehuikexue* 4 (1988); Teng Fu, "Five Theses on Traditional Cultural Thoughts" (*"Chuantong wenhua sixiang wulun"*), *Qiusuo* 2 (1988).

27. Yang Youquan, "The Yao-Liu Debate and the Predicament of Chinese Culture" (*"Yaoliu zhizheng yu zhongguo wenhua de kunjing"*), *Jianghanluntan* 6 (1986): 45.

28. Mao Zedong, *Selected Works of Mao Zedong* (*Mao Zedong Xuanji*), vol. 2 (Beijing: People's Press, 1977), p. 522.

29. Zhang Jian, "Three Issues in Confucian Studies" (*"Guanyu kongzi yanjiu de sange wenti"*), *Qiluxuekan* 4 (1986).

30. Sheng Duanming, "Self-closed Model of Taoyuan" (*Guanbizishou de taoyuan moshi*), *Jianghanluntan* 2 (1987): 51.

31. Chinese writers often criticize Confucianism for its archaism. See Shen Duanming, "Self-closed Model of Taoyuan"; Li Shuangbi, "The Great Cultural System: Observation of the Modern Chinese Historical System from a New Angle" (*"Da wenhua xitong: guancha zhongguo jingdashi tixi de xinshijiao"*), *Qiusuo* 3 (1988); Hao Yanrong, "Modernization and the Choice of Chinese Modern Intellectual Stratum" (*"Jindaihua yu zhongguo jindai zhishifenzi de xuanze"*), *Hebeixuekan* 3 (1989); on feudalism, see Shi Guang, "On Humanism, Humanistic

Centralism, and Humanitarianism" ("*Renwenzhuyi, renbenzhuyi ji rendaozhuyi bianzheng*"), *Qiusuo* 6 (1986); Chen Weipin, "Notes on the Paradox in the Confucian Thought System" ("*Lyuelun kongzi sixiang tixi de maodunxing*"), *Qiluxuekan* 1 (1985); Wang Weiguo, Fang Wei, and Song Jia, "The Completion of the Mission by the May Fourth New Cultural Movement and the Thriving of Commodity Economy" ("*Wusi xin wenhua yundong renwu de wancheng yu shangpin jingji de boxing*"), *Hebeixuekan* 3 (1989); Ding Shouhe, "Notes on Chinese Cultural Tradition" ("*Zhongguo wenhua chuantong shilun*"), *Qiusuo* 4 (1987); on rigidity, see Jiang Jianqiang, "The Five Spurious Phenomena in the Process of Sinifying Marxism" ("*Makesizhuyi zhongguohua de wu da shizheng*"), *Shehuikexuebao* (July 14, 1988); Guo Yi, "Confucius' Thinking Structures and Their Impact on the Traditional Chinese Thinking Pattern" ("*Kongzi de siwei jiegou ji qi dui zhongguo chuantong siwei fangshi de yingxiang*"), *Qiluxuekan* 3 (1986); Xu Suming, "The National Psychocultural Character as the Core of Each Cultural Mode" ("*Mingzu wenhuaxinli suzhi shi butong wenhua texing de jibenneihe*"), *Jianghanluntan* 10 (1986); and on lack of incentive and drive, see Zhu Laishan, "Inner Consciousness and Chinese Political Culture" ("*Neixing yishi yu zhongguo zhengzhi wenhua*"), *Jiangxidaxue xuebao* 2 (1986); Yu Wujing, "Inner Conflicts of the Contemporary Chinese Culture" ("*Dangdai zhongguo wenhua de neizai chongtu*"), *Fudanxuebao* 3 (1988); Cheng Weili, "The Ambiguity Complex in Contemporary Chinese Psychoculture" ("*Dangdai zhongguo de aihen zhenghouqun*"), *Fudanxuebao* 3 (1988).

32. Gu Xiaoming, "A Critique on the Cultural Mechanism of Propriety" ("*Dui li de wenhua jizhi benshen de pipan*"), *Fudanxuebao* 3 (1988).

33. Liu Zaifu and Lin Gang, "China's Traditional Culture and the Ah Q Model" ("*Zhongguo chuantong wenhua yu ah-q moshi*"), *Zhongguoshehuikexue* 3 (1988): 133–152.

34. However, there is the criticism that Confucianism sometimes impedes scientific thinking; see Li Xiaoming, "The Ancient Chinese Thinking Pattern and Its Modernization" ("*Zhongguo chuantong siwei moshi ji qi xiandaihua*"), *Jianghanluntan* 5 (1986); Zheng Xiaojiang, "Modern Reflections on the Principles of Ancient Chinese Thoughts" ("*Zhongguo gudai sikao yuanze de xiandai fansi*"), *Jiangxidaxue xuebao* 1 (1989); Yuan Yuehong, "Confucian Epistemology and Its Limitation" ("*Kongzi renshilun ji qi juxian*"), *Qiluxuekan* 4 (1985); Peng Jiurong, "Reflections on Traditional Chinese Thoughts in Literature" ("*Guanyu zhongguo chuantong wenxue sixiang de fansi*"), *Wenxuepinglun* 2 (1986).

35. Some believe that Confucianism encourages pragmatism, as affirmed in its stress of the golden mean; see Liu Zhengyi, "Exploring Confucius' Methodology" ("*Kongzi fangfalun chutan*"), *Qiluxuekan* 3 (1987). But others find that Mao Zedong disagreed; see Hou Xianlin, "Mao's Criticism and Application of the Principle of the Golden Mean" ("*Mao zedong dui zhongyung sixiang de pipan yu jicheng*"), *Qiluxuekan* 4 (1987).

36. For example, "Use righteousness to create wealth and use wealth to satisfy people"; "Measure the land to build the state and calculate the wealth to increase the population"; "The prince will enjoy sufficiency as long as the people do," Jiang, "Five Spurious Phenomena."

37. See the discussion in Zheng Ping and Feng Chungming, "Exploring the New Approach to Move Beyond Feudalistic Culture" ("*Tuozhan chaoyue fengjianzhuyi wenhua de xin jingdi*"), *Jiangxidaxue xuebao* 1 (1989); Lin Fang, "Exploring the Modern Value System in Our Country" ("*Wo guo xiandai jiazhi guan tantao*"), *Zhongguoshehuikexue* 3 (1989); Yu Yung, "Summary of the Seminar on

Confucius, Confucianism, and Contemporary Socialism" (*"Kongzi, lujia yu dang-dai shehuizhuyi xueshutaolunhui zongshu"*), *Qiluxuekan* 6 (1989).

38. See Ma Ming, "Exploring the Psychological Structures of Modern Chinese Merchants" (*"Zhongguo jindai shangren xinli jiegou chutan"*), *Zhongguoshe-huikexue* 5 (1986); Xu Suming, "On the Linkage Between Chinese Traditional Culture and Modernization" (*"Lun zhongguo chuantong wenhua yu xiandaihua de jiehebu"*), *Jianghanluntan* 2 (1988); Liu Jiancheng, "Mencius' Mercantilism Should Be Affirmed" (*"Mengzi zhongshangzhuyi ying yu kending"*), *Dongyuelun-cong* 2 (1982).

39. Although the political constraint on economic reform is a sensitive issue, Chinese scholars nonetheless touch upon it in a debate on why the May Fourth movement of 1919 failed. They focus on the relationship between Chinese culture and modernization. Some believe that the movement lacked the economic base, while others blame the movement for being culturally exotic. See Xie Xialing, "Reinterpreting the May Fourth Spirit, Absorbing the Confucian Thoughts" (*"Chongshi wusi jingshen, xishou luxue sixiang"*), *Fudanxuebao* 3 (1989); Li Wen, "Modernized Cultural Renaissance" (*"Xiandaihua de wenhua qimeng"*), *Fudanx-uebao* 3 (1989); Geng Jianxiung, "On the Political Mechanism of Broadcasting New Culture in China" (*"Lun xinwenhua zai zhongguo chuanbo de zhengzhi jizhi"*), *Fudanxuebao* 3 (1989); Geng Zhiyun, "Reevaluation of the May Fourth New Cultural Movement" (*"Wusi xinwenhua yundong de zairenshi"*), *Zhonggu-oshehuikexue* 3 (1989); Chen Sihe, "The May Fourth Movement and the Current Age" (*"Wusi yu dangdai"*), *Fudanxuebao* 3 (1989); Wang Furen, "In Pursuit of Modernization of the Entire Chinese Culture" (*"Dui quanbu zhongguo wenhua de xiandaihua zhuiqiu"*), *Zhongguoshehuikexue* 3 (1989); Zhu Wenhua, "The Trans-formation of Chinese Psychoculture Is the Premise of China's Modernization" (*"Gaizao zhongguoren de wenhuaxintai shi zhongguo xiandaihua de qianti"*), *Fu-danxuebao* 3 (1989); Zhou Zhenghe, "A Great Leap to Reevaluate the Traditional Culture" (*"Dui chuantong wenhua zairenshi de feiyao"*), *Fudanxuebao* 3 (1989).

40. For pros and cons on this position, see Xie Xialing, "On the Root of Dif-ference Between Chinese and Western Culture and the Trend of Contemporary Chinese Culture" (*"Lun zhong xi wenhua chayi zhi gen yu dangdai zhongguo wen-hua zhi quxiang"*), *Fudanxuebao* 3 (1988); Yang Shanming, "On Cultural Tradi-tion" (*"Wenhua chuantong lun"*), *Shandongdaxue xuebao* 3 (1988); Miao Rentian, "Introduction of Confucius' Concepts of Righteousness and Interest and Their Modern Implications" (*"Qianlun kongzi de yi li guan ji qi xiandai yiyi"*), *Qiluxu-ekan* 1 (1989); Li Shuyou, "The Neo-Confucian Ethos and Our Confucian Ethical Studies" (*"Xinluxue sichao yu women de lujia lunli yanjiu"*), *Nanjingdaxue xue-bao* 1 (1987).

41. Huning, Wang, "The Changing Structure of China's Political Culture" (*"Zhuanbianzhong de zhongguo zhengzhi wenhua"*), *Fudan xuebao* 3 (1988): 55–64.

42. The earliest signs appeared in 1956. See Cheng Chu-yuan, *Congressional Record* 133 (August 6, 1959): 6779–6780; Cheng Chu-yuan, "Basic Problems of Chinese Communists' Agricultural Collectivization" ("Zhonggong nongyie jitihua de jiben wenti"), *Mingzhu pinglun* 7, 11 (June 1956).

43. Earlier signs are discussed in Tien-chien Hwang, *Failures of Mao Tse-tung's Dictatorship, 1949–1963,* part 1 (Taipei: Asian Peoples' Anti-Communist League, 1963).

44. Western sources document the Chinese obsession with a unified, moral leadership in the PRC's earlier periods. See Zhou Enlai, "Report on Government Work"; Lu Dingyi, "Education Must Be Combined with Productive Labor"; Hebei

Provincial Committee of the Party, "On the Building of People's Communes"; Mao Zedong, "Speech at Moscow Celebration Meeting"; Central Committee, "Resolution on the Establishment of People's Communes in the Rural Areas," all in Robert R. Bowie and John K. Fairbank, eds., *Communist China, 1955–1959* (Cambridge: Harvard University Press, 1971).

45. See Central Committee, "Resolution on Some Questions Concerning the People's Communes," in Bowie and Fairbank, *Communist China, 1955–1959.*

46. See Hu Yinghang and Guan Yushu, "The 1959 Lushan Conference and Its Historical Lessons" (*"1959 nian lushan huiyi ji qi lishi jiaoxun"*), *Qiushixuekan* 2 (1985): 71–78.

47. For example, see the "Revised Later Ten Points," in Richard Baum and Frederick C. Teiwes, *Ssu-Ch'ing: The Socialist Education Movement, 1962–1966* (Berkeley: University of California Press, 1968), p. 105; also Li Tien-min, *Crisis of the Chinese Communist Regime—As Seen from Lien-chiang Documents* (Taipei: Asian Peoples' Anti-Communist League, 1964), pp. 31–34.

48. For early examples, see C. S. Chen and Charles P. Ridley, eds. and trans., *Rural People's Communes in Lien-chiang* (Stanford: Stanford University Press, 1969).

49. The moral responsibility of the cadres is somewhat different from that of the gentry. A cadre is supposed to convert the old society into a socialist one, whereas the gentry must maintain the existing one. Nonaction was required of the gentry (in order to suggest harmony); energy, courage, and a sense of direction were required of a cadre. According to Franz Schurmann, a cadre is young, not old; and he is a leader, not a conciliator. A cadre operates in the public realm, not in private. Above all, a good cadre resolutely carries out the party line, works independently, is willing to act positively, and does not seek private advantage. See Franz Schurmann, *Ideology and Organization in Communist China* (Berkeley: University of California Press, 1968), pp. 8, 164.

50. For a detailed discussion by Chinese scholars, see He Hongshang, ed., *Symposium of Deng Zihui's Thought on Agricultural Cooperative (Deng Zihui nongyehezuo sixiang xueshu taolunhui lunwenji)* (Beijing: Agricultural Publication, 1989); Hsu Li-chun, "Have We Already Reached the Stage of Communism," in Bowie and Fairbank, *Communist China, 1955–1959.*

51. Zhao Lin, "Only the Self is Absolute," *Chinese Sociology and Anthropology* (summer 1985). His original response appeared in *Zhongguo qingnian* 8 (1980): 4–6.

52. *Liaowang zhoukan* 2,1 (1984) complains that some party members and cadres have two attitude problems: insufficient faith and lack of self-awareness. One commentator quotes a comrade, saying that "the impurity of thought, style, and organization within the party is so serious, the situation is so complicated, can the party rectification this time really rectify well?" Despite official encouragement from party conservatives, the campaigns eventually died out. Authorities then decided to concentrate on a legal solution, with special attention paid to serious crimes (*daan* or *yaoan*), hoping to establish some form of deterrent. According to *Lilun yu shijian* 18 (1986): 17, for example, the city of Tielin investigated 245 serious crimes in 1986, 218 of which cases had been efficiently closed in the same year. Again, the effect on morality was moderate. *Xuexi yuekan*'s analysis (8 [1986]: 33) suggests that people psychologically resist altering political thought and consistently level negative judgments at any and all ideological education, their negative feeling becoming a "habit."

53. *Banyuetan* (8 [1988]: 52–53), a popular Chinese magazine, charges that society is a *baijiazi* (a child who squanders his or her parents' wealth). Although

there is no money to improve education, scientific research, and agriculture, the magazine says, social groups "multiply their purchasing power" and "luxury hotel complexes are springing up" and "imported cars are racing around." The article asks, "Where is discipline . . . . and where is a sense of responsibility?" It concludes that "a *baijiazi* cannot carry out construction work."

54. Wu Jiaxiang, "Control over Corruption," mimeograph.

55. In an article entitled "Cadres Cannot Cope," published in *Heilongjiang ribao* (January 31, 1988), Zhang expressed concern that "the quality of cadres cannot handle the situation." He acknowledges that China lacks "universal geniuses who are well versed in law, economics, and social management"; there is no sense of professionalism or notion of efficiency. Cadres have "a weak sense of responsibility and poor ideology and work style." It is not uncommon for cadres to "abuse their powers and seek personal gains, bend the laws for the benefit of relatives and friends, and harm the dignity . . . and the prestige of law enforcement organs." See "The Cadres' Corruption," *Chinese Law and Government* (fall 1988): 47.

56. A *Banyuetan* (13 [1987]: 11) interview reported a case in which a local authority infuriated peasants by appropriating fertilizer reserved for them. *Lilun yu shijian* (4 [1982]: 8) reported a case in which a criminal first arrested in 1962 had continued illegal commercial activities for the following two decades because he "had used cash and goods to pave the way" and had been shielded by party members and cadres in return. More than 100 people were involved.

57. In 1986, for example, Chen Yun, a senior party conservative, was quoted by *Xuexi yuekan* (5 [1986]: 25) as calling for tighter discipline and heavier penalties for those disobeying the party. Deng Xiaoping echoed this tough note in *Zhonggong wenti ziliao zhoukan* 253 (1987) on the issue of student demonstrations: The places where disturbances erupted were those where local authorities lacked a resolute attitude and clear-cut stand. See "Speech on the Current Problem of Student Disturbance," *Chinese Law and Government* (spring 1988): 18.

58. *Shihchie jipao* (New York), April 8, 1989, 16

59. Joseph W. Esherick and Jeffrey N. Wasserstrom, "Acting Out Democracy: Political Theater in Modern China," *Journal of Asian Studies* 49, 4 (November 1990): 835–865.

60. For a classic study of factionalism in Chinese, see Sa Mongwu, *History of Chinese Politics and Society* (*Zhongguo shehui zhengzhishi*), vols. 1–4 (Taipei: Sanmin, 1980).

61. For a case study in the Western literature, see Kenneth Lieberthal, *The Foreign Policy Debate in Peking as Seen Through Allegorical Articles, 1973–1976* (Santa Monica, Calif.: Rand, 1977); for a theoretical framework, see Lucian Pye, *The Dynamics of Chinese Politics* (Cambridge, Mass.: Oelgeschlager, Gunn & Hain, 1981); for a typical Western style of analysis, see Andrew Nathan, "A Factionalism Model for CCP Politics," *China Quarterly* 53 (1973).

62. The Western literature documents the policy-line struggle in China rather well. For a good argument about the two-line struggle, see Frederick C. Teiwes, *Leadership, Legitimacy, and Conflict in China* (Armonk, N.Y.: M. E. Sharpe, 1984), pp. 10–42; for an example of the three-line struggle, see Dorothy Solinger, ed., *Three Versions of Chinese Socialism* (Boulder, Colo.: Westview, 1984). Some consider policy disputes spurious— see Andrew Nathan, "Policy Oscillations in the People's Republic of China," *China Quarterly* 68 (1976); others disagree—see Tang Tsou, "Prolegomenon to the Study of Informal Groups in CCP Politics," *China Quarterly* 65 (1976) and Edwin Winckler, "Policy Oscillations in the People's Republic of China," *China Quarterly* 68 (1976).

63. On Chinese economists who were not really sure what to do with the Four Modernizations in the early stages, see Cyril Lin, "Interview of Wei and Zhao,"

*China Quarterly* 100 (December 1984). On how early stages were wasted, as people only cared about the image of modernization, see *Renmin ribao,* April 1, 1981.

64. To attack would be too technical for politicians to do. See Chao Kang, "Chinese Economic Reform Turns Westernization Irrevocably," (*"Zhonggong jinggai yi zoushang xihaude bugueilu"*) *United Daily,* December 14 and 15, 1990, 19.

65. For a summary of the technical nature of policy debate under reform, see Ruan Jianming et al., eds., *Dynamics of Economic Theory (Jingji lilun dongtai)* (Beijing: Chinese Economics Press, 1989).

66. Fang Lizhi, "China's Despair and China's Hope," *New York Review of Books* 36, 1 (February 2, 1989): 3–4; Fang Lizhi, "The Price China Has Paid: An Interview with Liu Binyan," *New York Review of Books* 35, 21 and 22 (January 19, 1989): 31–35.

67. *United Daily,* January 13, 1992.

68. Ding Junliang, *Where Is the Route? Reflections upon the Primary Stage of Socialism (Lu zai hefang—guanyu shehuizhuyi chuji jieduan de chensi)* (Changsha: Hunan University Press, 1989).

69. Fong Zhenggang, *On the Primary Stage of Socialism (Lun shehuizhuyi chuji jieduan)* (Changsha: Hunan University Press, 1989).

70. Yue Fubing, *On the Commodity Economy in the Primary Stage of Socialism (Shehuizhuyi chuji jieduan shangpin jingji lun)* (Beijing: China Prospect Press, 1989).

71. Jiang Xuemo, "New Light on Capitalism and Socialism—The Theoretical Foundation of Our Country's Economic Institutional Reform" (*"Dui zibenzhuyi han shehuizhuyi de zairenshi—wo guo jingji tizhi gaige de lilun jichu"*), in Shanghai Communist Party Propaganda Department, ed., *The First Wave (Diyici dachao)* (Shanghai: Sanlian Press, 1989).

72. Tan Naizhang et al., *On Six Major Issues in Economic Institutional Reform (Jingji tizhi gaige liu da yiti yanjiu)* (Beijing: Spring-Autumn Press, 1989), pp. 234–241.

73. Yue, *On the Commodity Economy,* pp. 90–91.

74. Some would agree that there are numerous routes for arriving at socialism. See Wu Boling, "On Economically Retarded Nations' Hopping over the Capitalist Stage of Development—The Basis of the Theory of the Primary Stage of Socialism in Our Country" (*"Jingji luohou guojia chaoyue zibenzhuyi fazhan jieduan wenti—woguo shehuizhuyi chuji jieduan lilun de yiju"*), in Shanghai Communist Party Propaganda Department, *First Wave.*

75. For further discussion, see Ma Hong, *The Prospect and Road of China's Socialist Modernization (Zhongguo shehuizhuyi xiandaihua de daolu han qianjing)* (Shanghai: People's Press, 1988), pp. 259–264; Wu Jiang, *A Few Problems of Contemporary Socialism (Dangdai shehuizhuyi luogan wenti)* (Beijing: Huaxia Press, 1989); Lu Yinglin and Fang Li, *Productive Force and Socialism (Shengchanli yu shehuizhuyi)* (Beijing: PLA Press, 1989); Gao Guang et al., *On Structures of Chinese Socialism in the Primary Stage (Zhongguo shehuizhuyi chuji jieduan jiegou yanjiu)* (Beijing: Chinese Communist Party Central School Press, 1988), pp. 298–299.

76. The regime cannot but correctly pursue its historical responsibility of engaging in commodity economy; see Chen Feng, "Double Categorization of Social Type and Socialism and Its Primary Stage—Also on the Theory of Productivity Standard, the Theory of Underdevelopment, the Theory of Taking the Course, the Theory of Empty Thought" (*"Shehui xingtai de liangchong huafen yu shehuizhuyi ji qi chuji jieduan—jian ping shenchangli biaozhuen shuo, buchengshou shuo, buke shuo han kong xiang shuo"*), in Shanghai Communist Party Propaganda Department, *First Wave.*

77. Socialism in China is different from the typical Leninist doctrine to the extent that it is peasant-based. See Tang Tsou, "Back from the Brink of Revolutionary-'Feudal' Totalitarianism," in V. Nee and D. Mozingo, eds., *State and Society in Contemporary China* (Ithaca: Cornell University Press, 1983).

## CHAPTER 2

1. I discuss the nature of moral regime in "The Decline of a Moral Regime: The Great Leap Forward in Retrospect," *Comparative Political Studies* (July 1994).

2. Wang Shubai, *The Chinese Gene in Maoism* (*Mao Zedong cixiang de zhongguo jiyin*) (Taipei: Jichitang Cultural Co., 1991).

3. See the concluding chapter of Hou Chiachu, *History of Chinese Economic Thought* (*Zhongguo jingji cixiang shi*) (Taipei: Chinese Cultural Renovation Commission, 1982).

4. Liu Zaifu and Lin Gang, "Chinese Traditional Culture and the Ah Q Model" (*Zhongguo chuantong wenhua yu ah-q moshi*), *Zhongguoshehuikexue* 3 (1988): 133–152.

5. Hou, *History,* p. 302.

6. Richard Solomon, *Mao's Revolution and the Chinese Political Culture* (Berkeley: University of California Press, 1971).

7. Zhang Dainian, *Studies of Chinese Ethical Thought* (*Zhongguo lunli sixiang yanjiu*) (Shanghai: Shanghai People's Press, 1989), p. 19.

8. Read the criticism by Hao Yanrong, "Modernization and the Choice of the Modern Chinese Intellectual Stratum" (*"Jindaihua yu jindai zhongguo zhishifenzi jiecen de xuanze"*), *Hebeixuekan* 3 (1989).

9. Lucian Pye, *The Mandarin and the Cadre* (Ann Arbor: Center for Chinese Studies, University of Michigan, 1988), p. 97.

10. Mao Zedong, *Selected Works of Mao Zedong* (*Mao Zedong xuanji*), vol. 2 (Beijing: People's Press, 1977), pp. 502–503.

11. Franz Schurmann, *Ideology and Organization in Communist China* (Berkeley: University of California Press, 1968), pp. 170–172.

12. K. Arrow, *Social Choice and Individual Values* (New York: Wiley, 1963).

13. Deng Zihui, "Report to the Meeting on Management of Agricultural Cooperatives," *Renmin ribao,* May 7, 1957.

14. Deng Zihui, "Speech to National Producers' Conference," *Gongren ribao,* May 8, 1956.

15. Deng Zihui, "The Great Implications of Village Cooperative Industry" (*"Xiang sheban gongye de weida yiyi"*), *Nongcun gongzuo tongxun*, October 1958.

16. Hao Mengbi and Duan Haoran, *The Sixty Years and Chinese Communism* (*Zhongguo gongchandang liushi nian*) (Beijing: PLA Press, 1984), pp. 538–540.

17. On the issue of high speed and proportion in the First Five-Year Plan, see *Wuhanxuebao* 5 (1959).

18. Liu Guangjie, *On China's Economic Development Strategy* (*Zhongguo jingji fazhan zhanlyue gailun*) (Beijing: Zhongguo Wuzi Press, 1989), pp. 65–66.

19. Yi Ran, "Mainland China Witnesses a Period of Power Decentralization" (*"Zhongguo dalu mianlin yige quanli fenhua de shiqi"*), *Studies of Chinese Communism* 24, 9–10 (September–October 1990).

20. Liu Yingtao and Luo Xiaoming, "On the Limitation of Applying Aggregate Analysis and Aggregate Policy in the Economic Theory and Practice in Our Country" (*"Lun zongliang fenxi yu zongliang zhengce zai wo guo jingji lilun yu jingji shijian zhong de juxianxing"*), *Jingji yanjiu* 6 (1987).

21. Social Science Academy, "Reflections on Economic Construction and Economic Reform in the Past Few Years" (*"Dui ji nian lai jingji jianshe yu jingji gaige de fanxi"*), *Jingji yanjiu* 3 (1987).

22. Li Yining, "Market, Resource Allocation, and Imbalance" (*"Shichang, ziyuan peizhi yu feijunheng"*), in Ding Shengjun and Wang Yibing, eds., *Regulate the Economic Environment and Establish the New Order for Circulation* (*Zhili jingji huanjing, jianli liutong xin zhixu*) (Beijing: Chinese Commercial Press, 1989), p. 54.

23. Ji Xiaopeng, "Developing Horizontal Economic Linkages, Promoting Economic Systemic Reform" (*"Fazhan henxiang jingji lianhe, cujin jingji tizhi gaige"*), *PLA Daily*, April 8, 1986.

24. Liu Peng and Zheng Lanxun, *New Conceptions—An Overview of Conceptual Reform* (*Xing guannian—guannian biange mianmianguan*) (Beijing: Overseas Chinese Press, 1989), p. 71.

25. Liu Wei et al., *Resource Allocation and Economic Systemic Reform* (*Ziyuan peizhi yu jingji tizhi gaige*) (Beijing: Chinese Finance and Economics Press, 1989), p. 233.

26. On municipal planning centers, see Guo Fengfeng and Li Xingshan, *Socialist Macroeconomic Management* (*Shehuizhuyi hongguanjingji guanlixue*) (Zhangjiako, Hebei: Chinese Communist Party Central School Press, 1989), pp. 40–59.

27. Ibid., pp. 144–146.

28. Liu Wei et al., *Resource Allocation*, pp. 241–256.

29. Yue Fubing, *On the Commodity Economy in the Primary Stage of Socialism* (*Shehuizhuyi chuji jieduan shangpin jingji lun*) (Beijing: China Prospect Press, 1989), pp. 130–132.

30. Zhang Yuanyuan, "On Export-oriented Economy Again" (*Zai lun waixiang jingji*), *Nanfang jingji* 6 (1985).

31. Liu Wei et al., *Resource Allocation*, p. 237. The Hoffman ratio is developed to measure the balance of industrial structure and the similarity in structure among different provinces.

32. Tong Dalin, "The Issues of Consumption and Market in Chinese Socialism" (*Zhongguo shehuizhuyi shichang han xiaofei wenti*), in Ding and Wang, *Regulate the Economic Environment and Establish the New Order for Circulation*, pp. 32–46.

33. Cao Fengqi, *The Theory and Practice of the Chinese Enterprise Stock System* (*Zhongguo qiye gufen zhi de lilun yu shijian*) (Beijing: Business Management Press, 1989), pp. 254–255.

34. Yue, *On the Commodity Economy*, pp. 296–297.

# CHAPTER 3

1. One lifetime student of Chinese economic thought straightforwardly calls the ruler's economy *tongzhi jingji* (literally, command economy). Obviously, dynastic rulers were unable to plan what was produced, unlike their contemporary socialist counterparts. Some scholars argue, however, that the way of thinking back in the dynastic periods is in line with the strategy of command economists. See Hou Chiachu, *History of Chinese Economic Thought* (*Zhongguo jingji sixiang shi*) (Taipei: Chinese Cultural Renovation Commission, 1982).

2. Concerning Chinese economic thought, see ibid. and the classical readings of Sa Mongwu, *History of Chinese Politics and Society* (*Zhongguo shehui zhengzhishe*), vols. 1–4 (Taipei: Sanmin, 1980).

3. Chih-yu Shih, "The Decline of a Moral Regime: The Great Leap Forward in Retrospect," *Comparative Political Studies* (July 1994).

4. Guo Fengfeng and Li Xingshan, *Socialist Macroeconomic Management (Shehuizhuyi hongguanjingji guanlixue)* (Zhangjiako, Hebei: Chinese Communist Party Central School Press, 1989), pp. 91–92.

5. Ibid., pp. 100–102.

6. Report on the Thirteenth National Congress of the Chinese Communist Party, 1987.

7. Tan Naizhang et al., *On Six Major Issues in Economic Institutional Reform (Jingji tizhi gaige liu da yiti yanjiu)* (Beijing: Spring-Autumn Press, 1989), p. 191.

8. Liu Wei et al., *Resource Allocation and Economic Systemic Reform (Ziyuan peizhi yu jingji tizhi gaige)* (Beijing: Chinese Finance and Economics Press, 1989), p. 8.

9. Chen Wenlin, *Introduction of China's Monetary Policy Reform (Zhongguo huobi zhengci gaige jianlun)* (Beijing: Chinese Finance and Economics Press, 1989), p. 36.

10. Guo and Li, *Socialist Macroeconomic Management,* pp. 228–229.

11. Ibid., pp. 46–47.

12. See Ronald H. Chilcote, *Theories of Development and Underdevelopment* (Boulder, Colo.: Westview, 1984), pp. 24–48.

13. Xu Guangjian, Wang Xiaobing, and Du Weichang, *Price Theory Under Reform (Gaige zhong de jiage lilun)* (Beijing: People's University Press, 1989), p. 55.

14. Guo and Li, *Socialist Macroeconomic Management,* p. 21.

15. Jiang Zeming, "Remarks on the Theoretical Seminar on Shanghai's First Memorial Decade of the Opening of the Third Plenary Session of the Central Committee of the Eleventh National Congress" *(Zai Shanghaishi jinian dang de shiyijie san zhongquanhui zhaokai shizhounian lilun taolunhui shang de jianghua)*, in Shanghai Communist Party Propaganda Department, ed., *The First Wave (Diyici dachao)* (Shanghai: Sanlian Press, 1989), p. 15.

16. See *Collection of Conference Documents of the Fourth Meeting of the Sixth National People's Congress (Diliujie quanguo renmin daibiaodahui disici huiyi wenjian huibian)* (Beijing: People's Press, 1986), p. 31.

17. Tan et al., *Six Major Issues,* p. 184.

18. See the discussion in Guo and Li, *Socialist Macroeconomic Management,* pp. 65–67.

19. Yue Fubing instead relies on the imagery of an airplane to describe such state investment. See *On the Commodity Economy in the Primary Stage of Socialism (Shehuizhuyi chuji jieduan shangpin jingji lun)* (Beijing: China Prospect Press, 1989), pp. 99, 105, and 241.

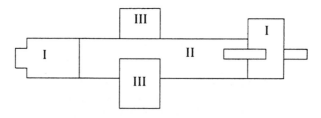

I: National Enterprises
II: Collective Enterprise
III: Other Enterprises

20. Tan et al., *Six Major Issues,* p. 257.

21. Guo and Li, *Socialist Macroeconomic Management,* p. 82.

22. Jiang Yingguang, "On Some Basic Theoretical Problems in Commercial Reform" (*Shangyie gaige de jige jiben lilun wenti*), in Ding Shengjun and Wang Yibing, eds., *Regulate the Economic Environment and Establish the New Order for Circulation* (*Zhili jingji huanjing, jianli liutong xin zhixu*) (Beijing: Chinese Commercial Press, 1989), pp. 87–91.

23. Qi Xingrong, "On Institutional Reform of Enterprise Leadership" (*"Lun qiyie lingdao tizhi gaige"*), in Shanghai Communist Party Propaganda Department, *First Wave,* p. 205.

24. Ibid., pp. 205–206.

25. Dong Furen, "On the Development of Our National Market" (*"Tan wo guo shichang de peiyu"*), in Ding and Wang, *Regulate the Economic Environment and Establish the New Order for Circulation,* p. 127.

26. Ma Heping, "Rectifying Networks of Regional Blocking and Sectorial Striping" (*"Zhengquechuli tiaotiao kuaikuai de guanxi"*), in *Historical Experiences in Our Country's Economic Institutional Reform* (*Wo guo jingji tizhi gaige de lishi jingyan*) (Beijing: People's Press, 1985), p. 173.

27. Liu Shuren, "Actively Promoting Economic Integration Through Horizontal Coordination" (*"Jiji tuijin hengxiang jingji lianhe"*), *Jingjiguanli* 1 (1986).

28. Liu et al., *Resource Allocation,* p. 240.

29. Susan L. Shirk, "The Politics of Industrial Reform," in E. J. Perry and C. Wong, eds., *The Political Economy of Reform in Post-Mao China* (Cambridge, Mass.: Council on East Asian Studies Harvard University Press, 1986), pp. 215–216.

30. Chen Shenshen, "The Key to Strengthening Reform Is to Restore Market Order" (*"Jianli shichang zhixu shi shenhua gaige de guanjian"*), in Shanghai Communist Party Propaganda Department, *First Wave,* p. 163.

31. Ibid., p. 164.

32. Xu Rongan, *Chinese Economics of City-Village Coordination* (*Zhongguo cheng xiang ronghe jingjixue*) (Beijing: Chinese Prospect Press, 1988), pp. 72–73.

33. Zhang Yi, *Introduction to China's Village Enterprises* (*Zhongguo xiangzheng qiye gailun*) (Shanghai: Shanghai Social Science Academy Press, 1988), pp. 47–48.

34. Victor Nee, "Between Center and Locality: State, Militia, and Village," in V. Nee and D. Mozingo, eds., *State and Society in Contemporary China* (Ithaca: Cornell University Press, 1983).

35. This is called "from heaven to earth"; see Elizabeth Croll, *From Heaven to Earth* (London: Routledge, 1994).

## CHAPTER 4

1. Alexander Eckstein, *China's Economic Revolution* (London: Cambridge University Press, 1981), pp. 54–58.

2. Yang Chung-fang, "On Chinese Moral Development: From the Perspective of Self-development" (*"Shilun zhongguoren de daode fazhan: yige ziwo fazhan de guandian"*); Huang Kwang-kuo, "The Notion of Justice in Confucianism" (*"Lujia sixiang zhong de zhengyi guan"*); Chen Shu-chuan, "Chinese Self-expression as Viewed Through the Sacrificing Act in the June Fourth Pro-democracy Movement" (*"Cong liu ci min yun de xisheng xingwei kan zhongguoren de ziwo biaoda"*), all in K. Yand and K. Huang, eds., *Chinese Psychology and Behavior*

(*Zhongguoren de xinli yu xingwei*) (Taipei: Department of Psychology, National Taiwan University, 1989).

3. See Chapter Three of this book.

4. Ronald Dore, *Taking Japan Seriously: A Confucian Perspective on Leading Economic Issues* (Stanford: Stanford University Press, 1987), pp. 169–192.

5. M. Therese Flaherty and Hiroyuki Itami, "Finance," in D. I. Okimoto et al., eds., *Competitive Edge: The Semi-conductor Industry in the United States and Japan* (Stanford: Stanford University Press, 1984), pp. 151–153.

6. Ronald Dore, *Flexible Rigidities: Industrial Policy and Structural Adjustment in the Japanese Economy, 1970–80* (Stanford: Stanford University Press, 1986), pp. 72–85.

7. Rodney Clark, *The Japanese Company* (New Haven, Conn.: Yale University Press, 1979), pp. 73–87.

8. Nakane Chie, *Japanese Society* (Berkeley: University of California Press, 1970).

9. Jun-ichi Kyogoku, *The Political Dynamics of Japan,* trans. Nobutaka Ike (Tokyo: University of Tokyo Press, 1987), pp. 63–95.

10. Ma Hong, "On Corporate Purchase" (*"Lun qiye maimai"*), in F. Tian, ed., *Theory and Practice of Corporate Purchase in China* (*Zhongguo qiye jianbing de lilun yu shijian*) (Beijing: Economic Management Club, 1989), p. 2.

11. Ibid., p. 3.

12. Ibid., p. 12.

13. Cao Siyuan, "Comparing the Institution of Corporate Purchase and the Institution of Bankruptcy" (*"Qiye jianbing yu qiye pochan zhidu de bijiao"*), in Tian, *Theory and Practice,* p. 65.

14. Ibid., p. 68.

15. Wang Bingyi and Shi Zhishuen, "Reflection and Retrospect on Corporate Purchase in the City of Baoding" (*"Dui baoding shi qiye jianbing de huigu yu sikao"*), in Tian, *Theory and Practice,* p. 79.

16. Shen Zhiyu and Xu Xiaojiu, "Analysis and Research on the Practice of Corporate Purchase in the City of Baoding" (*"Dui baoding shi qiye jianbing shijian de diaocha yu fenxi"*) in Tian, *Theory and Practice,* p. 92.

17. Yan Chengle, Hou Zhangjia, and Yu Qingying, "Reflection on the Upgrading of Corporate Purchase from the Primary to the Advanced Level" (*"Qiye jianbing you chuji xingtai xiang gaoji xingtai zhuanhuan de silu"*), in Tian, *Theory and Practice,* p. 101.

18. Capital Steel Corporation, "Developing Cross-sector, Cross-area, Cross-border Business Through Corporate Purchase" (*"Tongguo qiye jianbing fazhan kua hangye, kua dichu, kuaguo jingying"*), *Theory and Practice* in Tian, p. 144.

19. Cao Fongqi, *The Theory and Practice of the Chinese Enterprise Stock System* (*Zhongguo qiye gufen zhi de lilun yu shijian*) (Beijing: Business Management Press, 1989), pp. 213–217.

20. Ibid., p. 4.

21. Tan Naizhang et al., *On Six Major Issues of Economic Institutional Reform* (*Jingji tizhi gaige liu da yiti yanjiu*) (Beijing: Spring-Autumn Press, 1989), p. 106.

22. Cao, *Chinese Enterprise,* p. 203.

23. Office of Industry System, ed., *The Practices of Financial Groups* (*Qiye jituan shiwu*) (Beijing: Chinese Development Press, 1991), p. 31.

24. Cao, *Chinese Enterprise,* p. 209.

25. Ibid., pp. 208–209; italics added.

26. Ibid., p. 210.

27. Zhang Shengshu, Hu Wanrong, and Tang Mosen, *Economics of Raw Materials (Wuzi jingjixue)* (Beijing: Economics of Raw Materials Press, 1989), p. 124.

28. Chen Jiyuan and Xia Defang, *On the Models of Countryside Business (Xiangzheng qiye moshi yanjiu)* (Beijing: Chinese Social Science Academy Press, 1988), pp. 60–62.

29. Zhang Yi, *Introduction to China's Village Enterprises (Zhongguo xiangzheng qiye gailun)* (Shanghai: Shanghai Social Science Academy Press, 1988), pp. 109–112.

30. Xu Rongan, *Chinese Economics of City-Village Coordination (Zhongguo cheng xiang ronghe jingjixue)* (Beijing: China Prospect Press, 1988), pp. 354–355.

31. Chen and Xia, *Models,* p. 69.

32. Ibid., p. 84.

33. Yang Chengxun, *The Cooperative System and Family Economy Under Socialist Commodity Economy (Shehuizhuyi shangpin jingji xia de hezuo zhi yu jiating jingji)* (Beijing: Chinese Social Science Academy Press, 1988), p. 217.

34. Chen and Xia, *Models,* p. 94.

35. Ibid., p. 100.

36. Ibid., p. 101.

37. Ibid., pp. 113–116.

38. Also see the discussion by Su Dongshui, *Managing China's Village Economy (Zhongguo xiangzheng jingji guanlixue)* (Jinan: Shangdong People's Press, 1988), p. 25.

39. Zhang Yi, *Introduction,* p. 89.

40. Wang Weiguang, *Economic Interests, Political Order, Social Stability— The Deep Reflection on the Social Contradiction of Socialism (Jingji liyi, zhengzhi zhixu, shehui wending—shehuizhuyi shehui maodun de shenceng fanci)* (Beijing: Chinese Communist Party Central School Press, 1991), p. 186.

41. Ibid., p. 192.


## CHAPTER 5

1. Hou Chiachu, *History of Chinese Economic Thought (Zhongguo jingji cixiang shi)* (Taipei: Chinese Cultural Renovation Commission, 1982).

2. Lei Ting, "Chinese Self and Chinese Me: Metaphysics and Physics, New Grounds, and Psychology" (*"Zhongguoren de ziwo yu ziji: xingshang yu xingxia, xin li yu xinli"*), in K. Yang and K. Huang, eds., *Chinese Psychology and Behavior (Zhongguoren de xinli yu xingwei)* (Taipei: Department of Psychology, National Taiwan University, 1991), pp. 61–63.

3. Elsewhere I argue that a permanent moral decline actually started during the Great Leap Forward in 1958; see Chih-yu Shih, "The Decline of a Moral Regime: The Great Leap Forward in Retrospect," *Comparative Political Studies* (July 1994).

4. See Martin Carnoy, *The State and Political Theory* (Princeton: Princeton University Press, 1984), pp. 18–23.

5. For example, Roy Hofheinz Jr. and Kent E. Calder, *The Eastasia Edge* (New York: Basic Books, 1982), and Thomas Gold, *State and Society in the Taiwan Miracle* (Armonk, N.Y.: M. E. Sharpe, 1986), among others.

6. For example, see Jan Prybyla, "China's Economic Experiment: Back from the Market?" paper presented at the Western Political Science Association annual meeting, Salt Lake City, April 1989.

7. For example, Samuel Huntington, "Political Development and Political Decay," *World Politics* 17, 3 (1965): 386–430; Mark Kesselman, "Order or Movement? The Literature of Political Development as Ideology," *World Politics* 26, 1 (1973).

8. Max Weber, *The Religion of China,* trans. Hans H. Gerth (New York: Free Press, 1951).

9. Lucian Pye, *The Spirit of Chinese Politics* (Cambridge: MIT Press, 1968), pp. 12–35.

10. Tu Wei-ming, *Human Nature and the Cultivation and Growth of the Self* (*Renxing yu ziwo xiu zhang*) (Beijing: Chinese Peace Press, 1988); Yu Ying-shih, *Chinese Modern Religious Ethics and Merchant Spirit* (*Zhongguo jinshi zongjiao lunli yu shangren jingshen*); Thomas Metzger, *Escape from Predicament* (New York: Columbia University Press, 1977).

11. Ronald Dore, *Taking Japan Seriously* (Stanford: Stanford University Press, 1987).

12. Premier Li Peng mentioned stability more than ten times in his report on government work to the Third Plenary Session of the Seventh People's Congress. In fact, Premier Zhao Ziyang also supported the notion of neoauthoritarianism in China before he was purged in 1989.

13. Lucian Pye, *Asian Power and Authority* (Cambridge: Harvard University Press, 1985), pp. 228–236.

14. John Fei, "Prosperity and Stability in Hong Kong—A Cultural Approach," mimeograph, January 1987.

15. Chih-yu Shih, "Style Change in Chinese Macroeconomic Management During Reform and Opening" (*"Zhongguo dalu gaige kaifang zhong jinji tiaokong fangshi zhi bianqian"*), *Dongya jikan* (July 1991).

16. Liao Caihui and Li Wanqing, "On a Few Theoretical Questions of Socialist Market Economics" (*"Shehuizhuyi shichang jingji de jige lilun wenti"*), in Editorial Board of the Market Economy Seminar of Guangdong Province, ed., *Market Economy in the Primary Stage of Socialism* (*Shehuizhuyi chuji jieduan shichang jingji*) (Dalian: Northeastern School of Finance Press, 1988), pp. 77–78.

17. Remarks by the mayor of Shanghai quoted in Chih-yu Shih, "One Country, Two Systems as the Camouflage of Socialist Theme" (*"Yiguo liangzhi, shehuizhuyi zhutilun de baozhuang"*), *United Daily,* August 14, 1991.

18. Wang Songhsing, *The Turtle Mountain Island—On the Han Fishermen's Society* (*Guei shan dao—hanren yucun shehui zhi yanjiu*) (Nankang: Academia Sinica, 1967).

19. See Lucian Pye, *The Mandarin and the Cadre* (Ann Arbor: Center for Chinese Studies, University of Michigan, 1988).

20. See the discussion by Zheng Yingrong, "Bringing in Market, Building Market" (*"Yinjin shichang, jianzao shichang"*), in Editorial Board of the Market Economy Seminar, *Market Economy,* p. 161.

21. See Gu Ying et al., *Cooperative Business in Contemporary China* (*Dangdai zhongguo de gongxiaohezuo shiye*) (Beijing: Chinese Social Science Academy Press, 1990), pp. 40–58.

22. Ibid., pp. 78–80.

23. Yang Chengxun, *The Cooperative System and Family Economy Under Socialist Commodity Economy* (*Shehuizhuyi shangpin jingji xia de hezuo jingji yu jiating jingji*) (Beijing: Chinese Social Science Academy Press, 1988), p. 55.

24. Yang Changjun, "On the Scope of Socialist Market Economy" (*"Lun shehuizhuyi shichang jingji fanchou"*), in Editorial Board of the Market Economy Seminar, *Market Economy,* p. 40.

25. Qi Yungdong, "Socialist Market Economy and Its Operating Mechanism" ("*Shehuizhuyi shichang jingji ji qi yunxing jizhi*"), in Editorial Board of the Market Economy Seminar, *Market Economy*, pp. 113–114.

26. On the National Price Bureau, see Tong Wansheng, Li Zichao, and Chen Zumian, *Theory of Market Price (Shichang wujia xue)* (Beijing: Universal Aviation Press, 1989), pp. 142–143.

27. See the discussion in Yang Chengxun, *Cooperative System,* pp. 144–154.

28. Wu Shuqing, "From Criticism of the Responsibility System to Adherence and Perfection of the Responsibility System" ("*Cong dui chengbao zhi de pipan dao jianchi han wanshan chengbao zhi*"), in Research and Development of Capital Steel Corporation, ed., *Adhering to the Responsibility System, Enlivening the Large Enterprise (Jianchi chengbao zhi, gaohuo da qiye)* (Beijing: Chinese Democracy and Legal Institution Press, 1989).

29. He Jianzhang, "The Fundamental Dispute Centers on Whether or Not to Adhere to the Public Ownership of Means of Production" ("*Genben fenqi zai yu yao bu yao jianchi gong you zhi*"), in Research and Development of CSC, *Adhering.*

30. "Record of National Conference on Perfecting the Responsibility System" ("*Quanguo wanshan chengbao zhi yantaohui jiyao*"), in Research and Development of CSC, *Adhering.*

31. Xu Xiqian, "Use the Party's Basic Lines to Unify Thoughts" ("*Yao yung dangde jiben luxian tongyi sixiang*"), in Research and Development of CSC, *Adhering.*

32. Ding Caibing et al., *Commerce in Contemporary China (Dangdai zhongguo shangye)* (Beijing: Chinese Social Science Academy Press, 1988), pp. 153–154.

33. Ibid., pp. 160, 161.

34. Ibid., p. 202.

35. China Radio Station, April 30, 1991, Taipei.

36. Xu Chongzheng, *Overall Development of Men and Social Economy—Ethical Economics (Rende quanmian fazhan yu shehui jingji—lunli jingjixue)* (Hefei, Anhui: Anhui Education Press, 1990), p. 215.

37. *Guidelines of Political Economic Critics by Marx (Draft)*, vol. 3 (*Makeci Zhengzhi jingjixue pipan da gang [caogao]*) (Beijing: People's Press, 1963), 105.

38. Huang Shuding and Li Fan, *The Myth of Consumption in Contemporary China (Dangdai zhongguo xiaofai zhi mi)* (Rannan, Hebei: Chinese Commerce Press, 1990).

39. Li Xinjia, "Reconsidering Premature Consumption" ("*Guangyu xiaofei zaoshou de shangque*"), *Xiaofei jingji yanjiu ziliao* 1 (1985).

40. He Zhengyi, "Financial Policy That Controls the Excessive Increase in Consumption Fund" ("*Kongzhi xiaofei jijin zengzhang guomeng de caizheng zhengce*"), *Caizheng* 1 (1986).

41. Sun Xuewen, "The Existing Issues of Macromanagement in Our Country in the Past Six Years" ("*Wo guo jin liu nian lai hongguang guangli cunzai de wenti*"), *Cai jing guangli de lilun yu shijian* 5 (1985).

42. Zhu Liming, "Structural Elasticity of Demand and Income and Premature Consumption" ("*Shouru xuqiu jiego tanxing yu xiaofei zaoshou*"), *Xiaofei jingji* 1 (1986).

43. Yang Shengming, *Model Selection for Consumption with Chinese Characters (Zhongguoshi xiaofei moshi xuanze)* (Beijing: Chinese Social Science Academy Press, 1989), p. 117.

44. Ibid., p. 47.

45. Xu Chongzheng, *Overall Development,* pp. 241–242.

46. Wen Erxing, "Strictly Control Collective Consumption, Engage in Overall Price Management" (*"Yange kongzhi jituan xiaofei, dui wujia jinxing zonghe zhili"*), in Editorial Board of Market Economy Seminar, *Market Economy.*

47. Yang Chengxun, *Cooperative System,* pp. 353–354.

48. Ibid., p. 87.

49. Some believe that the best way to ensure future economic growth and a stable, expanding middle class is to build some rules and regulations into the system. Deputy Premier Zhu Rongji, who has a reputation of being a neo-Confucian, is one typical example here. Zhu was the mayor of Shanghai before rising to his current status, and this led many to think that regionalism has prevailed over centralism. Quite the contrary: Zhu actually developed his career in the ministerial/sectorial branches in his earlier days. By 1994 Zhu had become the major figure in China to urge for an orderly market, supposedly against the indiscriminate *fangquan rangli.*

## CHAPTER 6

1. Ren Chuanhong, *How to Do a Good Job on the Political Thought Work in Enterprises (Luhe zuohao qiye zhengzhi sixiang gongzuo)* (Shanghai: Shanghai People's Press, 1989), p. 7.

2. Ibid., pp. 8–9.

3. Ibid., p. 8.

4. Ibid., pp. 6, 9.

5. Li Qi and Zhao Yunxian, *The Building of an Enterprise Party (Qiyedang de jianshe)* (Beijing: Chinese Communist Party Central School Press, 1991), pp. 9–11.

6. Ibid., p. 115.

7. Ibid., p. 118.

8. Ibid., p. 79.

9. Ibid.

10. Ibid., p. 160.

11. Ren, *How to Do a Good Job,* p. 18.

12. Ibid., p. 27.

13. Interviewee No. 24.

14. Interviewee No. 27.

15. Interviewee No. 23.

16. Interviewee No. 28.

17. Ibid.

18. Ibid.

19. Interviewee No. 23.

20. Ibid.

21. Interviewee No. 27.

22. Interviewee No. 29.

23. Interviewee No. 30.

24. Ibid.

25. Interviewee No. 31.

26. Interviewee No. 30.

27. Ibid.

28. Interviewee No. 18.

29. Interviewee No. 2.
30. Interviewee No. 14.
31. Interviewee No. 16.
32. Interviewee No. 5.
33. Interviewee No. 17.
34. Interviewee No. 19.
35. Interviewee No. 3.
36. Interviewee No. 20.
37. Interviewee No. 15.
38. Interviewee No. 4.
39. Interviewee No. 25.
40. Ibid.
41. Interviewee No. 26.
42. Ibid.
43. Interviewee No. 25.

## CHAPTER 7

1. For a detailed discussion on the market-plan relationship, see Dai Yuancheng and Fang Liubi, *A New Thesis on Chinese Economy* (*Zhongguo jingji xinlun*) (Beijing: Chinese Social Science Academy Press, 1990), pp. 274–342.

2. For example, see Tong Wansheng, Li Zichao, and Chen Zumian, *Theory of Market Price* (*Shichang wujiaxue*) (Beijing: Universal Aviation, 1989); Xu Guangjian, Wang Xiaobing, and Du Weichang, *Price Theory Under Reform* (*Gaigezhong de wujia lilun*) (Beijing: People's University Press, 1989); Wu Renjian, "Inflation in China" (*"Zhongguo de tonghuo pengzhang"*), in Ruan Jianming et al., eds., *Dynamics of Economic Theory* (*Jingji lilun dongtai*) (Beijing: Chinese Economics Press, 1989), pp. 119–134; Liu Renhua and Hua Daozheng, "An Attempt to Integrate the Plan and the Market" (*"Shilun jihua yu shichang de neizai tongyi"*), in Propaganda Division, Headquarters of Political Department, ed., *Initial Exploration of the Theory on the Primary Stage of Socialist Development* (*Shehuizhuyi chuji jieduan lilun chutan*) (Beijing: PLA Press, 1988), pp. 241–246; Wang Zilin, *On National Enterprise* (*Guoyou zichanglun*) (Beijing: Chinese Finance Press, 1989), pp. 97–128; Zeng Muye et al., eds., *Market Economy of the Primary Stage of the Socialist Development* (*Shehuizhuyi chuji jieduan shichang jingji*) (Dalien: Northeastern Financial University Press, 1988).

3. Concerning the legitimacy of intervention, see Jiang Yingguang, "On Some Basic Theoretical Problems in the Commercial Reform" (*"Shangye gaigezhong de jige jiben lilun wenti"*), in Ding Shengjun and Wang Yibing, eds., *Regulate the Economic Environment and Establish the New Order for Circulation* (*Zhili jingji huanjing, jianli liutong xinzhixu*) (Beijing: Chinese Commercial Press, 1989).

4. Interviewee No. 31 repeated this point in his interview.

5. Interview with the Japanese-Chinese interpreter for the negotiations.

6. Chen Chang-ching, *Commodity Economy and the Chinese Communists' Socialist Road* (*Shangpin jingji yu zhonggong shehuizhuyi daolu*) (Taipei: Dandelion Press, 1988).

7. For example, see Wei Je, *Harmony Between Economic Freedom and Economic Control: On the Combination of Planning and Market* (*Jingji ziyou yu jingji*

*yueshu de hexie: jihua yu shichang de jiehe*) (Xi'an: Shanxi People's Press, 1991); of Capital Steel Research and Development Corporation, ed., *Adhering to the Responsibility System, Enliving the Large Enterprises (Jianchi chengbaozhi, gaohuo daqiye)* (Beijing: Chinese Legal Institution Press, 1990).

8. See Carl Riskin, *Chinese Political Economy* (New York: Oxford University Press, 1987), pp. 201–256.

## CHAPTER 8

1. Andrew Walder, *Communist Neo-Traditionalism* (Berkeley: University of California Press, 1986).

2. Nakane Chie, *Japanese Society* (Berkeley: University of California Press, 1970); Tadashi Fukutaki, *The Japanese Social Structure* (Tokyo: University of Tokyo Press, 1982).

3. On the psychological propensity of the Japanese toward dependent relationships, see Takeo Doi, *The Anatomy of Dependence* (Tokyo: Kodansha International, 1973).

4. On the notion of productive efficiency, see Ronald Dore, *Taking Japan Seriously* (Stanford: Stanford University Press, 1987).

5. Lucian Pye, *The Mandarin and the Cadre* (Ann Arbor: Center for Chinese Studies, University of Michigan, 1988).

6. For example, Union Research Institute, ed., *Collected Works of Liu Shao Ch'i, 1958–1967* (Hong Kong: Union Research Institute, 1968), p. 35; Wang Reipu and Cui Zifeng, *On the Party's Fundamental Lines on the Primary Stage of Socialism (Shehuizhuyi chuji jieduan dangde jibenluxian gailun)* (Beijing: Chinese Communist Party Central School Press, 1991), pp. 48–56.

7. Recent reform has allowed bankruptcy in order to force corrupt and inefficient state enterprises out of the market.

8. Frederick Mote, "Confucian Eremitism in the Yuan Period," in A. Wright, ed., *Confucianism and Chinese Civilization* (New York: Atheneum, 1965).

9. The other part of this research looks at the motivation of the general manager in making investment decisions. A tentative conclusion is that these socialist entrepreneurs work extremely hard only to promote their particular, personal goals. There is no general mechanism that can be identified as responsible for their eagerness and industry. Economic reform indeed provides an environment where they strive for achievement, but many more failures suggest that reform is not a sufficient condition to create highly motivated general managers.

10. On the new salary structure, see Bureau of Salary, Beijing Economic Commission, and Beijing Leather Manufacture, eds., *Salary Reform and the Structured Salary System (Gongzi gaige yu jiego gongzizhi)* (Beijing: Chinese Social Science Academy Press, 1985).

11. Interviewee No. 3.

12. The system of replacement smacks of feudalism. The system was canceled in many big cities but still applies in other locales. Information about the system of generation replacement is not consistent so far as I can tell.

13. Interviewee No. 14.

14. Interviewee No. 15.

15. Interviewee No. 1.

16. Interviewee No. 4.

17. Interviewee No. 7.

18. Interviewee No. 13.

19. Interviewee No. 2.

20. Interviewee No. 17.

21. Interviewee No. 19.

22. Interviewee No. 9.

23. Interviewee No. 5.

24. Interviewee No. 20.

25. See Walder, *Communist Neo-Traditionalism.*

26. Interviewee No. 21.

27. Interviewee No. 23.

28. New China News Agency, *High Way to Entrepreneurship (Qiye feiteng zhi lu)* (Beijing: China Prospect Press, 1985), pp. 118–119.

29. Luo Wen, *Case Analysis of Administrative Management at the Lowest Levels (Jiceng xingzheng guanli anli xuanxi)* (Guangxi: Guangxi Nations Press, 1990), p. 78.

30. Interviewee No. 4.

31. Interviewee No. 20.

32. Interviewee No. 14.

33. Interviewee No. 7.

34. Interviewee No. 5.

35. Interviewee No. 19.

36. Interviewee No. 1.

37. Interviewee No. 22.

38. Bureau of Enterprise System Reform, Commission on State System Reform, ed., *Handbook on Industrial Enterprise Management (Gongye qiye guanli shouce)* (Beijing: Economics Daily Press, 1988), p. 28.

39. Interviewee No. 28.

40. Interviewee No. 11.

41. Interviewee No. 12.

42. Interviewee No. 1.


# CHAPTER 9

1. Huang Shuding and Li Fan, *The Myth of Consumption in Contemporary China (Dangdai zhongguo xiaofei zhimi)* (Rannan, Hebei: Chinese Commercial Press, 1990).

2. Zhang Yi, *Introduction to China's Village Enterprises (Zhongguo xiangzheng qiye gailun)* (Shanghai: Shanghai Social Science Academy Press, 1988).

3. One noted professor of philosophy complains that it is a shame that the state fails to take good care of intellectuals and even push them to work for the market.

4. The third kind of business is extremely popular in the two cities and three prefectures I visited.

5. In general a national enterprise submits 55 percent of its profit. It still has to pay tax on the 45 percent it keeps. The negotiation between the enterprise and the state often centers on the issue of the tax base. The enterprise may be willing to pay 55 percent of only a small part of its profit by using various definitions of *profit.*

6. From interview scripts.

7. Ibid.

8. Ibid.

9. Ibid.

10. Ibid.

11. Lucian Pye, *The Dynamics of Chinese Politics* (Cambridge: Oelge-schlager, Gunn & Hain, 1981).

## CHAPTER 10

1. Some dislike the state-society differentiation. See Dorothy Solinger, *China's Transition from Socialism: Statist Legacies and Market Reforms, 1980–1990* (Armonk, N.Y.: M. E. Sharpe, 1993); Lowell Dittmer and Samuel Kim, eds., *China's Quest for National Identity* (Ithaca: Cornell University Press, 1992).

2. Some argue that reform has created a situation in which Chinese society has gained the upper hand in a game of power against the state. See Gordon White, *Riding the Tiger* (Stanford: University of Stanford Press, 1993).

3. See Andrew Walder, *Communist Neo-Traditionalism* (Berkeley: University of California Press, 1986).

4. See Brantly Womack, "Transfigured Community: Neo-Traditionalism and Work Unit Socialism in China," *China Quarterly* 126 (1991): 313–332.

5. Jean Oi, *State and Peasant in Contemporary China* (Berkeley: University of California Press, 1989).

6. Vivienne Shue, *The Reach of the State: Sketches of the Chinese Body Politic* (Stanford: Stanford University Press, 1988).

7. For a detailed account of policy cycles, see Susan Shirk, *The Political Logic of Economic Reform in China* (Berkeley: University of California Press, 1992).

8. This partially explains a leading China expert's claim that the Chinese have an unusual ability to tolerate inconsistency. See Lucian Pye, *The Mandarin and the Cadre* (Ann Arbor: Center for Chinese Studies, University of Michigan, 1988), pp. 36–74.

# BIBLIOGRAPHY

Ai Fei. "Confucian Ethics and Singapore Society" ("Rujia lunli yu xinjiapo she-hui"), *Nanjingdaxue xuebao* 1 (1987).

An Lan and Yang Furei. "Review of Confucian Research in the Past Ten Years" ("Shinianlai kongzi yanjiu pinghua"), *Jianghanluntan* 12 (1988).

Arrow, K. *Social Choice and Individual Values.* New York: Wiley, 1963.

Asian People's Anti-Communist League. *Rural People's Communes.* Taipei: Asian Peoples' Anti-Communist League, 1963.

Baum, Richard. *Prelude to Revolution.* New York: Columbia University Press, 1975.

Baum, Richard, and Frederick C. Teiwes. *Ssu-Ch'ing: The Socialist Education Movement, 1962–1966.* Berkeley: University of California Press, 1968.

Berger, Peter L., and Hsin-Huang Michael Hsiao, eds. *In Search of an East Asian Development Model.* New Brunswick: Transaction Books, 1988.

Bowie, Robert R., and John K. Fairbank, eds. *Communist China, 1955–1959.* Cambridge: Harvard University Press, 1971.

Bureau of Salary, Beijing Economic Commission, and Beijing Leather Manufacture, eds. *Salary Reform and the Structured Salary System* (Gongzi gaige yu jiego gongzizhi). Beijing: Chinese Social Science Academy Press, 1985.

Cao Deben. "On a Few Questions About Chinese Traditional Thoughts" ("Guanyu zhongguo chuantong sixiang de jige wenti"), *Jilindaxue shehuikexue xuebao* 2 (1989).

Cao Fongqi. *The Theory and Practice of the Chinese Enterprise Stock System* (Zhongguo qiye gufen zhi de lilun yu shijian). Beijing: Business Management Press, 1989.

Cao Siyuan. "Comparing the Institution of Corporate Purchase and the Institution of Bankruptcy" ("Qiye jianbing yu qiye pochang zhidu de bijiao"). In F. Tian, ed., *Theory and Practice of Corporate Purchase in China* (Zhongguo qiye jianbing de lilun yu shijian). Beijing: Economic Management Club, 1989.

Capital Steel Corporation. "Developing Cross-sector, Cross-area, Cross-border Business Through Corporate Purchase" ("Tongguo qiye jianbing fazhan kua hangye, kua dichu, kuaguo jingying"). In F. Tian, ed., *Theory and Practice of Corporate Purchase in China* (Zhongguo qiye jianbing de lilun yu shijian). Beijing: Economic Management Club, 1989.

Carnoy, Martin. *The State and Political Theory.* Princeton: Princeton University Press, 1984.

Central Committee. "Resolution on Some Questions Concerning the People's Communes." In Robert R. Bowie and John K. Fairbank, eds., *Communist China, 1955–1959.* Cambridge: Harvard University Press, 1971.

———. "Resolution on the Establishment of People's Communes in the Rural Areas." In Robert R. Bowie and John K. Fairbank, eds., *Communist China, 1955–1959.* Cambridge: Harvard University Press, 1971.

Chang Kuo-sin. *Mao Tse-tung and His China.* Hong Kong: Heinemann, 1978.

Chang, Parris H. "The Emergence of Reform Forces and Politics." In San-Woo Rhee, ed., *China's Reform Politics.* Seoul: Sogang University Press, 1986.

————. *Power and Policy in China.* University Park: Pennsylvania State University Press, 1975.

Chang Yachun. "Ideology and Social Control Under Deng Xiaoping" ("Deng Xiaoping luxian xia de yishixingtai yu shehui kongzhi"), Zhongguo dalu yanjiu 32, 11.

Chao Kang. "Chinese Economic Reform Turns Westernization Irrevocably" (Zhonggong jinggai yi zoushang xihuade bugueilu), *United Daily*, December 14 and 15, 1990.

Chen Bohai. "The Constructive Perspective on Chinese Cultural Spirit" ("Zhongguo wenhua jingshen zhi jiangou guan"), *Zhongguoshehuikexue* 4 (1988).

Chen, C. S., and Charles P. Ridley, eds., trans. *Rural People's Communes in Lienchiang.* Stanford: Stanford University Press, 1969.

Chen Chang-ching. *Commodity Economy and the Chinese Communists' Socialist Road* (Shangpin jingji yu zhonggong shehuizhuyi daolu). Taipei: Dandelion Press, 1988.

Chen, Feng. "Double Categorization of Social Type and Socialism and Its Primary Stage—Also on the Theory of Productivity Standard, the Theory of Underdevelopment, the Theory of Taking the Course, the Theory of Empty Thought" ("Shehui xingtai de liangchong huafen yu shehuizhuyi ji qi chuji jieduan—jian ping shenchangli biaozhuen shuo, buchengshou shuo, buke shuo han kong xiang shuo"). In Shanghai Communist Party Propaganda Department, ed., *The First Wave* (Diyici dachao). Shanghai: Sanlian Press, 1989.

Chen Jiyuan and Xia Defang. *On the Models of Countryside Business* (Xiangzheng qiye moshi yanjiu). Beijing: Chinese Social Science Academy Press, 1988.

Chen Shenshen. "The Key to Strengthening Reform Is to Restore Market Order" ("Jianli shichang zhixu shi shenhua gaige de guanjian"). In Shanghai Communist Party Propaganda Department, ed., *The First Wave (Diyici dachao).* Shanghai: Sanlian Press, 1989.

Chen Shu-chuan. "Chinese Self-expression as Viewed Through the Sacrificing Act in the June Fourth Pro-democracy Movement" ("Cong liu ci min yun de xisheng xingwei kan zhongguoren de ziwo biaoda"). In K. Yang and K. Huang, eds., *Chinese Psychology and Behavior* (Zhongguoren de xinli yu xingwei). Taipei: Department of Psychology, National Taiwan University, 1989.

Chen Sihe. "The May Fourth Movement and the Current Age" ("Wusi yu dangdai"), *Fudanxuebao* 3 (1989).

Chen Weipin. "Notes on the Paradox in the Confucian Thought System" ("Lyuelun kongzi sixiang tixi de maodunxing"), *Qiluxuekan* 1 (1985).

Chen Wenlin. *Introduction of China's Monetary Policy Reform* (Zhongguo huobi zhengce gaige jianlun). Beijing: Chinese Finance and Economics Press, 1989.

Cheng Chu-yuan. "Basic Problems of Chinese Communists' Agricultural Collectivization" ("Zhonggong nongye jitihua de jiben wenti"), *Mingzhu pinglun* 7, 11 (June 1956).

————. *Congressional Record* 133 (August 6, 1959).

————. "The Sharp Break and the Crisis of 'People's Commune'" ("Renmingongshe' de duncuo yu weiji"). In C. Cheng, ed., *Diagnoses of Chinese Communist Economy* (Zhonggong jingji de zhengduan). Taipei: Lianjing Publications, 1980.

Cheng Weili. "The Ambiguity Complex in Contemporary Chinese Psychoculture" ("Dangdai zhongguo de aihen zhenghouqun"), *Fudanxuebao* 3 (1988).

Chie, Nakane. *Japanese Society.* Berkeley: University of California Press, 1970.

Chilcote, Ronald H. *Theories of Development and Underdevelopment.* Boulder, Colo.: Westview, 1984.

Clark, Rodney. *The Japanese Company*. New Haven, Conn.: Yale University Press, 1979.

Commission on State System Reform, ed. *Handbook on Industrial Enterprise Management* (Gongye qiye guanli shouce). Beijing: Economics Daily Press, 1988.

*Collection of Conference Documents of the Fourth Meeting of the Sixth National People's Congress* (Diliujie quanguo renmin daibiaodahui disici huiyi wenjian huibian). Beijing: People's Press, 1986.

Confucius. "Confucius." In Ch'u Chai and Weinberg Chai, eds., *The Sacred Books of Confucius and Other Confucian Classics*. New Hyde Park, N.Y.: University Books, 1965.

Cottam, Martha. *Images and Intervention: United States' Policies Toward Latin America*. Pittsburgh: University of Pittsburgh Press, 1994.

Croll, Elizabeth. *From Heaven to Earth*. London: Routledge, 1994.

Dai Yuancheng and Fang Liubi. *A New Thesis on Chinese Economy* (Zhongguo jingji xinlun). Beijing: Chinese Social Science Academy Press, 1990.

Darlin, Alexander, and George W. Breslauer. *Political Terror in Communist Systems*. Stanford: Stanford University Press, 1970.

Deng Xiaoping. *Selected Readings of Deng Xiaoping* (Deng xiaoping wenxuan). Beijing: People's Press, 1983.

———. "Speech on the Current Problem of Student Disturbance," *Chinese Law and Government* (spring 1988).

Deng Zihui. "The Great Implications of Village Cooperative Industry" ("Xiang sheban gongye de weida yiyi"), *Nongcun gongzuo tongxun* (October 1958).

———. "Report to the Meeting on Management of Agricultural Cooperatives," *Renmin ribao,* May 7, 1957.

———. "Speech to National Producers' Conference," *Gongren ribao,* May 8, 1956.

Ding Caibing et al. *Commerce in Contemporary China* (Dangdai zhongguo shangye). Beijing: Chinese Social Science Academy Press, 1988.

Ding Junliang. *Where Is the Route?—Reflections upon the Primary Stage of Socialism* (Lu zai hefang—guanyu shehuizhuyi chuji jieduan de chensi). Changsha: Hunan University Press, 1989.

Ding Shengjun and Wang Yibing, eds. *Regulate the Economic Environment and Establish the New Order for Circulation* (Zhili jingji huanjing, jianli liutong xin zhixu). Beijing: Chinese Commercial Press, 1989.

Ding Shouhe. "Notes on Chinese Cultural Tradition" ("Zhongguo wenhua chuantong shilun"), *Qiusuo* 4 (1987).

Dittmer, Lowell. *China's Continuous Revolution*. Berkeley: University of California Press, 1987.

Dittmer, Lowell, and Samuel Kim, eds. *China's Quest for National Identity*. Ithaca: Cornell University Press, 1992.

Doi, Takeo. *The Anatomy of Dependence*. Tokyo: Kodansha International, 1973.

Dong Furen. "On the Development of Our National Market" ("Tan wo guo shichang de peiyu"). In Ding Shengjun and Wang Yibing, eds., *Regulate the Economic Environment and Establish the New Order for Circulation* (Zhili jingji huanjing, jianli liutong xin zhixu). Beijing: Chinese Commercial Press, 1989.

Dore, Ronald. *Flexible Rigidities: Industrial Policy and Structural Adjustment in the Japanese Economy, 1970–80*. Stanford: Stanford University Press, 1986.

———. *Taking Japan Seriously: A Confucian Perspective on Leading Economic Issues*. Stanford: Stanford University Press, 1987.

Eckstein, Alexander. *China's Economic Revolution*. London: Cambridge University Press, 1981.

Esherick, Joseph W., and Jeffrey N. Wasserstrom. "Acting Out Democracy: Political Theater in Modern China," *Journal of Asian Studies* 49, 4 (1990).

Fairbank, John King. *The United States and China.* Cambridge: Harvard University Press, 1983.

Fang Lin. "Chinese Modernization and Social Values." In D. Sinha and H. Kao, eds., *Social Values and Development.* Newbury Park, Calif.: Sage Publications, 1988.

Fang Lizhi. "China's Despair and China's Hope," *New York Review of Books* 36, 1 (February 2, 1989).

Fei, John. "Prosperity and Stability in Hong Kong—A Cultural Approach." Mimeograph, January 1987.

Feng Zhenggang. *On the Primary Stage of Socialism* (Lun shehuizhuyi chuji jieduan). Changsha: Hunan University Press, 1989.

Flaherty, M. Therese, and Hiroyuki Itami. "Finance." In D. I. Okimoto et al., eds., *Competitive Edge: The Semi-conductor Industry in the United States and Japan.* Stanford: Stanford University Press, 1984.

Fukutaki, Tadashi. *The Japanese Social Structure.* Tokyo: University of Tokyo Press, 1982.

Gao Guang et al. *On Structures of Chinese Socialism in the Primary Stage* (Zhongguo shehuizhuyi chuji jieduan jiegou yanjiu). Beijing: Chinese Communist Party Central School Press, 1988.

Geng Jianxiung. "On the Political Mechanism of Broadcasting New Culture in China" ("Lun xinwenhua zai zhongguo chuanbo de zhengzhi jizhi"), *Fudanxuebao* 3 (1989).

Geng Zhiyun. "Reevaluation of the May Fourth New Cultural Movement" ("Wusi xinwenhua yundong de zairenshi"), *Zhongguoshehuikexue* 3 (1989).

Gold, Thomas. *State and Society in the Taiwan Miracle.* Armonk, N.Y.: M. E. Sharpe, 1986.

Gu Xiaoming. "A Critique on the Cultural Mechanism of Propriety" ("Dui li de wenhua jizhi benshen de pipan"), *Fudanxuebao* 3 (1988).

Gu Ying et al. *Cooperative Business in Contemporary China* (Dangdai zhongguo de gongxiaohezuo shiye). Beijing: Chinese Social Science Academy Press, 1990.

Gui Fu. "Comments on Mencius' Thoughts of Benevolent Politics" ("Mengzi renzheng sixiang pingyi"), *Neimenggu shidaxuebao* 4 (1988).

*Guidelines of Political Economic Critics by Marx (Draft),* vol. 3 (Makeci Zhengzhi jingjixue pipan da gang [caogao]). Beijing: People's Press, 1963.

Guo Fongfong and Li Xingshan. *Socialist Macroeconomic Management* (Shehuizhuyi hongguanjingji guanli xue). Zhangjiako, Hebei: Chinese Communist Party Central School Press, 1989.

Guo Yi. "Confucius' Thinking Structures and Their Impact on the Traditional Chinese Thinking Pattern" ("Kongzi de siwei jiegou ji qi dui zhongguo chuantong siwei fangshi de yingxiang"), *Qiluxuekan* 3 (1986).

Hao Mengbi and Duan Haoran. *The Sixty Years and Chinese Communism* (Zhongguo gongchandang liushi nian). Beijing: PLA Press, 1984.

Hao Yanrong. "Modernization and the Choice of Chinese Modern Intellectual Stratum" ("Jindaihua yu jindai zhongguo zhishifenzi jie,cen de xuanze"), *Hebeixuekan* 3 (1989).

Harding, Harry. "From China, with Disdain: New Trends in the Study of China," *Asian Survey* 22, 10 (October 1982).

Harrison, Lawrence E. *Underdevelopment Is a State of Mind.* Lanham, Md.: Madison Books, 1985.

He Hongshang, ed. *Symposium of Deng Zihui's Thought on Agricultural Coopera-tive* (Deng Zihui nongyehezuo sixiang xueshu taolunhui lunwenji). Beijing: Agricultural Publication, 1989.

He Jianzhang. "The Fundamental Dispute Centers on Whether or Not to Adhere to the Public Ownership of Means of Production" ("Genben fenqi zai yu yao bu yao jianchi gong you zhi"). In Capital Steel Research and Development of Cor-poration, ed., *Adhering to the Responsibility System, Enlivening the Large En-terprise* (Jianchi chengbao zhi, gaohuo da qiye). Beijing: Chinese Democracy and Legal Institution Press, 1989.

He Zhengyi. "Financial Policy That Controls the Excessive Increase in Consump-tion Fund" ("Kongzhi xiaofei jijin zengzhang guomeng de caizheng zhengce"), *Caizheng* 1 (1986).

Hebei Provincial Committee of the Party. "On the Building of People's Com-munes." In Robert R. Bowie and John K. Fairbank, eds., *Communist China, 1955-1959*. Cambridge: Harvard University Press, 1971.

Hofheinz, Roy Jr., and Kent E. Calder. *The Eastasia Edge*. New York: Basic Books, 1982.

Hou Chiachu. *History of Chinese Economic Thought* (Zhongguo jingji sixiang shi). Taipei: Chinese Cultural Renovation Commission, 1982.

Hou Xianlin. "Mao's Criticism and Application of the Principle of the Golden Mean" ("Mao zedong dui zhongyung sixiang de pipan yu jicheng"), *Qiluxuekan* 4 (1987).

Hsu Li-chun. "Have We Already Reached the Stage of Communism." In Robert R. Bowie and John K. Fairbank, eds., *Communist China, 1955-1959*. Cambridge: Harvard University Press, 1971.

Hu Yinghang and Guan Yushu. "The 1959 Lushan Conference and Its Historical Lessons" ("1959 nian lushan huiyi ji qi lishi jiaoxun"), *Qiushixuekan* 2 (1985).

Huang Kwang-kuo. "Face and Favor: The Chinese Power Game," *American Jour-nal of Sociology* 97, 4 (1987).

———. "Modernization of the Chinese Family Business," *International Journal of Psychology* 25 (1990).

———. "The Notion of Justice in Confucianism" ("Lujia sixiang zhong de zhengyi guan"). In K. Yang and K. Huang, eds., *Chinese Psychology and Behavior* (Zhongguoren de xinli yu xingwei). Taipei: Department of Psychology, National Taiwan University, 1989.

Huang Shuding and Li Fan. *The Myth of Consumption in Contemporary China* (Dangdai zhongguo xiaofei zhi mi). Rannan, Hebei: Chinese Commerce Press, 1990.

Huntington, Samuel. "Political Development and Political Decay," *World Politics* 17, 3 (1965).

Hwang Tien-chien. *Failures of Mao Tse-tung's Dictatorship, 1949-1963*. Taipei: Asian Peoples' Anti-Communist League, 1963.

"The Issue of High-speed and Proportion in the First Five-Year Plan," *Wuhanxue-bao* 5 (1959).

Ji Xiaopeng. "Developing Horizontal Economic Linkages, Promoting Economic Systemic Reform" ("Fazhan henxiang jingji lianhe, cujin jingji tizhi gaige"), *PLA Daily*, April 8, 1986.

Jiang Jianqiang. "Five Spurious Phenomena in the Process of Sinifying Marxism" ("Makesizhuyi zhongguohua de wu da shizheng"), *Shehuikexuebao,* July 14, 1988.

Jiang Ronhai. "On Confucian Utilitarianism" ("Lun rujia de gonglisixiang"), *Bei-jingdaxue xuebao* 3 (1988).

Jiang Xuemo. "New Light on Capitalism and Socialism—The Theoretical Foundation of Our Country's Economic Institutional Reform" ("Dui Zibenzhuyi han shehuizhuyi de zairenshi—wo guo jingji tizhi gaige de lilun jichu"). In Shanghai Communist Party Propaganda Department, ed., *The First Wave* (Diyici dachao). Shanghai: Sanlian Press, 1989.

Jiang Yingguang. "On Some Basic Theoretical Problems in Commercial Reform" ("Shangye gaigezhong de jige jiben lilun wenti"). In Ding Shengjun and Wang Yibing, eds., *Regulate the Economic Environment and Establish the New Order of Circulation* (Zhili jingji huanjing, jianli liutong xin zhishu). Beijing: Chinese Commercial Press, 1989.

Jiang Zeming. "Remarks on the Theoretical Seminar on Shanghai's First Memorial Decade of the Opening of the Third Plenary Session of the Central Committee of the Eleventh National Congress" ("Zai Shanghaishi jinian dang de shiyijie san zhongquanhui zhaokai shizhounian lilun taolunhui shang de jianghua"). In Shanghai Communist Party Propaganda Department, ed., *The First Wave* (Diyici dachao). Shanghai: Sanlian Press, 1989.

Kazuo Koike. "Japan's Industrial Relations: Characteristics and Problems," *Japanese Economic Studies* (fall 1978).

Kesselman, Mark. "Order or Movement? The Literature of Political Development as Ideology," *World Politics* 26, 1 (1973).

Kuang Yaming. *On Confucius* (Kongzi pingzhuan). Shangdong: Qilu Bookstore, 1985.

Kyogoku Jun-ichi. *The Political Dynamics of Japan.* Trans. Nobutaka Ike. Tokyo: University of Tokyo Press, 1987.

Lei Ting. "Chinese Self and Chinese Me: Metaphysics and Physics, New Grounds, and Psychology" ("Zhongguoren de ziwo yu ziji: xingshang yu xingxia, xin li yu xinli"). In K. Yang and K. Huang, eds., *Chinese Psychology and Behavior* (Zhongguoren de xinli yu xingwei). Taipei: Department of Psychology, National Taiwan University, 1991.

Lenin, V. I. *Selected Readings of Lenin* (Liening xuanji). Beijing: People's Press, 1972.

Li Qi and Zhao Yunxian. *The Building of an Enterprise Party* (Qiyedang de jianshe). Beijing: Chinese Communist Party Central School Press, 1991.

Li Qiqian. "On the Value of Confucianism in the Modern Society" ("Lun kongzi sixiang zai xiandai shehui zhong de jiazhi"), *Qiluxuekan* 1 (1989).

Li Shuangbi. "The Great Cultural System: Observation of the Modern Chinese Historical System from a New Angle" ("Da wenhua xitong: guancha zhongguo jindaishi tixi de xinshijiao"), *Qiusuo* 3 (1988).

Li Shuyou. "The Neo-Confucian Ethos and Our Confucian Ethical Studies" ("Xinruxue sichao yu women de rujia lunli yanjiu"), *Nanjingdaxue xuebao* 1 (1987).

Li Tien-min. *Crisis of the Chinese Communist Regime—As Seen from Lien-chiang Documents.* Taipei: Asian Peoples' Anti-Communist League, 1964.

Li Wen. "Modernized Cultural Renaissance" ("Xiandaihua de wenhua qimeng"), *Fudanxuebao* 3 (1989).

Li Xiaoming. "The Ancient Chinese Thinking Pattern and Its Modernization" ("Zhongguo chuantong siwei moshi ji qi xiandaihua"), *Jianghanluntan* 5 (1986).

Li Xinjia. "Reconsidering Premature Consumption" ("Guanyu xiaofei zaoshou de shangchue"), *Xiaofei jingji yanjiu ziliao* 1 (1985).

Li Yining. "Market, Resource Allocation, and Imbalance" ("Shichang, ziyuan peizhi yu feijunheng"). In Ding Shengjun and Wang Yibing, eds., *Regulate the Economic Environment and Establish the New Order for Circulation* (Zhili jingji huanjing, jianli liutong xin zhixu). Beijing: Chinese Commercial Press, 1989.

Liao Caihui and Li Wanqing. "On a Few Theoretical Questions of Socialist Market Economics" ("Shehuizhuyi shichang jingji de jige lilun wenti"). In Editorial Board of the Market Economy Seminar of Guangdong Province, ed., *Market Economy in the Primary Stage of Socialism* (Shehuizhuyi chuji jieduan shichang jingji). Dalian: Northeastern School of Finance Press, 1988.

Leiberthal, Kenneth. *The Foreign Policy Debate in Peking as Seen Through Allegorical Articles, 1973–1976.* Santa Monica, Calif.: Rand, 1977.

Lifton, Robert J. *Revolutionary Immortality.* New York: Random House, 1968.

Lin, Cyril. "Interview of Wei and Zhao," *China Quarterly* 100 (December 1984).

Lin Fang. "Exploring the Modern Value System in Our Country" ("Wo guo xiandai jiazhi guan tantao"), *Zhongguoshehuikexue* 3 (1989).

Lindblom, Charles. *Politics and Market.* New York: Basic Books, 1977.

Liu Guangjie. *On China's Economic Development Strategy* (Zhongguo jingji fazhan zhanlyue gailun). Beijing: Zhongguo Wuzi Press, 1989.

Liu Jiancheng. "Mencius' Mercantilism Should Be Affirmed" ("Mengzi zhongshangzhuyi ying yu kending"), *Dongyueluncong* 2 (1982).

Liu Peng and Zheng Lanxun. *New Conceptions—An Overview of Conceptual Reform* (Xing guannian—guannian biange mianmianguan). Beijing: Overseas Chinese Press, 1989.

Liu Renhua and Hua Daozheng. "An Attempt to Integrate the Plan and the Market" ("Shilun jihua yu shichang de neizai tongyi"), in Propaganda Division, Headquarters of Political Department, ed., *Initial Exploration of the Theory on the Primary Stage of Socialist Development* (Shehuizhuyi chuji jieduan lilun chutan). Beijing: PLA Press, 1988.

Liu Shaoqi. "The Significance of the October Revolution." In Robert R. Bowie and John K. Fairbank, eds., *Communist China, 1955–1959.* Cambridge: Harvard University Press, 1971.

Liu Shuren. "Actively Promoting Economic Integration Through Horizontal Coordination" ("Jiji tuijin hengxiang jingji lianhe"), *Jingjiguanli* 1 (1986).

Liu Wei et al. *Resource Allocation and Economic Systemic Reform* (Ziyuan peizhi yu jingji tizhi gaige). Beijing: Chinese Finance and Economics Press, 1989.

Liu Weihua. "The Features of Evolution in Confucian Thought" ("Kongzi sixiang yanbian de tedian"), *Shehuikexue zhanxian* 3 (1985).

Liu Yingtao and Luo Xiaoming. "On the Limitation of Applying Aggregate Analysis and Aggregate Policy in the Economic Theory and Practice in Our Country" ("Lun zongliang fenxi yu zongliang zhengce zai wo guo jingji lilun yu jingji shijian zhong de juxianxing"), *Jingji yanjiu* 6 (1987).

Liu Zaifu and Lin Gang. "China's Traditional Culture and the Ah Q Model" ("Zhongguo chuantong wenhua yu ah-q moshi"), *Zhongguoshehuikexue* 3 (1988).

Liu Zhengyi. "Exploring Confucius' Methodology" ("Kongzi fangfalun chutan"), *Qiluxuekan* 3 (1987).

Liu Zuochang. "The Theory and the Progressive Implications of Mencius' Thoughts of Benevolent Politics" ("Mengzi de renzheng xueshuo jiqi jinbu yiyi"), *Shixueyuekan* 1 (1985).

Lu Dingyi. "Education Must Be Combined with Productive Labor." In Robert R. Bowie and John K. Fairbank, eds., *Communist China, 1955–1959.* Cambridge: Harvard University Press, 1971.

Lu Yinglin and Fang Li. *Productive Force and Socialism* (Shengchanli yu shehuizhuyi). Beijing: PLA Press, 1989.

Luo Wen. *Case Analysis of Administrative Management at the Lowest Levels* (Jiceng xingzheng guanli anli xuanxi). Guangxi: Guangxi Nations Press, 1990.

Ma Heping. "Rectifying Networks of Regional Blocking and Sectorial Striping" ("Zhengquechuli tiaotiao kuaikuai de guanxi"). In *Historical Experiences in Our Country's Economic Institutional Reform* (Wo guo jingji tizhi gaige de lishi jingyan). Beijing: People's Press, 1985.

Ma Hong. "On Corporate Purchase" ("Lun qiye maimai"). In F. Tian, ed., *Theory and Practice of Corporate Purchase in China* (Zhongguo qiye jianbing de lilun yu shijian). Beijing: Economic Management Club, 1989.

———. *The Prospect and Road of China's Socialist Modernization* (Zhongguo she-huizhuyi xiandaihua de daolu han qianjing). Shanghai: People's Press, 1988.

Ma Ming. "Exploring the Psychological Structures of Modern Chinese Merchants" ("Zhongguo jindai shangren xinli jiegou chutan"), *Zhongguoshehuikexue* 5 (1986).

MacFarquhar, Roderick. *The Origins of the Cultural Revolution, The Great Leap Forward, 1958–1960.* New York: Columbia University Press, 1983.

Madsen, Richard. *Morality and Power in a Chinese Village.* Berkeley: University of California Press, 1984.

Mao Zedong. *Selected Works of Mao Zedong* (Mao zedong xuanji). Beijing: People's Press, 1977.

———. "Speech at Moscow Celebration Meeting." In Robert R. Bowie and John K. Fairbank, eds., *Communist China, 1955–1959.* Cambridge: Harvard University Press, 1971.

Meisner, Maurice. *Mao's China: A History of the People's Republic.* New York: Free Press, 1977.

Mencius. "Mencius." In Ch'u Chai and Weinberg Chai, eds., *The Sacred Books of Confucius and Other Confucian Classics.* New Hyde Park, N.Y.: University Books, 1965.

Metzger, Thomas. *Escape from Predicament.* New York: Columbia University Press, 1977.

Miao Rentian. "Introduction of Confucius' Concepts of Righteousness and Interest and Their Modern Implications" ("Qianlun kongzi de yi li guan ji qi xiandai yiyi"), *Qiluxuekan* 1 (1989).

Morishima Michio. *Why Has Japan 'Succeeded'?* New York: Cambridge University Press, 1982.

Mote, Frederick. "Confucian Eremitism in the Yuan Period." In A. Wright, ed., *Confucianism and Chinese Civilization.* New York: Atheneum, 1965.

Nathan, Andrew. "A Factionalism Model for CCP Politics," *China Quarterly* 53 (1973).

———. "Policy Oscillations in the People's Republic of China," *China Quarterly* 68 (1976).

Nee, Victor. "Between Center and Locality: State, Militia, and Village." In V. Nee and D. Mozingo, eds., *State and Society in Contemporary China.* Ithaca: Cornell University Press, 1983.

Nee, Victor, and David Mozingo, eds. *State and Society in Contemporary China.* Ithaca: Cornell University Press, 1983.

New China News Agency. *Highway to Entrepreneurship* (Qiye feiteng zhi lu). Beijing: Chinese Prospect Press, 1985.

Office of Industry System, ed. *The Practices of Financial Groups* (Qiye jituan shiwu). Beijing: Chinese Development Press, 1991.

Ogden, Suzanne. *China's Unresolved Issues: Politics, Development, and Culture.* Englewood Cliffs, N.J.: Prentice-Hall, 1989.

Oi, Jean. *State and Peasant in Contemporary China.* Berkeley: University of California Press, 1989.

Pemple, P. J. *The Misunderstood Miracle.* Ithaca, N.Y.: Cornell University Press, 1988.

Peng Jiurong. "Reflections on Traditional Chinese Thoughts in Literature" ("Guanyu zhongguo chuantong wenxue sixiang de fansi"), *Wenxuepinglun* 2 (1986).

Prybyla, Jan. "China's Economic Experiment: Back from the Market?" Paper presented at the Western Political Science Association annual meeting, Salt Lake City, April 1989.

Pye, Lucian. *Asian Power and Politics.* Cambridge: Harvard University Press, 1985.

———. *The Dynamics of Chinese Politics.* Cambridge: Oelgeschlager, Gunn & Hain, 1981.

———. *The Mandarin and the Cadre.* Ann Arbor: Center for Chinese Studies, University of Michigan, 1988.

———. *The Spirit of Chinese Politics.* Cambridge: MIT Press, 1968.

———. "The State and the Individual: An Overview Interpretation," *China Quarterly* 127 (1992).

Qi Xingrong. "On Institutional Reform of Enterprise Leadership" ("Lun qiye lingdao tizhi gaige"). In Shanghai Communist Party Propaganda Department, ed., *The First Wave* (Diyici dachao). Shanghai: Sanlian Press, 1989.

Qi Yungdong. "Socialist Market Economy and Its Operating Mechanism" ("Shehuizhuyi shichang jingji ji qi yunxing jizhi"). In Editorial Board of the Market Economy Seminar of Guangdong Province, ed., *Market Economy in the Primary Stage of Socialism* (Shehuizhuyi chuji jieduan shichang jingji). Dalian: Northeastern School of Finance Press, 1988.

Ren Chuanhong. *How to Do a Good Job on the Political Thought Work in Enterprises* (Luhe zuohao qiye zhengzhi sixiang gongzuo). Shanghai: Shanghai People's Press, 1989.

Research and Development of Capital Steel Corporation ed. *Adhering to the Responsibility System, Enliving the Large Enterprises* (Jianchi chengbaozhi, gaohuo da qiye). Beijing: Chinese Legal Institution Press, 1990.

Riskin, Carl. *Chinese Political Economy.* New York: Oxford University Press, 1987.

Rosenau, James. *Turbulence in World Politics.* Princeton: Princeton University Press, 1990.

Ruan Jianming et al., eds. *Dynamics of Economic Theory* (Jingji lilun dongtai). Beijing: Chinese Economics Press, 1989.

Sa Mengwu. *History of Chinese Politics and Society* (Zhongguo shehui zhengzhishi). 4 vols. Taipei: Sanmin, 1980.

Schelling, Thomas. "Hockey Helmets, Daylight Saving, and Other Binary Choices." In Brian Barry and Russel Hardin, eds., *Rational Man and Irrational Society.* Beverly Hills: Sage, 1982.

Schurmann, Franz. *Ideology and Organization in Communist China.* Berkeley: University of California Press, 1968.

Selden, Mark, ed. *The People's Republic of China: A Documentary History of Revolutionary Change.* New York: Monthly Review Press, 1979.

Shen Zhiyu and Xu Xiaojiu. "Analysis and Research on the Practice of Corporate Purchase in the City of Baoding" ("Dui baoding shi qiye jianbing shijian de diaocha yu fenxi"). In F. Tian ed., *Theory and Practice of Corporate Purchase in China* (Zhongguo qiye jianbing de lilun yu shijian). Beijing: Economic Management Club, 1989.

Sheng Duanming. "Self-closed Model of Taoyuan" ("Guanbizishou de taoyuan moshi"), *Jianghanluntan* 2 (1987).

Shi Guang. "On Humanism, Humanistic Centralism, and Humanitarianism" ("Renwenzhuyi, renbenzhuyi ji rendaozhuyi bianzheng"), *Qiusuo* 6 (1986).

Shih Chih-yu. "The Decline of a Moral Regime: The Great Leap Forward in Retrospect," *Comparative Political Studies,* July 1994.

———. "One Country, Two Systems as the Camouflage of Socialist Theme" ("Yiguo liangzhi, shehuizhuyi zhutilun de baozhuang"), *United Daily,* August 14, 1991.

———. *The Spirit of Chinese Foreign Policy.* London: Macmillan, 1990.

———. "Style Change in Chinese Macroeconomic Management During Reform and Opening" ("Zhongguo dalu gaige kaifang zhong jingji tiaokong fangshi zhi bianqian"), *Dongya jikan,* July 1991.

Shirk, Susan L. *The Political Logic of Economic Reform in China.* Berkeley: University of California Press, 1992.

———. "The Politics of Industrial Reform." In E. J. Perry and C. Wong, eds., *The Political Economy of Reform in Post-Mao China.* Cambridge: Council on East Asian Studies, Harvard University, 1986.

Shue, Vivienne. *The Reach of the State: Sketches of the Chinese Body Politic.* Stanford: Stanford University Press, 1988.

Skinner, William. "Marketing and Social Structure in Rural China," *Journal of Asian Studies* 24, 3 (1965).

Skinner, William, and Edwin Winckler. "Compliance Succession in Rural Communist China: A Cyclical·Theory." In A. Etzioni, ed., *A Sociological Reader on Complex Organization.* New York: Holt, Rinehart, and Winston, 1969.

Social Science Academy. "Reflections on Economic Construction and Economic Reform in the Past Few Years" ("Dui ji nian lai jingji jianshe yu jingji gaige de fansi"), *Jingji yanjiu* 3 (1987).

Solinger, Dorothy. *China's Transition from Socialism: Statist Legacies and Market Reforms, 1980–1990.* Armonk, N.Y.: M. E. Sharpe, 1993.

———. *Chinese Business Under Socialism.* Berkeley: University of California Press, 1984.

———, ed. *Three Versions of Chinese Socialism.* Boulder, Colo.: Westview, 1984.

Solomon, Richard. *Mao's Revolution and the Chinese Political Culture.* Berkeley: University of California Press, 1971.

Su Dongshui. *Managing China's Village Economy* (Zhongguo xiangzheng jingji guanlixue). Jinan: Shangdong People's Press, 1988.

Su Wenning, ed. *Modernization—The Chinese Way.* Beijing: Beijing Review, 1984.

Sun Xuewen. "The Existing Issues of Macromanagement in Our Country in the Past Six Years" ("Wo guo jin liu nian lai hongguang guangli cunzai de wenti"), *Cai jing guangli de lilun yu shijian* 5 (1985).

Tai Hung-chao. "The Oriental Alternative: An Hypothesis on Culture and Economy." In H. Tai, ed., *Confucianism and Economic Development.* Washington, D.C.: Washington Institute Press, 1989.

Tai Kuo-hui. "Confucianism and Japanese Modernization." In H. Tai, ed., *Confucianism and Economic Development.* Washington, D.C.: Washington Institute Press, 1989.

Tan Naizhang et al. *On Six Major Issues of Economic Institutional Reform* (Jingji tizhi gaige liu da yiti yanjiu). Beijing: Spring-Autumn Press, 1989.

Teiwes, Frederick C. *Leadership, Legitimacy, and Conflict in China.* Armonk, N.Y.: M. E. Sharpe, 1984.

Teng Fu. "Five Theses on Traditional Cultural Thoughts" ("Chuantong wenhua sixiang wulun"), *Qiusuo* 2 (1988).

Tong Dalin. "The Issues of Consumption and Market in Chinese Socialism" ("Zhongguo shehuizhuyi shichang han xiaofei wenti"). In Ding Shengjun and Wang Yibing, eds., *Regulate the Economic Environment and Establish the New Order for Circulation* (Zhili jingji huanjing, jianli liutong xin zhixu). Beijing: Chinese Commercial Press, 1989.

Tong Wansheng, Li Zichao, and Chen Zumian. *Theory of Market Price* (Shichang wujia xue). Beijing: Universal Aviation Press, 1989.

Tsou, Tang. "Prolegomenon to the Study of Informal Groups in CCP Politics," *China Quarterly* 65 (1976).

Tu Wei-ming. *Human Nature and the Cultivation and Growth of the Self* (Renxing yu ziwo xiu zhang). Beijing: Chinese Peace Press, 1988.

"The Unavoidable Historical Route" ("Lishi biyou zhi lu"), *People's Liberation Army Daily*, September 19–23, 1991.

Union Research Institute, ed. *Collected Works of Liu Shao Ch'i, 1958–1967.* Hong Kong: Union Research Institute, 1968.

Van Ness, Peter, and Satish Raichur. "Dilemmas of Socialist Development: An Analysis of Strategic Lines in China, 1949–1981." In Peter Van Ness, ed., *Market Reform in Socialist Societies.* Boulder, Colo.: Lynne Rienner, 1989.

Walder, Andrew. *Communist Neo-Traditionalism.* Berkeley: University of California Press, 1986.

Wang Bingyi and Shi Zhishuen. "Reflection and Retrospect on Corporate Purchase in the City of Baoding" ("Dui baoding shi qiye jianbing de huigu yu sikao"). In F. Tian ed., *Theory and Practice of Corporate Purchase in China* (Zhongguo qiye jianbing de lilun yu shijian). Beijing: Economic Management Club, 1989.

Wang Furen. "In Pursuit of Modernization of the Entire of Chinese Culture" ("Dui quanbu zhongguo wenhua de xiandaihua zhuiqiu"), *Zhongguoshehuikexue* 3 (1989).

Wang, Huning. "The Changing Structure of China's Political Culture" ("Zhuanbianzhong de zhongguo zhengzhi wenhua"), *Fudanxuebao* 3 (1988).

Wang Reipu and Cui Zifeng. *On the Party's Fundamental Lines on the Primary Stage of Socialism* (Shehuizhuyi chuji jieduan dangde jibenluxian gailun). Beijing: Chinese Communist Party Central School Press, 1991.

Wang Ruowang. "Remarks on Social Problems in Reform." In *Selected Remarks by Fang Lizhi, Liu Binyan, and Wang Ruowang* (Fang Lizhi, Liu Binyan, Lan Wang Ruowang yanlun zhaiyao). Hong Kong: Shuguang, 1988.

Wang Shubai. *The Chinese Gene in Maoism* (Mao Zedong cixiang de zhongguo jiying). Taipei: Jichitang Cultural Co., 1991.

Wang Songhsing. *The Turtle Mountain Island—On the Han Fishermen's Society* (Guei shan dao—hanren yucun shehui zhi yanjiu). Nankang: Academia Sinica, 1967.

Wang Weiguang. *Economic Interests, Political Order, Social Stability—The Deep Reflection on the Social Contradiction of Socialism* (Jingji liyi, zhengzhi zhixu, shehui wending—shehuizhuyi shehui maodun de shenceng fanci). Beijing: Chinese Communist Party Central School Press, 1991.

Wang Weiguo, Fang Wei, and Song Jia. "The Completion of the Mission of the May Fourth New Cultural Movement and the Thriving of the Commodity Economy"

("Wusi xin wenhua yundong renwu de wancheng yu shangpin jingji de boxing"), *Hebeixuekan* 3 (1989).

Wang Zilin. *On National Enterprise* (Guoyou zichanglun). Beijing: Chinese Finance Press, 1989.

Weber, Max. *The Religion of China.* Trans. Hans H. Gerth. New York: Free Press, 1951.

Wei Je. *Harmony Between Economic Freedom and Economic Control: On the Combination of Planning and Market* (Jingji ziyou yu jingji yueshu de hexie: jihua yu shichang de jiehe). Xi'an: Shanxi People's Press, 1991.

Wen Erxing. "Strictly Control Collective Consumption, Engage in Overall Management of Price" ("Yange kongzhi jituan xiaofei, dui wujia jinxing zonghe zhili"). In Editorial Board of the Market Economy Seminar of Guangdong Province, ed., *Market Economy in the Primary Stage of Socialism* (Shehuizhuyi chuji jieduan shichang jingji). Dalian: Northeastern School of Finance Press, 1988.

White, Gordon. *Riding the Tiger.* Stanford: Stanford University Press, 1993.

Wilson, Dick. *The People's Emperor.* Garden City, N.Y.: Doubleday, Inc., 1980.

Wilson, Richard, ed. *Value Changes in Chinese Society.* New York: Praeger, 1979.

Winckler, Edwin. "Policy Oscillations in the People's Republic of China," *China Quarterly* 68 (1976).

Womack, Brantly. "Transfigured Community: Neo-Traditionalism and Work Unit Socialism in China," *China Quarterly* 126 (1991).

Wu Boling. "On Economically Retarded Nations' Hopping over the Capitalist Stage of Development—The Basis of the Theory of the Primary Stage of Socialism in Our Country" ("Jingji luohou guojia chaoyue zibenzhuyi fazhan jieduan wenti—wo guo shehuizhuyi chuji jieduan lilun de yiju"). In Shanghai Communist Party Propaganda Department, ed., *The First Wave* (Diyici dachao). Shanghai: Sanlian Press, 1989.

Wu Jiang. *A Few Problems of Contemporary Socialism* (Dangdai shehuizhuyi luogan wenti). Beijing: Huaxia Press, 1989.

Wu Jiaxiang. "Control over Corruption." Mimeograph.

Wu Renjian. "Inflation in China" ("Zhongguo de tonghuo pengzhang"). In Ruan Jianming et al., eds., *Dynamics of Economic Theory* (Jingji lilun dongtai). Beijing: Chinese Economics Press, 1989.

Wu Shuqing. "From Criticism of the Responsibility System to Adherence and Perfection of the Responsibility System" ("Cong dui chengbao zhi de pipan dao jianchi han wanshan chengbao zhi"). In Research and Development of Capital Steel Corporation, ed., *Adhering to the Responsibility System, Enlivening the Large Enterprise* (Jianchi chengbao zhi, gaohuo da qiye). Beijing: Chinese Democracy and Legal Institution Press, 1989.

Xiao Gongqing. "The Three Historical Archetypes of Confucianism and the Modern Chinese Political Culture" ("Luxue de sanzhong lishixingtai yu dangdai de zhongguo zhengzhi wenhua"), *Chinese Culture Monthly*, October 1989.

Xie Xialing. "On the Root of Difference Between Chinese and Western Culture and the Trend of Contemporary Chinese Culture" ("Lun zhong xi wenhua chayi zhi gen yu dangdai zhongguo wenhua zhi quxiang"), *Fudanxuebao* 3 (1988).

———. "Reinterpreting the May Fourth Spirit, Absorbing the Confucian Thoughts" ("Chongshi wusi jingshen, xishou ruxue sixiang"), *Fudanxuebao* 3 (1989).

Xu Chongzheng. *Overall Development of Men and Social Economy—Ethical Economics* (Rende quanmian fazhan yu shehui jingji—lunli jingjixue). Hefei, Anhui: Anhui Education Press, 1990.

Xu Guangjian, Wang Xiaobing, and Du Weichang. *Price Theory Under Reform* (Gaigezhong de wujia lilun). Beijing: People's University Press, 1989.

Xu Rongan. *Chinese Economics of City-Village Coordination* (Zhongguo cheng xiang ronghe jingjixue). Beijing: China Prospect Press, 1988.

Xu Suming. "The National Psychocultural Character as the Core of Each Cultural Mode" ("Minzu wenhuaxinli suzhi shi butong wenhua leixing de jibenneihe"), *Jianghanluntan* 10 (1986).

————. "On the Linkage Between Chinese Traditional Culture and Modernization" ("Lun zhongguo chuantong wenhua yu xiandaihua de jiehebu"), *Jianghanluntan* 2 (1988).

Xu Xiqian. "Use the Party's Basic Lines to Unify Thoughts" ("Yao yung dangde jiben luxian tongyi sixiang"). In Research and Development of Capital Steel Corporation, ed., *Adhering to the Responsibility System, Enlivening the Large Enterprise* (Jianchi chengbao zhi, gaohuo da qiye). Beijing: Chinese Democracy and Legal Institution Press, 1989.

Xu Zhixiang. "Forty Years of Research on Confucianism, 1949–1989" ("Kongzi yanjiu sishinian, 1949–1989"), *Qiluxuekan* 6, 1989.

Xue Muqiao. *China's Socialist Economy.* Beijing: Foreign Language Press, 1981.

Yan Chengle, Hou Zhangjia, and Yu Qingying. "Reflection on the Upgrading of Corporate Purchase from the Primary to the Advanced Level" ("Qiye jianbing you chuji xingtai xiang gaoji xingtai zhuanhuan de silu"). In F. Tian, ed., *Theory and Practice of Corporate Purchase in China* (Zhongguo qiye jianbing de lilun yu shijian). Beijing: Economic Management Club, 1989.

Yang Changjun. "On the Scope of Socialist Market Economy" ("Lun shehuizhuyi shichang jingji fanchou"). In Editorial Board of the Market Economy Seminar of Guangdong Province, ed., *Market Economy in the Primary Stage of Socialism* (Shehuizhuyi chuji jieduan shichang jingji). Dalian: Northeastern School of Finance Press, 1988.

Yang Chengxun. *The Cooperative System and Family Economy Under Socialist Commodity Economy* (Shehuizhuyi shangpin jingji xia de hezuo zhi yu jiating jingji). Beijing: Chinese Social Science Academy Press, 1988.

Yang Chung-fang. "On Chinese Moral Development: From the Perspective of Self-development" ("Shilun zhongguoren de daode fazhan: yige ziwo fazhan de guandian"). In K. Yang and K. Huang, eds., *Chinese Psychology and Behavior* (Zhongguoren de xinli yu xingwei). Taipei: Department of Psychology, National Taiwan University, 1989.

Yang Shanming. "On Cultural Tradition" ("Wenhua chuantong lun"), *Shandongdaxue xuebao* 3 (1988).

Yang Shengming. *Model Selection for Consumption with Chinese Characters* (Zhongguoshi xiaofei moshi xuanze). Beijing: Chinese Social Science Academy Press, 1989.

Yang Youquan. "The Yao-Liu Debate and the Predicament of Chinese Culture" ("Yaoliu zhizheng yu zhongguo wenhua de kunjing"), *Jianghanluntan* (1986).

Yi Ran. "Mainland China Witnesses a Period of Power Decentralization" ("Zhongguo dalu mianlin yige quanli fenhua de shiqi"), *Studies of Chinese Communism* 24, 9–10 (September–October 1990).

Yu Wujing. "Inner Conflicts in Contemporary Chinese Culture" ("Dangdai zhongguo wenhua de neizai chongtu"), *Fudanxuebao* 3 (1988).

Yu Ying-shih. "Between Tao and the Regime" ("Daotong yu zhengtong zhijian"), *Zhonghua wenhua yuekan* 60 (1984).

————. *Chinese Modern Religious Ethics and Merchant Spirit* (Zhongguo jinshi zongjiao lunli yu shangren jingshen). Taipei: Lianjing Publications, 1987.

Yu Yung. "Summary of the Seminar on Confucius, Confucianism, and Contemporary Socialism" ("Kongzi, rujia yu dangdai shehuizhuyi xueshutaolunhui zongshu"), *Qiluxuekan* 6 (1989).

Yuan Yuehong. "Confucian Epistemology and Its Limitation" ("Kongzi renshilun ji qi juxian"), *Qiluxuekan* 4 (1985).

Yue Fubing. *On the Commodity Economy in the Primary Stage of Socialism* (Shehuizhuyi chuji jieduan shangpin jingji lun). Beijing: China Prospect Press, 1989.

Zeigler, Harmon. *Pluralism, Corporatism, and Confucianism*. Philadelphia: Temple University Press, 1986.

Zeng Muye et al., eds. *Market Economy of the Primary Stage of the Socialist Development* (Shehuizhuyi chuji jieduan shichang jingji). Dalian: Northeastern Financial University Press, 1988.

Zhang "The Cadres' Corruption," *Chinese Law and Government* (fall 1988).

Zhang Dainian. *Studies of Chinese Ethical Thought* (Zhongguo lunli sixiang yanjiu). Shanghai: Shanghai People's Press, 1989.

Zhang Jian. "Three Issues in Confucian Studies" ("Guanyu kongzi yanjiu de sange wenti"), *Qiluxuekan* 4 (1986).

Zhang Shengshu, Hu Wanrong, and Tang Mosen. *Economics of Raw Materials* (Wuzi jingjixue). Beijing: Economics of Raw Materials Press, 1989.

Zhang Xiqing. "How Did Modern Chinese Bourgeois Thinkers Treat Western Capitalist Civilization?" ("Zhongguo jindai zichanjieji sixiangjia shi ruhe duidai xifang zibenzhuyi wenming de"), *Qiushixuekan* 2 (1986).

Zhang Yi. *Introduction to China's Village Enterprises* (Zhongguo xiangzheng qiye gailun). Shanghai: Shanghai Social Science Academy Press, 1988.

Zhang Yuanyuan. "On Export-oriented Economy Again" ("Zai lun waixiang jingji"), *Nanfang jingji* 6 (1985).

Zhao Lin. "Only the Self Is Absolute," *Chinese Sociology and Anthropology* (summer 1985).

Zheng Ping, and Feng Chungming. "Exploring the New Approach to Move Beyond Feudalistic Culture" ("Tuozhan chaoyue fengjianzhuyi wenhua de xin jingdi"), *Jiangxidaxue xuebao* 1 (1989).

Zheng Xiaojiang. "Modern Reflections on the Principles of Ancient Chinese Thoughts" (Zhongguo gudai sikao yuanze de xiandai fansi), *Jiangxidaxue xuebao* 1 (1989).

Zheng Yingrong. "Bringing in Market, Building Market" ("Yinjin shichang, jianzao shichang"). In Editorial Board of the Market Economy Seminar of Guangdong Province, ed., *Market Economy in the Primary Stage of Socialism* (Shehuizhuyi chuji jieduan shichang jingji). Dalian: Northeastern School of Finance Press, 1988.

Zhou Enlai. "Report on Government Work." In Robert R. Bowie and John K. Fairbank, eds., *Communist China, 1955–1959*. Cambridge: Harvard University Press, 1971.

Zhou Zhenghe. "A Great Leap to Reevaluate the Traditional Culture" ("Dui chuantong wenhua zairenshi de feiyao"), *Fudanxuebao* 3 (1989).

Zhu Laishan. "Inner Consciousness and Chinese Political Culture" ("Neixing yishi yu zhongguo zhengzhi wenhua"), *Jiangxidaxue xuebao* 2 (1986).

Zhu Liming. "Structural Elasticity of Demand and Income and Premature Consumption" ("Shouru xuqiu jiego tanxing yu xiaofei zaoshou"), *Xiaofei jingji* 1 (1986).

Zhu Wenhua. "The Transformation of Chinese Psychoculture Is the Premise of China's Modernization" ("Gaizao zhongguoren de wenhuaxintai shi zhongguo xiandaihua de qianti"), *Fudanxuebao* 3 (1989).

# INDEX

Ah Q, 6
Arrow, Kenneth J., 23

bankruptcy, 26, 54, 100, 123
Baoding (municipality), 55
Beijing: as central planner, 24; as conservative control, 155; leadership in 46, 50; as planning center, 27, 49; tour to, 150
Beijing massacre, 9, 155, 163
Beijing Print and Dye Company, 135, 137, 138
bloc. *See kuaikuai*
Boxer Rebellion, 20
Bureau of Education, 150
Bureau of Finance, 104
Bureau of Industry, 104
Bureau of Tax, 104

cadre: in assembly, 136, 137, 138; background of, 164; between party and enterprise, 90; collective identity and, 126; as conservative, 99; as consumer, 79; dress of, 125; dual roles of, 102; as educator, 84, 151, 152; in factory, 60; function of, 134, 159; ideology of, 44; intellectual level of, 98; interest distribution and, 156; life of, 131, 132; local leadership of, 7; of low level, 142; manager and, 109, 127; in market, 64; moral sense of, 82; problem of, 97; profit-consciousness of, 135; protectionism and, 158; of purchased enterprise, 55; as rascal, 161; regime and, 8; resource of, 82; role in enterprise, 88; as state employee, 84; under socialism, 65; vested interest of, 104
Capital Steel Corporation, 55, 76, 77, 120
central bank, 37, 38
Central Party School, 36
Changzhou (municipality), 60
Chicago School of Economics, 81
China: aggregate supply, 25; authoritarianism in, 68; bonus sharing in, 111; capitalism in, 39; collectivism in, 85; colonialism in, 20; command economy in, 34; compared with

Asia, 40; compared with Japan, 65, 66; consumption in, 81; corporatism in, 5; economic history of, 33; enterprise in, 29; enterprise-state relation in, 100; entrepreneurship in, 104; in history, 67; identity in, 139; industrial development of, 60; in information age, 42; legitimacy claim in, 43; local leadership in, 152; manager in, 105; marketing style in, 147; neo-Confucianism in, 4; opportunity cost concept in, 15; patriarchal tradition in, 12; political change in, 28; political culture, 20, 53; political economy of, 13, 14, 155; productive factor in, 49; reform in, 44, 62, 141; relation with Japan, 50; school enterprise in, 153; short-term development in, 26; socialism in, 31, 39, 119; socialist enterprise in, 138; song in, 131; state of, 156, 158, 164; state planner in, 71; technology level in, 110; traditional wisdom in, 126; tradition in, 84, 129, 142, 151; underdevelopment of, 38; value system in, 93; worker in, 127
Chinese Communist Party: authoritarianism of, 85; cooperative division in, 73; corporate purchase and, 56; disgust toward, 112; duty of, 94; economic development and, 22; economic role of, 91; as educator, 43; in enterprise, 87, 93, 97; enterprise policy of, 54; factory identity and, 134; function of, 101; as indoctrinator, 42; leadership of, 44, 48; legitimacy of, 109, 123, 132; opportunity cost and, 19; political campaign by, 71; preference management by, 41; as proletariat, 119; recruitment by, 135; rectification campaign of, 89; relation with enterprise, 90; relation with state, 98; role in enterprise, 99; in rural enterprise, 60; in school enterprise, 149; socialism, 11; under socialism, 156; in state, 158; as target of Maoism, 66; task of, 88; under threat, 105; toward cooperativism, 72
Chongqing (municipality), 58

201

# ABOUT THE BOOK
# AND THE AUTHOR

As China's reforms take root, the differences between the traditional value of harmony and the socialist norm of class struggle are becoming increasingly obscured. Chinese citizens are, in fact, theoretically allowed—even encouraged—to be socialist and profit-driven at the same time.

Chih-yu Shih looks at this precarious dyad, demonstrating what reform has done to the country's political and economic mechanisms and, equally significant, how the coexistence of collectivism and individualism continues to dominate the thinking of China's reformers. Considering the issue from cultural, moral, political, and ideological perspectives, Shih addresses the popular questions of whether Chinese socialism has died.

In the second part of the book, the results of Shih's insightful private interviews with planners, general managers, party cadres, and ordinary workers reveal the delicate and complex interrelationships among them. Also of special value is the author's comprehensive bibliography of Chinese-language sources on economic reform.

**Chih-yu Shih** is associate professor of political science at National Taiwan University. His publications include *China's Just World: The Morality of Chinese Foreign Policy* (Lynne Rienner 1993).